AN
ANNE TYLER
COMPANION

AN
ANNE TYLER
COMPANION

❧

Robert W. Croft

GREENWOOD PRESS
Westport, Connecticut • London

Library of Congress Cataloging-in-Publication Data

Croft, Robert W. (Robert Wayne), 1957–
    An Anne Tyler companion / Robert W. Croft.
        p.   cm.
    Includes bibliographical references (p.   ) and index.
    ISBN 0–313–28999–9 (alk. paper)
    1. Tyler, Anne—Criticism and interpretation.   2. Women and
literature—United States—History—20th century.   I. Title.
PS3570.Y45Z633   1998
813'.54—dc21   97–33137

British Library Cataloguing in Publication Data is available.

Library of Congress Catalog Card Number: 97–33137
ISBN: 0–313–28999–9

First published in 1998

Greenwood Press, 88 Post Road West, Westport, CT 06881
An imprint of Greenwood Publishing Group, Inc.

Printed in the United States of America

∞™

The paper used in this book complies with the
Permanent Paper Standard issued by the National
Information Standards Organization (Z39.48–1984).

10 9 8 7 6 5 4 3 2 1

As always,
For my family,
Melody, Britanny, and Christian—
My anchors
and
for two true friends,
Jeff and Jeannie Davis

Contents

Preface

This book grew out of a need that I discovered as I was working on my dissertation on Anne Tyler. Although Tyler is a major contemporary novelist with thirteen published novels and almost fifty short stories, I soon discovered that no reference guide to her works existed. So, as I was researching my earlier book, *Anne Tyler: A Bio-Bibliography*, I began to work on such a reference guide so that information on Tyler's works would be more readily accessible to future Tyler scholars and aficionados.

In particular, Tyler's many short stories, published over a period of more than thirty years in a wide range of publications, some of them obscure and virtually inaccessible, are sometimes hard to locate. To make matters worse, Tyler herself has no plans to collect her short stories any time soon. Therefore, the short story entries, which synopsize and comment upon her short stories, should be very helpful to those interested in extending their knowledge of Tyler's work beyond her novels.

This book begins with a short introductory chapter on Tyler's life, followed by a second chapter discussing her major themes and motifs. Those interested in a fuller treatment of her life should consult my earlier book.

The main section of the book consists of encyclopedic entries, arranged alphabetically, on each of Tyler's novels and short stories. At the end of the entries on her novels are suggestions for further reading, as well as a selected list of book reviews on that novel. The entries on novels mainly focus on commentary rather than providing exhaustive plot summary. For the short story entries, however, I included both commentary and a detailed synopsis of each short story. This more detailed treatment of Tyler's short stories is necessary because they are less accessible than her novels.

In addition to the entries on her fictional works, this section of the book interweaves entries, alphabetically arranged along with the novel and short story entries, on all of Tyler's fictional characters, as well as entries on her major themes and motifs. Following each of these entries (in parentheses) is an abbreviation (from the key at the beginning of this book) noting which novels and/or short stories the character or theme appears in. Please note that some characters' nicknames, maiden names, or first names not commonly used in the work are placed in parentheses. Furthermore, cross-references are given for female characters whose names change after they marry. In such cases, I used the name a character is called during the bulk of the novel or short story for the main entry for that character. For example, Elizabeth Abbott (from *The Clock Winder*) is listed as such, even though her name changes to Emerson at the end of the novel. Entries on themes and motifs are also cross-referenced in some cases to avoid duplication and to connect similar concepts.

The reference section of the book consists of a Primary Bibliography listing Tyler's novels (in order of publication, as well as paperback reprints), her short stories (also in order of publication), and a selected bibliography of her nonfiction (including an annotated selected list of some of her more revealing book reviews). Following that is a Selected Secondary Bibliography (including all the books and some of the more interesting articles written about her work, as well as interviews with Tyler). After the bibliographical section come the Appendices, consisting of a map of Baltimore noting some of the places and streets used in Tyler's novels, a list of places referred to in Tyler's novels (with asterisks beside actual Baltimore locations), and a list of songs mentioned in Tyler's novels. Finally, there is an Index, indexing Tyler's works, characters, themes, and motifs.

During the time that I have been working on this book I have received a great deal of help and encouragement from a number of people. I would first like to thank George Butler at Greenwood Press for his excellent editorial help, as well as Arlene Belzer and Megan Brown Hull of Coastal Editorial Services. In addition, I would like to thank the fine staff at the Gainesville College library, especially Priscilla Rankin. At the University of Georgia, thanks to cartographer Brian Davis for his help with the map of Baltimore. And thanks to Anne Tyler herself for her assistance and good wishes.

Most of all, I want to thank my family for their love and support. Britanny, Christian, and Melody, you are the reason for my writing and my life. I love you.

Abbreviations

NOVELS

AT	*The Accidental Tourist*
BL	*Breathing Lessons*
CN	*Celestial Navigation*
CW	*The Clock Winder*
DHR	*Dinner at the Homesick Restaurant*
EP	*Earthly Possessions*
IMEC	*If Morning Ever Comes*
LY	*Ladder of Years*
MP	*Morgan's Passing*
SC	*Searching for Caleb*
SDL	*A Slipping-Down Life*
SM	*Saint Maybe*
TCT	*The Tin Can Tree*

SHORT STORIES

"Artificial"	"The Artificial Family"
"As the Earth"	"As the Earth Gets Old"

"Average"	"Average Waves in Unprotected Waters"
"Baltimore"	"The Baltimore Birth Certificate"
"Base-Metal"	"The Base-Metal Egg"
"Bride"	"The Bride in the Boatyard"
"Bridge"	"The Bridge"
"Common"	"The Common Courtesies"
"Country"	"The Country Cook"
"Dry"	"Dry Water"
"Feather"	"The Feather Behind the Rock"
"Flaw"	"A Flaw in the Crust of the Earth"
"Foot-Footing"	"Foot-Footing On"
"Genuine"	"The Genuine Fur Eyelashes"
"Geologist"	"The Geologist's Maid"
"Half-Truths"	"Half-Truths and Semi-Miracles"
"Holding"	"Holding Things Together"
"I'm Not Going"	"I'm Not Going to Ask You Again"
"I Never Saw"	"I Never Saw Morning"
"I Play"	"I Play Kings"
"Knack"	"A Knack for Languages"
"Laps"	"Laps"
"Laura"	"Laura"
"Lights"	"The Lights on the River"
"Linguistics"	"Linguistics"
"Misstep"	"A Misstep of the Mind"
"Neutral"	"Neutral Ground"
"Nobody"	"Nobody Answers the Door"
"Outside"	"Outside"
"People"	"People Who Don't Know the Answers"
"Rerun"	"Rerun"
"Respect"	"Respect"
"Runaway"	"The Runaway Wife"
"Saints"	"The Saints in Caesar's Household"
"Some Sign"	"Some Sign That I Ever Made You Happy"
"Spending"	"Spending"
"Street"	"A Street of Bugles"
"Tea-Machine"	"The Tea-Machine"
"Teenage"	"Teenage Wasteland"

"Two People"	"Two People and a Clock on the Wall"
"Uncle"	"Uncle Ahmad"
"Under Tree"	"Under the Bosom Tree"
"Who Would Want"	"Who Would Want a Little Boy?"
"With Flags"	"With All Flags Flying"
"Woman"	"A Woman Like a Fieldstone House"
"Your Place"	"Your Place is Empty"

Chronology of
Anne Tyler's Life

1941	Anne Phyllis Tyler is born October 25 in Minneapolis, MN
1948	Tyler family moves to Celo Community in mountains of North Carolina
1953	Tyler family moves to Raleigh, NC, where Anne attends Broughton High School
1958–61	Tyler attends Duke University in Durham, NC, majors in Russian, and publishes her first short stories in the campus literary magazine, *Archive*
1961–62	Tyler pursues a master's degree in Russian at Columbia University, but returns home to North Carolina without completing her thesis
1963	Tyler marries Taghi Modarressi, an Iranian medical student specializing in child psychiatry; after a trip to Iran to visit relatives, the couple moves to Montreal, where Taghi completes his residency
1964	*If Morning Ever Comes* is published by Knopf
1965	*The Tin Can Tree* is published by Knopf; first daughter, Tezh, is born
1967	Second daughter, Mitra, is born; family moves to Baltimore
1970	*A Slipping-Down Life* is published by Knopf
1972	*The Clock Winder* is published by Knopf; Tyler's first book review appears in the *National Observer*
1974	*Celestial Navigation* is published by Knopf; Gail Godwin's highly favorable review of the novel appears in the *New York Times Book Review*
1975	*Searching for Caleb* is published by Knopf; John Updike's review of the novel in the *New Yorker* calls Tyler "not merely good, . . . [but] *wickedly* good"

1976   Tyler's first book reviews in the *New York Times Book Review* appear
1977   *Earthly Possessions* is published by Knopf; Tyler receives citation of merit from the American Academy and Institute of Arts and Letters
1980   *Morgan's Passing* is published by Knopf; Tyler is awarded the Janet Heidinger Kafka Prize
1982   *Dinner at the Homesick Restaurant* is published by Knopf; Tyler wins Pen/Faulkner Award for Fiction
1983   Tyler is elected a member of the American Academy and Institute of Arts and Letters; *Dinner at the Homesick Restaurant* is a finalist for the Pulitzer Prize for Fiction
1985   *The Accidental Tourist* is published by Knopf; the novel wins the National Book Critics Circle Award
1986   *The Accidental Tourist* is a finalist for the Pulitzer Prize for Fiction
1988   *Breathing Lessons* is published by Knopf; film version of *The Accidental Tourist*, starring William Hurt and Kathleen Turner, premieres; film nominated for an Academy Award the next year
1989   *Breathing Lessons* wins the Pulitzer Prize for Fiction
1991   *Saint Maybe* is published by Knopf
1995   *Ladder of Years* is published by Knopf

Anne Tyler's Life

Following Anne Tyler's birth in Minneapolis, Minnesota, on October 25, 1941, her Quaker activist parents, Lloyd Parry Tyler—a chemist—and Phyllis Mahon Tyler—a social worker—moved around the Midwest for several years. Then in 1948, they moved to a cooperative community in the mountains of North Carolina called Celo.

In this small community, Anne and her younger brother Israel (nicknamed Ty) were taught at home but attended the local school for one year. The isolation of the community developed in Tyler both a sense of distance and the habit of observing the world objectively as an outsider. When Lloyd Tyler's income proved insufficient to support his growing family (another son, Seth, was born in 1949), Lloyd and Phyllis moved their family to Raleigh, North Carolina, in 1953, where a year later their last child, Jonathan, was born.

In Raleigh, Anne had the good fortune to attend Broughton High School, where a great English teacher, Mrs. Phyllis Peacock, encouraged Anne's writing talent, as she had a previous student, Reynolds Price. During this period, Anne also discovered her greatest literary influence, Eudora Welty, whose stories taught her the importance of carefully chosen details and showed her the possibilities of writing about ordinary life.

Upon graduating high school at the age of 16, Anne continued her studies at nearby Duke University in Durham, North Carolina, where she had won a full scholarship. There, again, she encountered teachers who recognized and encouraged her writing talent. One of those teachers was Reynolds Price, who had just begun his teaching career that year. At Duke,

Anne's major was Russian, although she did participate in several plays and contribute several short stories ("The Lights on the River," "Laura," "The Bridge," "I Never Saw Morning," and "The Saints in Caesar's Household") to the campus literary magazine, *Archive*.

After Duke, Anne headed north to New York City, where she attended graduate school at Columbia University to pursue a master's degree in Russian. A year later she returned home to work as a bibliographer in Duke's library, having left Columbia without finishing her master's thesis. During this time, Anne met Taghi Modarressi, an Iranian medical student who was specializing in child psychiatry. When Taghi asked Anne to marry him, she replied (like so many of Tyler's young women when they get proposals), "Oh, well. Why not?" They were married in May 1963. Soon afterward Anne accompanied Taghi on a trip to Iran to meet his relatives—more than two hundred of them. The prospect of meeting so many people scared Anne, but she spent the time before the visit learning as much Persian as possible, and the visit went well.

Because Taghi's visa was expiring, the couple moved to Montreal, Canada, where Taghi had obtained a residency in child psychiatry. At first Anne could not find a job herself, so she worked on completing her first novel, *If Morning Ever Comes* (1964). Eventually, she obtained a job at the McGill University Law Library, but still had plenty of time to write at night and completed her second novel, *The Tin Can Tree* (1965), within a year. Both of these novels, as well as all of Tyler's subsequent novels, were published by Alfred A. Knopf. Anne was also lucky in beginning a long-lasting writer/ editor relationship with Judith Jones, who was to remain her editor for the next thirty years.

After her second novel, however, a big change occurred in Tyler's life— motherhood. Her first daughter, Tezh, was born in 1965, followed two years later by her second daughter, Mitra. With the demands of motherhood, Tyler's pace of writing slowed down. The one novel she produced during this period, *Winter Birds, Winter Apples*, proved a disappointment and remains unpublished.

The year 1967 brought about another significant change in Tyler's life, a change that proved extremely influential to her writing. When Taghi finished his residency, he received a job offer from the University of Maryland Medical School in Baltimore. Thus the Modarressi family moved to Baltimore, where they have lived ever since. Once settled in Baltimore, Anne began to write once again, as much as her motherly duties would allow. At first, all she could manage was a series of several short stories, although these were published in national periodicals such as *McCall's*, the *New Yorker*, and *Ladies' Home Journal*. Despite the demands of motherhood and the interruption of her writing routine, Tyler enjoyed these years of caring for infants. In her most telling personal essay, "Still Just Writing," Tyler credits the experience of motherhood with making her grow "richer and deeper" and giving her "more of a self to speak from."

By 1970, when Tyler's younger daughter started nursery school, Tyler's novel writing was back on track, and she published *A Slipping-Down Life*. Although it is the shortest of Tyler's novels, it was soon followed by *The Clock Winder* (1972), Tyler's first novel set in Baltimore. It seemed that Tyler had finally become familiar enough with her adopted city to set her novels there. And it is clear that Tyler had set up a strict writing routine that allowed her to juggle her roles of mother, wife, and writer successfully. In "Still Just Writing," she explains how she would live two different lives: writing during the day while her children were away at school and then picking up the string of her other life when her daughters would come home each afternoon.

Using this technique, Tyler was able to produce a prodigious number of books over the next few years, as well as a number of short stories. First came *Celestial Navigation* in 1974, significant because its hero, the agoraphobic artist Jeremy Pauling, is the character closest to Tyler's own personality, although she is much more socially adept and efficient than Jeremy. A year later, Tyler produced *Searching for Caleb*, the novel in which she tackles the longest timeframe of any of her novels—nearly a hundred years. Then in 1977 she published *Earthly Possessions*, the closest work to a feminist novel that Tyler has ever written. Yet to call the novel even partially feminist is to mislabel it, for at heart Tyler is always a humanist, favoring neither sex over the other and often switching the viewpoint in her novels back and forth between male and female characters, so as to present a more balanced view of the whole of life. With such a unique, almost genderless viewpoint, she was definitely swimming against the critical current of the day.

During this period Tyler launched a third career as a book reviewer. In 1972, she wrote her first review for the *National Observer*, eventually becoming a regular reviewer in 1975. Within a few years she was reviewing for publications ranging from the *New Republic* and *Saturday Review* to the *New York Times Book Review* and the *Washington Post Book World*, as well as other newspapers all over the country. Her reviews were generally favorable. She always searched for, and usually found, something worthwhile to praise in each book that she reviewed, although she was capable of condemning an author who broke the unwritten pact between writer and reader by making his or her writing too obscure or by not remaining faithful to the spirit of a book's characters. Over the next twenty years, Tyler produced over 250 reviews. (Note: Commentary on some of the more interesting and revealing of these reviews is included in the primary bibliography on pages 260–64.)

Tyler's productivity soon brought her a flurry of critical attention. Gail Godwin noted her talent in a glowing review of *Celestial Navigation*, while John Updike called her "*wickedly* good" in his review of *Searching for Caleb*.

Additional honors came in the form of a citation of merit from the American Academy and Institute of Arts and Letters in 1977, followed by membership in 1983.

Still, commercial success continued to elude Tyler. None of her novels sold more than about 10,000 copies, although paperback sales were stronger and helped build up her reading audience. This period in the late 1970s was difficult for other reasons. She and her family felt many of the pressures related to the Iranian Revolution. Consequently, Tyler's next novel, *Pantaleo*, was a disappointment, which, to the credit of her artistic integrity, she declined to publish. Her next novel, *Morgan's Passing* (1980), although expected to be her breakthrough novel, again proved a commercial disappointment. The novel is interesting, nevertheless, for its main character, Morgan Gower, an inveterate imposter who takes on various identities throughout the novel. In her 1976 *Washington Post* essay, "Because I Want More Than One Life," Tyler confessed a similar motivation for her writing.

Then in 1982 came *Dinner at the Homesick Restaurant*. For the first time an Anne Tyler novel sold well. The novel garnered critical praise, as well as a nomination as a finalist for the Pulitzer Prize for Fiction. The novel emphasizes Tyler's main theme, the family and the individual's conflicting relationship to the family. Three years later, Tyler proved that she could only get better. *The Accidental Tourist* received another nomination as a finalist for the Pulitzer and won the coveted National Book Critics Circle Award. In 1988, it was made into a motion picture starring William Hurt, Kathleen Turner, and Geena Davis, who won an Academy Award as Best Supporting Actress for her portrayal of Muriel Pritchett.

The year 1988 also brought the publication of Tyler's most honored novel, *Breathing Lessons*, which was awarded the Pulitzer Prize for Fiction the following year. The novel, one of Tyler's funniest, chronicles a day in the life of an "ordinary" marriage. Within the Aristotelian timeframe of the novel, Tyler convinces us that no day is ordinary and certainly no marriage is. In fact, in a book review she wrote in 1987, while she was composing *Breathing Lessons*, Tyler asserted that "an ordinary, run-of-the-mill marriage has in many ways a more dramatic plot than any thriller ever written."

Sticking to her Baltimore home, Tyler then wrote *Saint Maybe* (1991). Unusual for its attention to the subject of religion, *Saint Maybe* nevertheless maintains Tyler's interest in exploring the tension between an individual's conflicting needs for freedom and connection to others, especially family. Then in 1995 came *Ladder of Years*, Tyler's latest exploration of the circular nature of time. In this novel, the heroine, Delia Grinstead, escapes from her family only to return to them a year and a half later, having learned that she was really just struggling to accept the loss of her own children, who are growing up and moving away from her.

Who knows what Tyler will produce next? Whatever she comes up with, though, it will be human and moving and, probably, very funny. For Anne

Tyler is a novelist with a tragicomic vision, someone who sees the sadness of life and yet can still find something to laugh about. Or perhaps, like her characters, she has simply learned that that is the best way to get through life.

Anne Tyler's Themes

Almost everything that Anne Tyler has ever written contains an inherent paradox. On the one hand, the world she writes about is an ordinary world, a circumscribed world, limited to home and family, and she rarely ventures far from those subjects. Yet the journeys her characters make are nevertheless far-ranging, for they are journeys of self-exploration. During these journeys Tyler's characters attempt to learn more about themselves and their places in the world.

The chief vehicle that Tyler uses to express this contradictory vision of life is the family. The human family is the basic unit of all society. It is the one common construct that all societies share. Even so, the reaction of people to their families is uniquely individual for each person. Tyler loves to explore the tension between an individual character and his or her family, exploring the ways in which family relationships are formed; how, if ever, they change; and the ways in which each member of a family affects other family members. Oddly, on the one hand, the family is nurturing, giving the individual his or her very identity. Because of the day-to-day contact between the individual and the family, however, the individual sometimes begins to feel restricted or even imprisoned.

Such is the case in *Saint Maybe*, where Ian Bedloe feels these contradictory emotions. At first Ian is a 17-year-old boy eager to conquer the world. Yet Ian's guilt over causing his brother Danny's death causes him to return to his family and take over the responsibility for them for the rest of his life. After some soul-searching, however, Ian eventually works through his feelings of restrictedness and accepts his position in the family. At other times the effects of family can almost paralyze a person, as in the case of Macon Leary of *The Accidental Tourist*. Returning to the clutches of his baked potato–eating family, Macon remains there, at first literally immobilized in a cast, until Muriel Pritchett comes along and frees him. Or take the case of *Dinner at the Homesick Restaurant*, whose title suggests the contradictory effects of family on the individual. On the one hand, the family nurtures and provides a base for the individual so that when a person is away, he or she does miss home, thus producing a feeling of homesickness. At the same time, if the family does not provide the right influences or the proper measure of nurturing, then the home can produce psychological and emotional sicknesses in its members. Cody Tull, for instance, cannot overcome the effects of his father's desertion. He spends his whole life viewing time only as a commodity useful for making more money. Cody's sister, Jenny Tull, who suffers the most debilitating effects from her mother Pearl's abuse, becomes anorexic. Worse still, she repeats the cycle of child abuse with her own daughter Becky. Finally, Ezra Tull, whose restaurant provides the scene for many of the unfinished family dinners in the novel, fails to maintain the one relationship that would have connected him to the rest of the world and made his break from his family successful. Instead, Cody runs away with Ezra's fiancée, Ruth Spivey, leaving Ezra to attempt to recreate a substitute family in the guise of a series of family dinners that never quite come off. Essentially, he spends the rest of his life alone, never leaving his mother's home and living only through the lives of the people who work and eat in his restaurant.

In response to the family's restrictiveness, many of Tyler's characters dream about escape. They yearn for the freedom that they think they will find out on their own in the world. Yet what usually develops in Tyler's novels is a sort of escape/return paradigm. Her characters run away from home but then return later to their original situations. In *The Clock Winder*, Elizabeth Abbott flees the neediness of the Emerson household only to return and marry into it, thus permanently assuming both the Emerson name and identity. In *Earthly Possessions*, when Charlotte Emory decides to leave her stultifying family, she receives some outside help in the guise of her bumbling bank robber/kidnapper, Jake Simms. Later, however, on her own initiative, she decides to return home. In Tyler's latest novel, *Ladder of Years*, Delia Grinstead walks off down the beach to escape her family only to return at the end of the novel, having realized that she was really running away from herself.

Even those characters who seem to make successful breaks from their families don't really change their situations as much as they think they do. Justine Peck, in *Searching for Caleb*, who spends her whole life trying to escape her Peck ancestry, marries her own cousin and winds up joining a traveling carnival and telling fortunes, just as she has always done. Although Morgan Gower, in *Morgan's Passing*, leaves his wife Bonny, he only winds up replacing Leon Meredith as Emily Meredith's husband and fellow puppeteer. In effect, he is merely playing another role, as he has all his adult life. And Macon Leary, in *The Accidental Tourist*, after breaking away from his marriage to Sarah, quickly attaches himself to Muriel Pritchett, another woman with a child.

Another recurrent theme in Tyler's work is her fascination with art. As a writer herself, Tyler understands the tension between the outside world and the inner creative world of the artist, whether he or she be a writer, painter, sculptor, or musician, or any of a number of other crafts that provide Tyler's characters with creative outlets. In *The Tin Can Tree*, James Green is a photographer whose pictures attempt to impose an order on the world both of the subject and the photographer. More important, for a moment, these photographs stop the passage of time, giving the artist an opportunity to view the world at a moment in which the flux of the world has been arrested so that it can be examined. This order imposed by the artist is his or her unique vision of the world. It gives the artist tremendous power. At the end of *The Tin Can Tree*, when Joan Pike replaces James as photographer, she realizes this artistic power to capture the lives of the characters she has been trying to understand, unsuccessfully, over the course of the novel. Yet, in this one instant of time, as she focuses the camera's lens on her subjects, she is able to capture and, perhaps, comprehend them for the first time.

In *Earthly Possessions*, Charlotte Emory uses this same technique of photography. Having inherited her father's photography studio, Charlotte spends a lifetime taking pictures of strangers. Unlike her father, however, Charlotte allows her customers to wear whatever outfits they like. Usually, the customers, thinking that they are hiding their true identities, choose outlandish costumes. What Charlotte discovers, though, is that these disguises ultimately reveal much more than they conceal about her subjects' lives.

Other types of artists that Tyler incorporates into her works include writers, such as Macon Leary in *The Accidental Tourist*, who writes a series of guidebooks for travelers who don't like to leave home. On the surface, Macon's concern as a writer is rather mundane, chronicling as he does the deterioration of various hotels and restaurants. Yet, in the actual task of writing, Macon is an artist fascinated with points of grammar and diction. Thus, in his books he creates another world, a place ordered according to his unique vision of life.

Still other characters gain satisfaction from other creative outlets. Ira Moran, in *Breathing Lessons*, is a framemaker who frames the ordinary works of other people, such as needlepoint and photographs. In a way this activity hardly seems an art. In her novels, however, this is exactly what Tyler attempts to do: capture the ordinary aspects of life and reveal how unordinary they really are. This process makes her, as a writer, not so much a commentator on life in the last half of the twentieth century as an observer of life. Ira's simple job of framing these ordinary artifacts shows his own attempts to create order and to comprehend the ordinary. In *Saint Maybe*, Ian's job as a furniture maker creates a sense of his craftsmanship and his unique ability to order his world. In his mind, having caused the death of his brother Danny, Ian does not want to work on any furniture that does not have straight lines that can easily be mended if he messes them up, unlike human lives. By the end of the novel, however, he has grown as an individual and as an artisan. Thus, by the time he is expecting his son Joshua, Ian's attitude toward furniture-making has changed. As he works on a cradle for his son, Ian begins to appreciate the curves of the cradle as they bend off beyond the horizon of his thoughts.

The most important artist figure in all of Tyler's fiction is Jeremy Pauling of *Celestial Navigation*, the character who she has admitted is perhaps the closest to her own personality, although she herself is neither as reclusive nor as ineffectual as Jeremy. Over the course of the novel, Jeremy's sculptures grow from small, flat structures to fully rounded, three-dimensional creations. His sensibility of looking at the world and noticing texture and form more than character is Tyler's attempt to recreate the workings of the mind of the artist. In fact, the agoraphobic Jeremy can make sense of the outer world only by first ordering it and then translating it into an artistic creation.

Besides art, Tyler's characters attempt to impose order on their worlds in other ways. Macon Leary's systems in *The Accidental Tourist* are his attempt to create an orderly world safe from the dangers of the outside world, which has taken the life of his son Ethan. Mrs. Emerson's clocks in *The Clock Winder*, all ticking in synchronization, or at least as close as she can manage until Elizabeth Abbott shows up to set them straight, are another symbol of the attempt to achieve and maintain order. In addition, Mrs. Emerson's letters, dictated first into a dictaphone so that she can organize her thoughts, are still another example of a character's attempt to bring order into his or her chaotic life. Another set of letters, the Pecks' obligatory bread-and-butter thank you notes, imprint an order on the behavior of the members of the Peck family. Even Caleb, who has been away from the rest of the family for sixty years, feels compelled to send one of these cryptic missives to Justine after he leaves.

The world, however, is not an orderly place. Often Tyler's characters must face that fact and try to cope with this chaos in a variety of different ways. Many of them have fascinations with games that are played according to rules and have definite winners and losers. Cody Tull, in *Dinner at the Homesick Restaurant*, loves Monopoly, at which he cheats to win. In *Breathing Lessons*, Ira plays solitaire. In *Saint Maybe*, Ian Bedloe plays parcheesi with his niece and nephew after the death of his brother. But the dice that roll in that game provide further evidence of the chanciness of life.

Many of Tyler's characters depend on various versions of luck or chance, even fortunetellers, to help them chart their courses through life. In *Dinner at the Homesick Restaurant*, Jenny Tull visits a fortuneteller before she marries for the first time. The fortuneteller advises her to marry to avoid having love destroy her. Justine Peck, in *Searching for Caleb*, actually becomes a fortuneteller herself. Her advice to most of her customers is to accept change, to take risks, to launch out into new ventures, and to get outside themselves. Strangely, many of Justine's customers don't take her advice, although at the end of the novel Justine, whose whole life has been one long move from one town to the next following her husband Duncan, finally accepts change as an integral part of life and settles down in a traveling carnival show.

What to do in a world of change becomes a critical question for Tyler's characters. Ever since her first novel, Tyler has been fascinated with exploring and re-exploring this theme. In *If Morning Ever Comes*, Ben Joe Hawkes, after caring for his family of women, has finally moved on with his life, having left North Carolina for New York, where he attends Columbia Law School. But when a family crisis arises, his sister Joanne's leaving her husband and coming home, Ben Joe feels compelled to return home to Sandhill, North Carolina, to look after his family. When he arrives, however, what he discovers is that his family really no longer needs him. In the end, it is he who takes a piece of home and his past, in the form of his old girlfriend Shelley Domer, back to New York, where he plans to continue his life. In *The Tin Can Tree*, Joan Pike goes through a similar crisis and resolution. Unable to help her Aunt Lou, whose daughter Janie Rose has just died, and unable to convince her longtime fiance, James Green, to abandon his hypochondriacal brother Ansel and marry her, Joan finally leaves. On the bus, however, Joan realizes that she must return home. Ironically, when she returns, she learns that another crisis has occupied the attention of her family: her young cousin Simon's running away. Therefore Joan fits seamlessly back into the flow of their lives, with no one except Simon and Ansel ever realizing that she has been gone. In *A Slipping-Down Life*, Evie Decker yearns for change. Thinking that she has found it in the form of rebel rock singer Drumstrings Casey, Evie goes so far as to cut his name on her forehead. In the end, however, she discovers that Drum is an ordinary person and an undependable provider. Thus, for the benefit of her coming child, Evie returns to her father's house to establish a life for her baby.

Another key element in Tyler's fiction is her treatment of time. For Tyler, time is circular and reflexive. Her characters move along the flow of time, almost unaware of its passage, until through their memories they reflect back on the enormous changes that time has brought about, or, in some cases, the lack of change that time has produced. Since time is circular, characters often find themselves back where they started. In *Saint Maybe*, as Ian walks downstairs to present his new son Joshua to his family, he thinks back to the time when his brother Danny had presented his new daughter Daphne, now a grown young woman, to the family. In *The Accidental Tourist*, Macon Leary finds himself buying clothes for another little boy and getting as much pleasure from Alexander's enthusiastic response as Macon had with his son Ethan a few years earlier.

Tyler's greatest exploration of time occurs in *Breathing Lessons*, with its Aristotelian one-day timeframe. Through memory, Tyler manages to present Maggie and Ira Moran's 28-year marriage in its entirety, revealing what has made them the people they are and how their marriage has evolved and endured. In *Searching for Caleb*, Tyler's timeframe expands to nearly a century, but her message remains the same as the old French saying: "The more things change, the more they remain the same." Thus, in the Peck family, everything imaginable happens, but the essential nature of the Pecks remains constant through several generations.

In the midst of all this passage of time, Tyler manages to infuse her novels with a unique sense of humor. Her humor has often been praised, but rarely understood for its complexity. Tyler's humor encompasses a unique blend of the comic and the tragic. She cannot seem to make up her mind whether life is essentially a comic farce or a tragedy that we must laugh at to endure. What results then is a type of self-abnegating humor that, on the surface, is hysterically funny, yet which, underneath, contains a contradictory serious-ness. Each of Tyler's comic scenes presents a unique blend of the quirky and the eccentric. Underneath, however, always lurks that dark, tragic pa-thos representing the underside of the human experience.

In *Ladder of Years*, Adrian Bly-Brice's mother-in-law interrupts the Grin-steads' family dinner to accuse Delia Grinstead of breaking up her daughter's marriage. Everyone present, except Delia, who knows that the woman is speaking the truth, considers even the possibility of Delia having an affair absurd. In *Saint Maybe*, Daphne Bedloe relates her "dream" of a fat stranger chasing her uncle Ian. In *Breathing Lessons*, Maggie Moran lurches out into the street in a newly repaired car straight into the path of an oncoming Pepsi truck. In *The Clock Winder*, Timothy Emerson and Elizabeth Abbott run around chasing a turkey.

While all of these scenes are quite funny on the surface, they nevertheless reveal, on closer inspection, a tragic underside. The reader's sympathy is aroused by the elderly mother-in-law's confusion after Delia denies her charges in *Ladder of Years*. Furthermore, Delia's own conflicting feelings of relief (at not having been found out) and anger (at her family's dismissive attitude) stir up emotions that will ultimately cause her to walk out on her family. In *Saint Maybe*, everyone at the dinner table is sobered by Daphne's humiliation of the unsuspecting Sister Harriet. In *Breathing Lessons*, the injury that Maggie barely avoids only highlights the haphazard fashion in which she lives her life and the unrealistic manner in which she confronts, or fails to confront, the problems in her life. And in *The Clock Winder*, the turkey's escape is only temporary. More disturbing, the turkey's bloody death reveals the underlying tension in Timothy's (and the other Emerson children's) relationship with his mother. Thus, Tyler's humor, while making us laugh, almost immediately also sobers us and makes us think.

Ultimately, however, Tyler's humor illustrates the endurance of the human spirit. The foreigners' shenanigans in *Saint Maybe* provide a good example of this aspect of Tyler's humor. As they struggle to make their way in a foreign land, negotiating the language and customs of another culture, they nevertheless manage to retain a joy for living that cannot be quenched by a few burning radios or an errant garage door opener.

This endurance of the foreigners is typical of many Tyler characters. Ordinary life presents challenges and obstacles to each of them that could be, but usually somehow aren't, overwhelming. For instance, Tyler's characters often struggle with issues of dependency. As parents, they worry about the tremendous responsibility, expense, and time that raising children requires. Some characters feel overburdened by the responsibility. Pearl Tull in *Dinner at the Homesick Restaurant*, Ian Bedloe in *Saint Maybe*, and Macon Leary in *The Accidental Tourist* all worry and strain to meet the physical and emotional needs of their children. Although they are not always completely successful, they usually manage to fulfill their responsibilities as parents. The only character who completely fails to uphold his parental obligations is Jeremy Pauling in *Celestial Navigation*, whose artistic vision won't allow him the latitude to relate to children on their level.

From the opposite perspective, the children of these struggling parents often experience similar conflicting feelings toward their parents. The Emerson children in *The Clock Winder* are all devoted to their overbearing mother, even as they attempt to escape, unsuccessfully, from her influence. In *Saint Maybe*, perhaps Tyler's most insightful portrayal of children's viewpoints, she shows the struggles of Agatha Bedloe as she attempts to cope with her mother's emotional breakdown, Thomas Bedloe as he tries to grow up without his mother, and Daphne Bedloe as she searches for an identity in the family. All three children come to view their uncle, Ian Bedloe, very differently as they grow older. At first, he is their hero; later he becomes an embarrassment and a worry until he meets Rita diCarlo and establishes his own family. And in *Dinner at the Homesick Restaurant*, Cody, Ezra, and Jenny Tull all blame their mother in varying degrees for their problems, yet, as Jenny points out, they all turn out all right in the end. So how bad could their childhood really have been? It seems that most of Tyler's children ultimately come to accept Elizabeth Abbott's somewhat awed view of the parent/child relationship in *The Clock Winder*. As she watches a parade outside in the street and notices the crowd of people watching it, Elizabeth realizes that each person on the face of the earth must have had a parent to get him or her through childhood. That knowledge gives her the courage to tackle parenthood herself.

The most complex relationship that Tyler explores, however, is marriage.

In *Breathing Lessons*, Maggie Moran's friend Serena Gill tells her that marriage is not like a movie. It is too real to be summed up in such a facile fantasy. Through the years, Maggie and Ira Moran's marriage changes and grows as they experience their share of highs and an equal number of lowpoints. Often Maggie and Ira get on each other's nerves. After all, marriage is a closer relationship than even parent and child. Even so, as Ira notes, after being married to Maggie for over twenty years, neither he nor she can really tell how deeply they are tied to each other by their common experience and by love. In The *Accidental Tourist*, a slightly different view of marriage is posited, one of a marriage whose roots have not managed to extend deep enough to bridge the gap that opens between Macon and Sarah Leary following their son Ethan's death. In *Earthly Possessions*, Charlotte Emory's final acceptance of her husband Saul occurs only after her "escape" has taught her that living with Saul all these years has bound her to him in spirit more than all the houses and furniture in the world ever could.

Marriage, thus, for Tyler is real, no fairy tale. Yet she often uses fairy tales as a foundation for her stories. *Morgan's Passing*, for instance, opens with a puppet version of Cinderella. By the end of the novel, Morgan has become Emily's Prince Charming, albeit a very different sort of prince. These fairy tales appeal to Tyler and to us because they offer simple explanations for the complex questions of life. But what Tyler shows us in her work is that beneath the simple, ordinary fabric of life is a mixture of the sublime and the ridiculous and the real that both transcend and extend the imaginative reach of any fairy tale. The bitter truth is that real life may not always offer a happy ending. That doesn't matter, though, because the true adventure is the journey itself. And Tyler's novels take us along on those fascinating journeys.

Works, Characters, Themes, and Motifs

A

Christopher Abbott. (MP) Molly Gower Abbott's son; Morgan and Bonny Gower's grandson.

Elizabeth Priscilla Abbott. (CW) young woman who becomes a handyman to Mrs. Emerson; she marries Matthew Emerson.

Reverend John Abbott. (CW) Elizabeth Abbott's father; minister of Faith Baptist Church in Ellington, North Carolina.

Mrs. Julia Abbott. (CW) Elizabeth Abbott's mother.

Molly Gower Abbott. (MP) See MOLLY GOWER.

Uncle Abbott. ("Dry") Liz Anders' brother, who lives with her family and works at a saw shop.

abortion. (BL, MP) Tyler tackles the complex issue of abortion in *Breathing Lessons* when Maggie prevents Fiona from going through with her abortion. Despite her success with Fiona, however, Maggie, citing "constitutional permission" (BL 242), confronts the protestors at the abortion clinic. Ironically, the protestors' objective in this case is the same as hers—to convince Fiona not to have the abortion. Thus, while abortion in principle seems acceptable to Tyler, in practice, however, she seems not to approve of it in individual cases. In *Morgan's Passing*, Emily Meredith also rejects abortion as an option when Morgan Gower gets her pregnant.

Jo Ann Dermott Abrams. (BL) friend of Maggie Moran and Serena Gill's who reads the Kahlil Gibran passage about death at Max Gill's funeral, just as she had read the passage on marriage at his and Serena's wedding; she had married Nat Abrams.

Nat Abrams. (BL) a classmate of Ira Moran's, who was a few years ahead of Maggie and Serena's class; he stays to himself at the funeral; he had married Jo Ann Dermott.

absent fathers. ("As the Earth," AT, "Average," BL, CN, CW, DHR, "Dry," IMEC, SM, "Street," "Two People," "Who Would Want") Many of Tyler's characters are fatherless due to death or desertion. Sammy in "A Street of Bugles," Jason Schmidt in "Who Would Want a Little Boy," the Tull children in *Dinner at the Homesick Restaurant*, the Learys in *The Accidental Tourist*, the Emerson children in *The Clock Winder*, the Paulings in *Celestial Navigation*, and the Hawkes children in *If Morning Ever Comes* are all functioning without a male parent. In other cases, although a father is present, he is often either ineffectual or dependent on his children, as in the case of Doug Bedloe in *Saint Maybe* or Sam Moran in *Breathing Lessons*. Perhaps this lack of paternal support is one reason why so many of Tyler's characters often feel isolated from themselves and others and why they struggle so hard to establish identities for themselves.

The Accidental Tourist. One of Tyler's funniest novels, *The Accidental Tourist* is also her one novel that has been made into a major motion picture. Lawrence Kasdan's 1988 film version of the novel starred William Hurt as Macon Leary, Kathleen Turner as Sarah Leary, and Geena Davis as Muriel Pritchett, a role for which she won an Academy Award.

The novel's title is one of Tyler's best, for it perfectly expresses her philosophy of life. The possibility for order, change, and choice in anyone's life is uncertain; therefore, like the Learys in the novel, many people pull in their horns and isolate themselves for fear of getting hurt. Yet, whether they like it or not, the process of time and life puts everyone on a journey that encompasses all those elements. Everyone is a tourist. Macon Leary is simply a tourist who attempts to reconcile these conflicting desires for change and stability.

At the start of the novel, Macon is stagnating in his search for order. His reaction to his son Ethan's death is to retreat into his Macon Leary Body Bag and ignore the rest of the world. Ultimately, he insulates himself even further by falling down his basement stairs and breaking his leg, thus prompting his physical encasement in a cast. Then he retreats even deeper into himself by returning to the insular Leary family home, run by his sister Rose, whose obsessive alphabetizing and caregiving to neighbors and Macon's other two divorced brothers, who have retreated home before him, only serve to highlight her own repressed life.

In order to break out of the stagnation of this life, Macon needs the aid of an outsider, someone who does not fit into the Leary world in which his family plays a game called Vaccination with rules so arcane that only the Leary siblings can grasp them. That aid comes in the form of frizzy-haired Muriel Pritchett, a dog trainer who takes on the task of helping Ethan's dog, Edward, overcome his anger at being abandoned, in addition to facilitating Macon's working through his own grief over Ethan's death. For a while, Macon succeeds in reaching outside himself as he becomes more and more involved in Muriel's life, as well as the life of her son Alexander. Unfortunately, Macon falters, succumbing to his fear of change and settling back into his familiar life with his wife Sarah, from whom he had been separated. In the end, however, Muriel Pritchett's persistence pays off. After Muriel follows Macon to Paris, he finally realizes that Muriel offers him his one chance to escape his restrictive past, so he decides to leave Sarah again and live with Muriel. Although his life will now contain all the dangers and uncertainties of change that he has avoided his entire life, in making this decision, Macon is taking a positive step. His decision to move on with his life completes his psychological healing and frees him to risk loving another person again.

For Further Reading

Almond, Barbara R. "The Accidental Therapist: Intrapsychic Change in a Novel." *Literature and Psychology* 38 (Spring-Summer 1992): 84–104.

Croft, Robert W. *Anne Tyler: A Bio-Bibliography.* Westport, CT: Greenwood Press, 1995. 76–81.

English, Sarah. *"The Accidental Tourist* and *The Odyssey." Anne Tyler as Novelist.* Ed. Dale Salwak. Iowa City: University of Iowa Press, 1994. 155–61.

Evans, Elizabeth. *Anne Tyler.* New York: Twayne, 1993.

Freiert, William K. "Anne Tyler's Accidental Ulysses." *Classical and Modern Literature* 10 (Fall 1989): 71–79.

Humphrey, Lin T. "Exploration of a Not-So-Accidental Novel." *Anne Tyler as Novelist.* Ed. Dale Salwak. Iowa City: University of Iowa Press, 1994: 147–54.

Petry, Alice Hall. *Understanding Anne Tyler.* Columbia: University of South Carolina Press, 1990. 210–32.

Voelker, Joseph C. *Art and the Accidental in Anne Tyler.* Columbia: University of Missouri Press, 1989. 147–64.

Selected Book Reviews

Eder, Richard. *Los Angeles Times Book Review* 15 Sept. 1985: 3+.

Mars-Jones, Adam. "Despairs of a Time-and-Motion Man." *Times Literary Supplement* 4 October 1985: 1096.

Mathewson, Joseph. "Taking the Anne Tyler Tour." *Horizon* Sept. 1985: 14. [Reprinted in *Critical Essays on Anne Tyler*. Ed. Alice Hall Petry. New York: G.K. Hall, 1992: 123–25.]

McMurtry, Larry. "Life Is a Foreign Country." *New York Times Book Review* 8 September 1985: 1+. [Reprinted in *Critical Essays on Anne Tyler*. Ed. Alice Hall Petry. New York: G. K. Hall, 1992: 132–36.]

Olson, Clarence E. "The Wonderfully Wacky World of Anne Tyler." *St. Louis Post-Dispatch* 8 Sept. 1985: B4.

Prescott, Peter S. "Watching Life Go By." *Newsweek* 9 Sept. 1985: 92. [Reprinted in *Critical Essays on Anne Tyler*. Ed. Alice Hall Petry. New York: G. K. Hall, 1992: 117–18.]

Updike, John. "Leaving Home." *New Yorker* 28 Oct. 1985: 106–8+. [Reprinted in *Critical Essays on Anne Tyler*. Ed. Alice Hall Petry. New York: G. K. Hall, 1992: 126–31.]

Yardley, Jonathan. "Anne Tyler's Family Circles." *Washington Post Book World* 25 Aug. 1985: 3. [Reprinted in *Critical Essays on Anne Tyler*. Ed. Alice Hall Petry. New York: G. K. Hall, 1992: 119–22.]

accidents. (AT, BL, SM, MP, TCT) Accidents occur unexpectedly in Anne Tyler's fiction, just as they do in real life. Unlike real life, however, Anne Tyler can sometimes turn these mishaps into humor, as in the case of Macon Leary's tumble down the basement stairs in *The Accidental Tourist* or Maggie Moran's fender bender with a Pepsi truck in *Breathing Lessons*. In other cases, however, only tragedy results, such as Danny Bedloe's fatal car crash in *Saint Maybe* or Janie Rose Pike's deadly tractor accident in *The Tin Can Tree*. In these instances, Tyler's gaze turns away from the tragedy itself and concentrates on the aftermath of the event and how it affects those who remain alive.

advertisements. (AT, BL, EP, MP, SC) Like Flannery O'Connor's road signs, Anne Tyler's use of popular culture, especially advertising, adds an immediacy to her work, as well as a layer of social commentary. Tyler's characters sing the latest jingles and notice bumper stickers as they drive along. Perhaps the most influential instance of this phenomenon occurs in *Earthly Possessions*, where Charlotte Emory's cereal box message becomes her life motto: "Keep on Truckin'."

affairs. (IMEC, LY, MP) The affairs in Anne Tyler's novels are very civilized. In *If Morning Ever Comes*, Phillip Hawkes' long-term relationship with Lili Belle Mosely is never openly challenged by his wife. Eventually, Phillip and Lili Belle even produce a child together. In *Morgan's Passing*, Morgan Gower and Emily Meredith conduct an ongoing affair that also produces a child, a complication that precipitates Morgan's switch from his life with his wife Bonny to a new life with Emily, a life in which he simply replaces Emily's old husband Leon. In *Ladder of Years*, Delia Grinstead's unconsummated affair with Adrian Bly-Brice produces only humor from their first meeting in a grocery story to the hilarious visit of Adrian's mother-in-law when she crashes Delia's family dinner. Ultimately, the affair is less about romance and more about Delia's ineptitude, as well as her restless search to accept the changes in her life.

African American characters. (BL, CW, "Common," "Geologist," IMEC, LY, "Misstep," SC, SDL, TCT) Although Tyler has sometimes been criticized for the scarcity of African American characters in her most recent work, the truth is that Tyler's stories and novels do contain many African American characters. Recent works do seem to place these characters in minor roles, such as Rick Rackley in *Ladder of Years*, but in *Breathing Lessons* one of the major characters is Mr. Otis, whose commentary on married life reinforces the novel's ongoing theme: what makes a happy marriage.

Earlier novels and stories, especially those with North Carolina settings, however, do incorporate more African American characters. Although many of these characters are maids, they nonetheless serve important roles. In *A Slipping-Down Life*, Clotelia acts as a mother substitute for Evie Decker. In "The Geologist's Maid," Bennett Johnson lives vicariously through his maid Maroon's more colorful life. In *The Tin Can Tree*, Missouri expresses the novel's theme: "Bravest thing about people . . . is how they go on loving mortal beings after finding out there's such a thing as dying" (TCT 106).

For Further Reading

Petry, Alice Hall. "Bright Books of Life: The Black Norm in Anne Tyler's Novels." *Southern Quarterly* 31 (Fall 1992): 7–13.

Mr. Aggers. (AT) manager of the Buford Hotel that Macon Leary visits in New York City.

aging. (BL, CW, "Feather," IMEC, LY, MP, SC, SM, "With All Flags," "Woman") Anne Tyler once said that she thought she could spend her whole life writing about old men. Her interest in and compassion for the elderly are readily apparent throughout her entire oeurve. From Gram, in her first novel, *If Morning Ever Comes*, to Nat Moffat in her latest novel, *Ladder of Years*, Anne Tyler presents her older characters with great dignity. In *The Clock Winder*, Elizabeth Abbott nurses the dying Mr. Cunningham. In *Breathing Lessons*, Mr. Daniel Otis elicits Maggie's sympathy. In *Saint Maybe*, Doug Bedloe struggles to adjust to retirement. This dignity that Tyler's elderly characters strive for is highlighted in "With All Flags Flying," where Mr. Carpenter chooses to move into an old folks' home rather than become a burden to his family. The most comprehensive treatment of an elderly character, however, occurs in *Searching for Caleb*, where Daniel Peck, a character modeled after Tyler's own grandfather, searches valiantly for his long-lost brother Caleb.

agoraphobia. (BL, CN, "Holding") In *Celestial Navigation*, Jeremy Pauling suffers from a debilitating case of agoraphobia. Sheltered by his mother as he was growing up, Jeremy retreats further and further into the family boardinghouse and, ultimately, into his own world of art. Eventually he feels like he is "marooned on some island" (CN 100). Even Mary Tell cannot permanently rescue him from his self-imposed isolation.

Aileen. (LY) Senior City resident who attends Nat and Binky Moffat's wedding.

airplanes. (AT, DHR) Airplanes play a role in *The Accidental Tourist* by providing the cocoon-like travel mode necessary for a man like Macon Leary, who would rather stay home than travel to other places. Ironically, however, thanks to the airplane, Macon ventures further away from home than any of Tyler's other characters—all the way to Paris. In another use of the airplane motif, at the end of *Dinner at the Homesick Restaurant*, Cody Tull remembers an airplane droning overhead, providing a bird's-eye view of time, as the arrow that he had caused his brother Ezra to shoot off course sailed toward their mother.

Chuck Akers. (LY) young policeman who comes to check up on Delia Grinstead in Bay Borough.

Al. ("Dry") one of Jonas Anders' friends who helps with the plan to scatter Uncle Wurssun's ashes.

Herbie Albright. (BL) childhood friend of Jesse Moran's.

John Albright. (AT) Sarah Leary's divorce attorney.

alcoholism. (EP, "Outside," SM, TCT) None of Tyler's major characters fall prey to this disease. A few minor characters, however, such as Mr. Kitt in *Saint Maybe*, Mr. Douglas in "Outside," Ansel Green in *The Tin Can Tree*, and some of Saul Emory's recovering church members in *Earthly Possessions*, do have drinking problems.

Mr. Alden. (BL) Maggie Moran and Serena Gill's high school civics teacher.

Alexander. (DHR) bagboy at Sweeney Brothers Grocery when Pearl Tull first starts working there in 1944.

Alicia. (DHR) Ezra Tull's cat who knows how to yawn.

Myrtle Allingham. (LY) older neighbor and patient of Sam Grinstead's with a bad hip who invites the Grinsteads to dinner; she later dies of a stroke.

alphabetizing. (AT, SDL) See ORDER.

Alvareen. (CW) the African American maid Mrs. Emerson hires to replace Emmeline Babcock; her husband suffers from arthritis.

Mr. Ambrose. (SC) Justine and Duncan Peck's Semple, Virginia, neighbor, who helps Duncan load their mattresses when they move to Caro Mill, Maryland.

Mrs. Ambrose. (SC) Mr. Ambrose's wife.

Lacey Debney Ames. (EP) Charlotte Emory's obese mother; a former first grade teacher.

Murray Ames. (EP) Charlotte Emory's father; a photographer.

Arthur Amherst. (MP) stable history professor Bonny Gower starts dating after Morgan Gower leaves her.

Silas Amsel. (SC) fat, bearded owner of the Blue Bottle Antique shop in Caro Mill, Maryland, who gives Duncan Peck a job; he is Lucy Peck's sister's brother-in-law.

Arn Anders. ("Dry") Liz Anders' 6-year-old son.

Jonas Anders. ("Dry") Arn Anders' 13-year-old brother, who usually wakes him up; he runs away from home repeatedly.

Liz Anders. ("Dry") Arn, Jonas, and Samuel Anders' mother; a beautician whose ne'er-do-well husband was accidentally run over and killed while he was loafing in front of the feed store.

Lucille Anders. ("Dry") Walston Anders' long-suffering wife, who sends his family his ashes.

Samuel Anders. ("Dry") Arn Anders' oldest brother, age 17, who has a paper route and works at a garage.

Walston Anders. ("Dry") Arn Anders' uncle (his dead father's brother), who was nicknamed "Wurssun" because he was the worst of the lot; he kills himself and requests that his ashes be scattered on Penobscot Bay in Maine.

Andrew. (SM) one of Ian Bedloe's best friends when he is a teenager; he eventually goes to graduate school at Tulane.

Angie. (SM) Thomas Bedloe's fiancée; a rather bossy woman of whom the other family members do not really approve, but say nothing about out of consideration for Thomas.

Anna. (EP) daughter of the dark-haired European immigrant woman who kidnapped Charlotte Emory at the fair when Charlotte was a young girl.

Anna. ("Knack") Mark Sebastiani's older, married sister.

anorexia. (DHR, EP) In *Dinner at the Homesick Restaurant*, Jenny Tull suffers from anorexia, a symptom of the lack of emotional support her mother, Pearl, gives to her while she is growing up. Unfortunately, this cycle of child abuse continues into the next generation. Jenny's daughter Becky also receives too little emotional support from Jenny, who is raising Becky during the time when she is going through medical school, having just been abandoned by her second husband. Becky's case of anorexia is even more severe than Jenny's.

Mrs. Apple. (MP) Victor Apple's mother, who owns Crafts Unlimited, the store above which Emily and Leon Meredith live in a third-floor apartment.

Victor Apple. (MP) member of Off the Cuff improvisational group, whose mother lives in Baltimore.

appliances. (BL, CN) See GADGETS.

archery. (DHR) A pivotal motif in *Dinner at the Homesick Restaurant*, the fateful picnic during which Cody causes Ezra's arrow to stray off course and hit Pearl provides the reason for Cody's life-long guilt at causing his father's desertion.

Ahmad Ardavi. ("Uncle") Hassan Ardavi's wealthy, larger-than-life Iranian uncle, who looks like a 7-foot tall "Mr. Clean."

Ali Ardavi. ("Your Place") Hassan Ardavi's older brother, who died four years earlier of a brain hemorrhage; he was always weak and a cause of constant worry for his mother.

Babak Ardavi. ("Your Place") Hassan Ardavi's younger brother, whose marriage Mrs. Ardavi has recently arranged.

Elizabeth Ardavi. ("Uncle," "Your Place") Hassan Ardavi's American wife, who caters to Uncle Ahmad and her mother-in-law at first but then grows tired of their demands and interference as their visits grow longer.

Hassan Ardavi. ("Uncle," "Your Place") Elizabeth Ardavi's Iranian husband, a doctor who has lived in America for several years; in "Uncle Ahmad," his favorite relative, Uncle Ahmad, comes for an extended visit; in "Your Place is Empty," Hassan's mother stays for almost five months.

Hilary Ardavi. ("Uncle," "Your Place") Elizabeth and Hassan Ardavi's oldest daughter, who is not quite two when her grandmother comes to visit in "Your Place is Empty." In "Uncle Ahmad" she thinks of Uncle Ahmad as a magician.

Jenny Ardavi. ("Uncle") Elizabeth and Hassan Ardavi's younger daughter, who thinks of Uncle Ahmad as a magician.

Mr. Ardavi. ("Your Place") Hassan Ardavi's father, who died of a liver ailment six years after he married Mrs. Ardavi, forcing her to move back in with her family to raise their three sons.

Mrs. Ardavi. ("Your Place") Hassan Ardavi's widowed mother, who visits from Iran.

Mr. Armistead. (AT) the sculptor Sarah Leary studies with on Saturdays.

army. (CW, DHR, SM) Tyler's characters' experience with anything military is extremely limited, perhaps stemming from her own Quaker pacifism. When a character does go off to the army, more often than not he returns quickly and safely, as is the case with Ezra Tull in *Dinner at the Homesick Restaurant*, whose sleepwalking gains him a quick discharge, and Ian Bedloe in *Saint Maybe*, whose convenient heart murmur keeps him out of the service altogether. Only Peter Emerson, in *The Clock Winder*, actually serves time in Vietnam, but even he returns unhurt. In fact, he seems more affected by his Emerson upbringing than by any negative war experiences.

art. ("Bridge," CN, CW, IMEC, TCT) Tyler has a keen interest in art, especially in *Celestial Navigation*, where her artist figure, Jeremy Pauling, the character who is most like herself, views the world through an artist's eyes. In "The Bridge," an early short story, Tyler uses Harriet Landing as an artist figure who attempts to break through the isolation of her life. Ironically, however, the very act of creating art serves only to isolate her further. Thus, Harriet's paintings become increasingly abstract, and her portrait of a little girl remains faceless.

"The Artificial Family." *Southern Review* NS 11 (Summer 1975): 615–21. This story highlights three of Tyler's favorite themes. First, Mary feels restricted by her marriages: her first, which she ran away from for reasons that she won't talk about, and her second to Toby, who begins to smother her with his possessiveness. Second, the story reveals Tyler's view of motherhood, which is filled with so many endless responsibilities as to seem overwhelming sometimes. Yet, at the same time, a mother feels an unbreakable bond to her child that makes it impossible not to fulfill those maternal duties. Finally, when Mary and Samantha leave, they travel light, a favorite motif of Tyler's, suggesting that objects act contrary to freedom, the more essential principle in a person's life. Therefore, Tyler's characters often leave carrying what seems like very little. Actually, however, they always carry with them what they consider their most important possessions.

Synopsis: When Toby meets Mary at a party and asks her out, she immediately tells him that she has a daughter. He begins to date her and to go on outings that include her daughter, Samantha. Mary does not reveal much about her previous marriage, just that she had run away after two years, taking nothing but Samantha with her. As Toby becomes increasingly involved in their lives, he offers to start babysitting for Samantha so that Mary won't have to keep paying a sitter. But Mary declines his offer.

After only five months Toby and Mary get married. Because of the ready-made family, Toby's parents don't approve. Their disapproval, however, only brings Samantha, Toby, and Mary closer together. Toby becomes increasingly attached to Mary. As his love grows, though, he begins to fear that she might leave him. He also begins to love Samantha as his own child and starts showering her with attention.

For her part, Mary dislikes Toby's spoiling Samantha since that forces her to have to play the heavy in disciplining the child. Although Toby explains that he just wants to give her and Samantha all kinds of things because he loves them so much, Mary responds, "Men are the only ones who have that much feeling left to spare. . . . Women's love gets frittered away; every day a thousand little demands for milk and bandaids and swept floors and clean towels" (16).

At Easter, Toby buys Samantha a big Easter basket, but Mary is not pleased because Toby is changing their traditions. In spite of Samantha's obvious delight with the basket, Mary's face becomes mask-like, and she begins to become increasingly distant from Toby.

Then one Monday evening in June, Toby arrives home to find a note ("I've gone"). He is devastated, but recalls that Samantha has an art class that is scheduled for Mondays. So he runs frantically to the class, hoping to catch Samantha and Mary, but they're not there. Upon his return home, he finds all their belongings still in the apartment and realizes that all "they would have taken with them . . . was their long gingham gowns and each other" (18).

artists. ("Bridge," CN) As a child, Anne Tyler wanted to become an artist. Her reviews of art books, as well as her own fiction, reveal that she has not lost the artist's eye for detail. Her greatest artist character, Jeremy Pauling in *Celestial Navigation*, exhibits the quintessential artistic sensibility. Totally focused on his art, Jeremy's unique perspective incorporates everything he sees and everyone he meets into his growing sculptures.

For Further Reading

Inman, Sue Lile. "The Effects of the Artistic Process: A Study of Three Artist Figures in Anne Tyler's Fiction." *The Fiction of Anne Tyler.* Ed. C. Ralph Stephens. Jackson: University Press of Mississippi, 1990: 55–63.

"As the Earth Gets Old." *New Yorker* 29 Oct. 1966: 60–64. In this story, Tyler presents two different mother/daughter relationships. Each has its own dynamics and set rules just as much as the chief motif—the Scrabble game—does. Mrs. Brauw and her daughter, Beatrice, have been playing a battle of wits for years, simulated by the Scrabble game in which Mrs. Brauw cheats just as she has worked to control Beatrice's whole life. For her part, Beatrice takes great pleasure in circumventing her mother's machinations, even in her death, which, ironically, frees her from her mother's clutches.

The second mother/daughter relationship, between Joanna Hope and Mrs. Hope, does not come without its own obligations and demands. Eventually, Joanna must acquiesce to her mother's request, almost as completely as Beatrice had. Real change, it seems, as always in Anne Tyler's work, remains only a remote possibility.

Synopsis: The Hopes (16-year-old Joanna and her mother) often go over to play Scrabble with their neighbor Mrs. Brauw and her spinster daughter, Beatrice, partly out of pity and partly out of obligation. They pity Mrs. Brauw because she is old and infirm, due to an accident long ago that had killed her husband. Additionally, they feel obligated because Mrs. Brauw has rented them the house next to hers for half price since Mr. Hope is in a sanatorium.

Mrs. Brauw, who used to play Monopoly, looks forward to her neighbors' visits immensely, especially their Scrabble games, at which she cheats. Joanna notices the old woman's cheating, but Mrs. Hope tells Joanna not to say anything about it. Once Joanna tries to cheat by feeling the letters the way Mrs. Brauw does, but she can't recognize the letters by touch.

At any rate, the real contest is always between Mrs. Brauw and Beatrice, not the Hopes. Somehow Beatrice always manages to win, even though she sometimes takes fifteen minutes to think of a word to top her mother's. Therefore the Hopes are actually "incidental to the real game" (61).

One night, however, after Mrs. Brauw chastises Joanna for filling up a space she had wanted to use with an "ordinary word" (61), Joanna confronts the old woman about her cheating: "How did you work it in Monopoly?" (61), to which Beatrice replies, "She was the one who kept the bank" (61). Not having thought that Beatrice knew about her mother's cheating, the Hopes are amazed at the soft-spoken woman's reaction.

That night Joanna tells her mother she's not ever going back to the Brauws'. For a while Mrs. Hope stops going as well. Three weeks later Beatrice calls to invite them over, but they make excuses. A week later, in April, Mrs. Brauw herself calls, and Mrs. Hope relents. Within a month Joanna has started accompanying her mother again because she feels sorry for her having to go alone. While they play, once again in their old positions around the card table, Joanna looks at their unchanging reflections in the window.

One night in early June, Joanna wakes up to find the Brauws' house on fire. Worried because Mrs. Brauw can't walk with her injured hip, the Hopes call the fire department and rush over to check on the Brauws. Although they call out to the women, no answer comes from the silent house.

When the firemen finally arrive, they immediately spot Mrs. Brauw in a second-story window. It takes two firemen to carry her down the ladder. Joanna thinks she sees Beatrice briefly in a window, but it's too late. Beatrice dies in the flames. Ironically, Mrs. Brauw seems impassive.

When Mrs. Hope offers to let Mrs. Brauw spend the night at her house, the old woman accepts. Forced to have to sleep with her mother, Joanna spends the night trying to recall something worth remembering about Beatrice but can think of nothing.

The next day when Joanna comes home from school, Mrs. Brauw is still there. Mrs. Hope has promised that Joanna would play Scrabble with her, so the two begin to play. Mrs. Brauw's mind isn't really on the game, though. She rambles on about her fears and dislikes: "As the earth gets older, there are more and more things one has to steel one's mind against" (64). She is particularly upset that Beatrice, who had promised she would look after her mother, has left her alone, and concludes that it was "a cheat from beginning to end" (64).

Although Joanna expresses her sympathy about Beatrice's death, she immediately regrets doing so because Mrs. Brauw replies resignedly, "Well, there's no way I can try to change things anymore, is there?" (64).

auctions. ("Tea-Machine") The auction of seemingly worthless objects allows young John Paul Bartlett the opportunity to examine the value of material possessions as he contemplates spending his own life following in his father's footsteps rather than striking out on his own.

Sister Audrey. (SM) unwed teenaged mother who had put her baby in a Dempsey Dumpster; she helps out at Camp Second Chance as penance.

automobiles. (AT, BL, CW, DHR, EP, "Holding," LY) Many scenes in Tyler's work take place in an automobile. And in two novels, *Breathing Lessons* and *Earthly Possessions*, the majority of the action takes place in a car. The automobile, with its constant motion and its ability to transport a person to another place, allows Tyler to explore the possibility of change without really changing the lives of her characters. Additionally, the car represents another modern machine that, although it has become indispensable to our lives, has also added more responsibility and stress to our existence, as evidenced in "Holding Things Together."

"Average Waves in Unprotected Waters." *New Yorker* 28 Feb. 1977: 32–36. One of Tyler's most widely anthologized stories, "Average Waves in Unprotected Waters" presents a typical Tylerian situation—a person attempting to endure the hand that life has dealt him or her. Bet Blevins' steadfastness in caring for her son and in standing in the waves as long as she could both attest to her inner strength. Outwardly, however, this strength takes a great toll on her. In order to endure the pain of loss, she detaches herself and becomes an observer of life rather than a participant.

The story also illustrates Tyler's skillful use of memory to create character. Through Bet's memories, as she rides along in the train, the reader becomes aware of the hardships and isolation that this brave woman has had to endure. Thus, Bet's decision to give up her son for his own good becomes more sympathetic and her action an act of heroism.

Synopsis: On the day she is to institutionalize her mentally handicapped son, Arnold, Bet Blevins wakes up in her shabby rented room. At age 9 Arnold has become too much for Bet to handle anymore. While she dresses and feeds her son this last time, she agonizes over her decision and wonders whether the boy understands what is happening. As Bet and Arnold head out the door, her neighbor Mrs. Puckett, who is crying, gives her cookies for Arnold, but he runs out without acknowledging the woman who used to babysit him.

On the train, while Arnold sleeps, Bet remembers him as a baby, how her husband Avery had left when they learned that their son was mentally handicapped, and how she had married too young against her parents' wishes. She also wonders whether the gene that caused Arnold's disability came from Avery or from her. She suspects that it came from her because she has always felt that "she never could do anything as well as most people" (33). Up until now, however, she has had one constant virtue: her steadfastness. She remembers how she used to stand in the water letting the waves slam into her when her family had lived next to the shore. And even after Avery left, she had stayed on in the apartment for a while, not waiting for his return, but just taking "some comfort from enduring" (34). Then Arnold wakes up, and Bet has to entertain him. He laughs at an old lady who has sneaked onto the train and is fighting with the conductor.

In Parkinsville Bet and Arnold take a taxi to Parkins State Hospital. Even though Arnold begs for a cookie, Bet hesitates to give him one because she is afraid he will get messy. She cannot bear for the people at the hospital to think of him as "ordinary and unattractive"; rather, she wants them "to see how small and neat he was, how somebody cherished him" (34). To keep him from throwing a tantrum, though, she breaks off a small piece of cookie and gives it to him. When they arrive at the hospital, Bet asks the taxi driver several times to wait for her outside the hospital. He assures her that he will not leave.

Inside the hospital a nurse takes Bet on a tour. As she shows Bet the room where Arnold will sleep, Bet tries to tell the nurse about Arnold. Assuring Bet that her son will be well cared for, the nurse informs Bet that she will not be able to visit him for six months while he is getting adjusted to his new home. After leaving Arnold his favorite blanket, Bet says good-bye.

In tears, Bet rushes out of the hospital to the waiting cab and urges the driver to hurry back to the station. She has timed her departure so that she will not have to wait any longer than necessary for the train. At the station, however, she learns that the train will be twenty minutes late. Nearly desperate, she wonders how she will ever make it through those interminable minutes. Just then the town's mayor arrives on the platform to give what he says will be a twenty-minute speech. Greatly relieved, Bet believes that he has come just for her sake and imagines that "from now on, all the world was going to be like that—just something on a stage, for her to sit back and watch" (36).

Avery. (BL) Crystal Stuckey's beefy boyfriend who helps move Fiona Moran's belongings out of the Morans' house after Fiona and Jesse split up; Crystal later marries him, but he dies six weeks later in a construction accident.

Driscoll Avery. (LY) Susie Grinstead's longtime boyfriend; she agrees to marry him at the end of the novel.

Louise Avery. (LY) Driscoll Avery's mother, who is more concerned about the reception than the postponement of the wedding.

Malcolm Avery. (LY) Driscoll Avery's father.

Spence Avery. (LY) Driscoll Avery's sister, who is a bridesmaid in Driscoll and Susie Grinstead's wedding.

B

Emmeline Babcock. (CW) Mrs. Emerson's longtime maid, whom she had fired for running down the batteries on her transistor radio.

babies. (BL, "Common," CN, DHR, LY, SDL, SM) Anne Tyler remembers her own daughters' early years with fondness, recalling in her most revealing personal essay, "Still Just Writing," that, although having children did curtail her literary output for a few years, that she had "more of a self to speak from" once her daughters were old enough to go to school, after which time she could devote more of her energies to writing. In her novels, therefore, babies are welcome events. In *Celestial Navigation*, Mary Tell is an earth mother figure, producing offspring every other year. In *Breathing Lessons*, Leroy's early years help bond Maggie and Fiona and leave a lasting impact on Maggie. In *Saint Maybe*, despite his knowledge of the tremendous responsibilities of parenting, Ian Bedloe looks forward to the birth of his son.

Adar Bagned. (DHR) the model Sam Wiley moves in with after leaving Jenny Tull.

Harley Baines. (DHR) Jenny Tull's first husband; an obsessive/compulsive genetics genius.

Jenny Baines. (DHR) See JENNY MARIE TULL.

Joseph Ballew. (SDL) rock singer from Pulqua who sings angry songs.

Sandy Ballew. ("Dry") a friend of Jonas Anders who helps with the plan to scatter Uncle Wurssun's ashes.

"The Baltimore Birth Certificate." *Critic* Feb. 1963: 41–45. Significant in the Tyler canon as the first story to mention Baltimore (although only in the title, not as a setting), "The Baltimore Birth Certificate" is also Tyler's first story to be published in a national publication, the *Critic*.

The story introduces several themes and techniques that, like her Baltimore settings in her mature works, were to become Tylerian standards. Her obvious sensitivity to the plight of the elderly Miss Penney in this story suggests a deeper understanding of the need for all individuals to establish and maintain their own separate identities. Miss Penney's quest for her birth certificate is a universal struggle that all individuals must face as they attempt to find validation for their existence in a hostile world. Another element common to Tyler's later work is the technique of using memory as a means of arresting time, just as Miss Penney's niece, Betsy, holds back the doors of the subway car.

Synopsis: Miss Penney, a 62-year-old retired salesclerk, begins thinking about obtaining a copy of her birth certificate. The thought becomes "like the thought of a person she was lonely for" (41). Finally, she writes off to Baltimore for her birth certificate, but the officials there reply that they can find no record of her birth. This unexpected turn of events unsettles Miss Penney. For over a month she is at loose ends.

Then, in August, Miss Penney decides to take action. First she makes a list of people who might be able to help her locate her birth certificate. After discounting her neighbors, whom she does not associate with because they are Puerto Rican or black, as well as her brother Warren in North Carolina because he would laugh at her for even wanting a birth certificate, she finally decides to ask her niece Betsy to help. Miss Penney calls Betsy's office and leaves a message for Betsy to come over on her lunch hour.

When Betsy arrives, Miss Penney tells her niece that she has written to Baltimore, where she was born sixty-two years ago, but that no record of her birth exists. To explain her desire to locate her birth certificate, Miss Penney says: "People get born, you know, each one separate; each one got his own separate birth certificate. They don't come all in one big group off a subway platform; it's one by one, and every one of them with a certificate to prove it" (43).

Because Miss Penney cannot afford a regular lawyer on her limited income, Betsy suggests that they go to Legal Aid for help in locating her birth certificate. Although Betsy says she does not have enough time, Miss Penney insists that they go immediately to the Legal Aid office. Betsy relents, yet Miss Penney feels suddenly frightened by the prospect of the subway ride uptown. She remembers feeling the same way twenty-five years earlier when she had ridden the train down to North Carolina at Betsy's birth.

On the train ride uptown, Miss Penney admires the way Betsy manages. As they exit the subway car, Betsy catches the door and holds it open (as if stopping the whole train) until Miss Penney can get off. At the Legal Aid office, however, the receptionist is not encouraging. She tells Miss Penney that she can wait to see the lawyer, but that he is probably not going to be able to help her because she was born at home and the birth was perhaps not even recorded. Miss Penney is adamant, however: "But I was born, wasn't I?" (45).

Betsy, who is on her lunch hour, has to leave her aunt. Though her niece's decision upsets Miss Penney at first, she finally allows Betsy to leave. Determined to prove that she was born, Miss Penney continues to wait tearfully for her turn to see the lawyer. As she waits, she thinks admiringly of how Betsy had held the train back so deliberately. This thought gives Miss Penney courage, and she sits patiently waiting for "the man to bring her birth certificate" (45).

Bando. (EP) boy who works at the Texaco station who comes in to have Charlotte Emory take his photograph every month.

bank robbery. (EP, SC) In *Earthly Possessions,* Jake Simms' botched robbery provides Charlotte Emory with her opportunity to escape from her family.

Joe Barker. (CW) Mrs. Barker's husband, who likes to eat meat.

Mrs. Barker. (CW) woman Elizabeth Abbott calls pretending to be conducting a survey for the gas company.

Barley twins. (BL) Jeannie and her sister are old friends of Maggie Moran and Serena Gill's; despite Serena's pleading, they refuse to sing at Max Gill's funeral.

Barney. ("Street") Sammy's older boss, who accompanies him when he tests out the boat, the *Odessa.*

Joe Barrett. (CW) medical student from whose test Timothy Emerson cheats.

Joelle Barrett. (BL) nursing assistant at Silver Threads Nursing Home.

Mr. Barrett. (BL) Serena Gill's father, who lived in Guilford in a fine brick colonial house with stone lions at the end of the sidewalk; he got Serena's mother, Anita Palermo, pregnant and then deserted her.

Mrs. Barrett. (AT) one of the old people Rose Leary looks out for; she eats Thanksgiving dinner with the Learys.

Bartlett. (CW) hero of the western novel Elizabeth Abbott reads to Mr. Cunningham.

Bill Bartlett. ("Tea-Machine") John Paul Bartlett's older brother, who also works for their father, Homer Bartlett; he and his wife, Katy, live with his parents.

Homer Bartlett. ("Tea-Machine") John Paul and Bill Bartlett's auctioneer father; he is overweight and suffers a stroke.

John Paul Bartlett. ("Tea-Machine") Homer Bartlett's dissatisfied 21-year-old son, who works at his father's auction house.

Katy Bartlett. ("Tea-Machine") Bill Bartlett's wife, who also works at the auction house.

Nick Bascomb. (SM) a friend of Daphne Bedloe's; Rita diCarlo lives with him until she meets Ian Bedloe.

baseball. (BL, DHR, "I'm Not Going," LY) Tyler is a baseball fan herself. In *Dinner at the Homesick Restaurant*, Ezra Tull takes his blind mother, Pearl, to an Orioles game. In *Ladder of Years*, Delia Grinstead watches a game played in the fog.

"The Base-Metal Egg." *Southern Review* NS 9 (Summer 1973): 682–86. In this unusually titled story, Tyler probes into the mind of a young woman who is just coming of age. What Mary Beth is discovering is that the forces of society and tradition (in the form of her mother and her boyfriend) run contrary to her individual sense of identity. Thus, she desires not the white pearls, so traditional and so perfectly round and enclosing, but a base-metal locket that would set her apart from everyone else and open up to reveal her true self.

At the end of the story, however, Mrs. Polk buys Mary Beth the pearls anyhow because Mary Beth is afraid to open up and reveal her true feelings or, perhaps, because she feels that her mother would not understand her if she did attempt to communicate her feelings. At any rate, Mary Beth's true self, like most people's, remains hidden.

Synopsis: Mary Beth Polk accompanies Darwin Two (her present boyfriend) and her mother (Mrs. Polk) to buy a string of pearls for her graduation. Mary Beth's appearance has suddenly turned beautiful, but she dresses too casually to suit her fastidiously fashionable mother, who has to tell her daughter to put on a bra. Darwin Two, who also dresses well, wonders if Mary Beth likes him only because his name is the same as her previous boyfriend's.

Outside the jewelry store, Mary Beth notices their reflection in the window. They look like "one of those engaged-couples-plus-mother-in-law out shopping for china" (684). Darwin Two keeps asking Mary Beth if she would like him if he had a different name. Absentmindedly, Mary Beth doesn't respond.

Mary Beth doesn't really care for any of the pearls she sees. Instead she secretly wishes for an egg made of some base-metal which would open like a locket, because everyone would identify such an unusual object with her. Even if it were lost, everyone would know to return it to her.

Finally, at another jewelry store Mrs. Polk and Darwin Two pick out some pearls for Mary Beth. Mrs. Polk tells her, "There's so much *ahead* for you! And all of it wonderful" (686). But Mary Beth seems lost in thought. Darwin Two asks if she's thinking of someone else. She replies no and keeps thinking of how the base-metal egg would have given her an identity all her own, different from the roles she's slowly being forced into.

Laura Pauling Bates. (CN) Jeremy Pauling's widowed sister from Richmond.

Mr. Bates. (CN) Laura Bates' hemophiliac husband, who died after cutting his finger on a Campbell's soup can.

Grandpa Baum. (SC) Laura Baum Peck's father, a German cutler.

George Pendle Bay. (LY) founder of Bay Borough; his statue adorns the town square; he founded the town in the middle of the Civil War when he dreamed that an angel told him, "Ye are sitting in the barber's chair of infinity" (LY 86).

Jim Bayles. ("Some Sign") evening pharmacist at Sam Simmons' drug store.

beach. (AT, BL, DHR, LY, MP) See VACATIONS.

Calvin (Cal) Beadle. ("Teenage") hip tutor whom a psychologist recommends that Daisy and Matt Coble hire to work with their troubled son Donny.

Becky. (AT) Macon Leary's travel agent.

Bee Bedloe. (SM) the optimistic mother of the Bedloe clan; a former fourth grade teacher; she suffers from arthritis; she dies of a stroke in 1988.

Danny Bedloe. (SM) Ian Bedloe's older brother, almost 30 (in 1965); he works in the post office, marries Lucy Dean, and finally commits suicide by running his car into a stone wall.

Daphne Bedloe. (SM) daughter of Lucy Dean (and probably Howard Belling); she is born in 1966 on her uncle Ian Bedloe's birthday (January 2); she remains in Baltimore.

Doug Bedloe. (SM) Ian Bedloe's father; a high school algebra teacher/ baseball coach at Poe High School who eventually retires.

Ian Bedloe. (SM) a 17-year-old boy interested in baseball and girls at the start of the novel who undergoes a religious transformation and takes on the task of raising his brother Danny's wife's children over the next twenty years; he marries Rita diCarlo.

Joshua Bedloe. (SM) Ian and Rita Bedloe's son.

Lucy Dean Dulsimore Bedloe. (SM) a young divorcée with two children who marries Danny Bedloe; she dies in October 1966 of an overdose of sleeping pills.

Rita diCarlo Bedloe. (SM) Clutter Counselor who marries Ian Bedloe; mother of Joshua Bedloe.

Thomas Dulsimore Bedloe. (SM) Thomas, who is three at the start of the novel, is a carefree child, although he misses his mother (Lucy Dean Bedloe) after her death; popular in school, he grows up to be a designer of children's video games and becomes engaged to Angie.

Agatha Dulsimore Bedloe-Simms. (SM) Agatha, who is six at the start of the novel, is a serious child who acts as a confidant to her mother (Lucy Dean Bedloe); she grows up to be an oncologist in Los Angeles and marries another doctor, Stuart Simms.

Bee. ("Holding") Lucy Simmons' old college friend, who is going to lunch with her when Lucy's car develops trouble.

Aunt Alice Bell. (SC) Margaret Rose Peck's aunt, who has been to Paris.

Dory Bell. ("Spending") Joe Bell's wife, who receives a check for $1,000 from her daughter, Lindy.

Joe Bell. ("Spending") Dory Bell's husband; an old man who is retired from working in a hardware store; he and Dory receive a $1,000 check from their daughter, Lindy.

Mr. Bell. (SC) Margaret Rose Peck's father, who refuses to allow her to live with him after she leaves Daniel Peck.

Mrs. Walter Bell. (CW) Mrs. Emerson's neighbor.

Howard Belling. (SM) the lawyer who handled Lucy Dean's divorce from Tom Dulsimore; he is married; nevertheless, he brings Lucy and the children to Baltimore, sets Lucy up in an apartment, and then abandons her; he is probably Daphne Bedloe's biological father.

Ben. ("Two People") Melinda's father, who sends her to stay with his sister Sony Elliott.

Ben. ("Woman") Corey's husband, who works for Northeastern Life Insurance Company.

Eugene Bennett. ("Genuine") Bridget Muggins' boyfriend; he comes from a large family.

John Paul Bennett. ("Genuine") Eugene Bennett's younger brother, who brings a camera to their sister Maggie's graduation.

Joshua Bennett. (MP) neighbor of Morgan Gower's; an antique dealer.

L. D. Bennett. ("Genuine") Eugene Bennett's older brother, who rides in the back of the pickup.

Maggie Bennett. ("Genuine") Eugene Bennett's sister who is graduating from ninth grade at a training (i.e., reform) school; she requests false eyelashes for her graduation present.

Mary Bennett. (TCT) the woman who works the shift after Tommy Jones in the Larksville drug store.

Mary Jean Bennett. (BL) classmate whom Serena Gill had forgotten to invite; she appears in the chorus when Serena shows the movie of her wedding.

Mr. Bennett. ("Genuine") Eugene Bennett's father; a tenant farmer.

Mrs. Bennett. ("Genuine") Eugene Bennett's pregnant mother.

Pansy Bennett. ("Genuine") one of Eugene Bennett's younger sisters; she shows Bridget Muggins the false eyelashes the Bennetts have bought for Maggie Bennett's graduation present.

Mrs. Benning. (SC) neighbor who offers to let Meg Peck stay with her in Semple, Virginia, until the schoolyear is out.

Pig Benson. (SM) one of Ian Bedloe's best friends when he is a teenager; he enlists in the army.

Mr. Bentham. (EP) alcoholic from Holy Basis Church who lives with the Emorys.

Carol Bentley. (IMEC) Joanne and Gary Bentley's 2-year-old daughter with curly red hair.

Gary Bentley. (IMEC) Joanne Hawkes Bentley's tall, red-haired husband, a former Marine and now a salesman, who is originally from Georgia.

Joanne Hawkes Bentley. (IMEC) Ben Joe Hawkes' older sister, who leaves Gary Bentley, her husband of seven years, and returns home.

Helena Berger. (MP) neighbor of Emily Meredith's who helps with Emily's daughter, Gina.

Bernard. ("Bridge") a poet who lives in the apartment below Harriet Landing; her one confidant, he tries but never quite succeeds in drawing her out of herself emotionally.

Bernice. (LY) Binky Moffat's sister.

Bertha. (SDL) character on the soap opera Clotelia watches.

Cousin Bertha. (DHR) Pearl Tull's sickly cousin who carries a bottle of scented crystals in case of fainting spells.

Bessie. (BL) dog Mr. Otis used to have.

Aunt Bessie. (DHR) relative of Pearl Tull's who might be the woman in the blouse at the picnic in the photograph Ezra Tull describes for his blind mother.

Betsy. (DHR) Jane Lowry's young daughter.

Betty Catherine. ("Lights") young girl who tries to comprehend the drowning deaths of her father and brother.

Billy. (CW) son of Mary Emerson and Morris; Mrs. Emerson's grandson.

birth. (BL, CN, "Common," MP, SM) Life renewing itself through the birth of children is a recurrent theme in Tyler's work. In *Breathing Lessons*, Maggie Moran's granddaughter Leroy represents a chance for Maggie to correct the mistakes that she made raising her own children. In *Saint Maybe*, the birth of Ian Bedloe's son Joshua reconnects Ian to the cycle of time and completes the circle begun by the birth of Daphne Bedloe earlier in the novel. In "The Common Courtesies," the birth of Mrs. Lorna Love Johnson's grandson also forces her to accept the passage of time with all its inherent changes and dangers.

birthday parties. (SC, SM, "Under Tree") In addition to their festive nature, birthday parties serve as markers of the passage of time. In *Saint Maybe*, several parties mark different stages in characters' lives: childhood, middle age, retirement.

Sateen Bishop. (BL) worker at Silver Threads Nursing Home who helps Bertha Washington push Maggie Moran around in a laundry cart.

Howell Blake. (TCT) a man who works in tobacco for Mr. Terry.

Mr. Blake. (CW) pastor at Faith Baptist Church prior to Rev. Abbott.

Mrs. Nancy Bledsoe. (CW) a woman who gives Rev. Abbott a collie in appreciation for his help during her mother's death.

Arnold Blevins. ("Average") Bet and Avery Blevins' mentally handicapped 9-year-old son.

Avery Blevins. ("Average") Bet Blevins' husband, who deserted her a few weeks after learning of their son Arnold's mental handicap.

Bet Blevins. ("Average") a single, lower-class mother struggling to raise her mentally handicapped son, Arnold; eventually she must institutionalize him.

blindness. (DHR, SC) Pearl Tull's blindness in *Dinner at the Homesick Restaurant* and Daniel Peck's deteriorating sight in *Searching for Caleb* force both of these characters to depend more on others and to rely on another inner vision, memory, to negotiate their way through life toward the end of their lives.

Adrian Bly-Brice. (LY) 32-year-old man who has an unconsummated affair with Delia Grinstead; he writes newsletters.

Rosemary Bly-Brice. (LY) Adrian Bly-Brice's estranged wife; owner of a catering firm ironically called The Guilty Party; she is having an affair with their accountant, Skipper.

boardinghouses. (BL, CN, DHR, EP, MP) The boardinghouse, with its multidimensional familial construct, is a useful tool in Tyler's work. Most tellingly, in *Celestial Navigation*, the Paulings' boardinghouse provides the agoraphobic Jeremy Pauling his one opportunity to engage other people and to establish human connections. Without the boardinghouse, Jeremy's life would be one of sterility, centered only in his art, which would have eventually suffered from the absence of human contact.

boats. ("Bride," CN, "Street") With all their romantic connotations of travel and escape, boats prove to be less effectual in Tyler's work. In *Celestial Navigation*, Jeremy Pauling can't sail out of the constricted circle of his life. In "A Street of Bugles," Sammy heads out to sea only to be called back by the ties that hold him to the town of Balton.

Bobby. (BL) Mabel's oldest son, whom she made move out after he complained about her tuna casserole.

Bobby. ("Lights") Betty Catherine's brother, whose body is found in the Savannah River.

Bobby. (SC) Alonzo Divich's fourth wife's stepson, who continues to work in Alonzo's carnival even after his mother divorces Alonzo.

Miss Bohannon. (EP) the nurse who teaches the childcare class Mindy Callender attends at the Dorothea Whitman Home for Wayward Girls in Linex, Georgia.

Garner Bolt. (AT) Macon Leary's elderly neighbor who brings Macon his mail.

Biddy Bond. ("Laps") Mrs. Bond's youngest child.

Buck Bond. ("Laps") Mrs. Bond's husband, who works too late to come to the pool.

Lindy Bond. ("Laps") Mrs. Bond's 14-year-old daughter, who swims laps in the pool.

Mrs. Bond. ("Laps") narrator of the short story "Laps"; a mother who brings her three children to swim in the neighborhood pool for the day with her friend Sue Ellen and her children.

Nicholas Bond. ("Laps") Mrs. Bond's son, who gets kicked in the stomach by some older boys.

Book Reviewing. Beginning in 1972, Anne Tyler launched another career as a book reviewer. Her first review appeared in the *National Observer* in 1972. Three years later she was asked to become a regular reviewer for that periodical and was soon contributing a monthly review. In 1976 she also began reviewing for the *New York Times Book Review*, in 1977 for the *Washington Post Book World*, in 1978 for *New Republic*, and eventually for a wide range of newspapers across the nation.

Tyler reviewed books ranging from art books to short story collections, eventually producing over 250 reviews by the time she stopped reviewing in 1991, having lost her "capacity for enthusiasm" for reviewing. Her reviews reveal her to be an astute and immensely fair critic who delights in the authorial successes of the writers whose books she reviews. She is most impressed with aptly chosen details and with vividly drawn, credible characters to whom a reader can relate. She can, however, be quite blunt in stating her displeasure with an author who fails to support his or her imaginative fictional forays with plausible detail or who obfuscates and obscures the reader's understanding of a story.

For Further Reading

Crowe, Brenda Stone. "Anne Tyler: Building Her Own 'House of Fiction.' " Diss. University of Alabama, 1993.
Evans, Elizabeth. " 'Mere Reviews': Anne Tyler as Book Reviewer." *Critical Essays on Anne Tyler*. Ed. Alice Hall Petry. New York: G. K. Hall, 1992: 233–42.

Black Emma Borden. (SC) Red Emma Borden's late husband's cousin, who works at the Caro Mill Diner in the afternoons.

Red Emma Borden. (SC) morning waitress/short order cook at the Caro Mill Diner; later, on Justine Peck's advice, she takes a job as a mail carrier.

Lafleur Boudrault. (SC) Justin Montague Peck's Creole gardener, who introduces Caleb Peck to ragtime.

Sulie Boudrault. (SC) Lafleur Boudrault's wife; she works as the Pecks' maid for over sixty years and takes over the care of the Peck children after their mother, Margaret Rose Peck, leaves; Sulie is the only person who knows where Caleb Peck is, but she doesn't tell what she knows until someone asks her—sixty years later.

Nick Bourne. (BL) old classmate of Maggie Moran and Serena Gill's who had sung "True Love" at Serena's wedding, but couldn't come to Max Gill's funeral because of the distance.

Tom Bowen. ("Outside") one of the only friends Jason McKenna makes in Pulmet, New Hampshire; he works at a repair shop; it is he who tells Jason the truth about Mr. and Mrs. Douglas.

Eliza Bowers. ("Two People") Sony Elliott's neighbor, who attempts to figure out the cause of Melinda's sleepwalking; she has seven children.

Boyd. (DHR) one of Cody Tull's best friends in ninth grade; he and Cody are in the same homeroom.

Mr. Bragg. (LY) Teensy Rackley's prejudiced and increasingly senile father, who disapproves of his black son-in-law, Rick Rackley; nevertheless, he eventually comes to live with Teensy and Rick.

Billy Brandon. (TCT) Simon Pike's friend who has a new chemistry set.

Mindy Brant. (BL) a friend of Leroy Moran's.

Mr. Brant. (SM) deaf cabinetmaker who hires Ian Bedloe to work at his shop.

Mrs. Brant. (SM) Mr. Brant's younger wife; she has been deaf since birth and attended Gallaudet; she has many friends and eventually runs off with her next-door neighbor.

Beatrice Brauw. ("As the Earth") Mrs. Brauw's middle-aged daughter; a spinster who battles with her mother at Scrabble and always wins; she dies in a house fire.

Mrs. Brauw. ("As the Earth") the Hopes' overweight landlady who cheats at Scrabble.

Breathing Lessons. *Breathing Lessons,* Anne Tyler's Pulitzer Prize–winning novel, is her fullest exploration of one of her major themes: marriage. Using an Aristotelian one-day timeframe, Tyler, through memory, carries the reader through the twenty-eight year marriage of Maggie and Ira Moran. Along the way, for this novel is also a journey—to the funeral of the husband of Maggie's friend, Serena Gill—Maggie and Ira run the gamut of emotions and crises that a married couple can face. Love and loss, birth and death, hope and disappointment, all of these are woven into the fabric of the Morans' lives.

Maggie, the main character, whose haphazard, meddling approach to life so infuriates her husband and her family, nevertheless manages to rise to every occasion and keeps pushing for what she considers her ultimate goal: to reunite her son Jesse with his ex-wife, Fiona, and their daughter, Leroy. Somehow, through all her exploits Maggie keeps this goal firmly in mind. Ira, whose perspective is given in Part II of the novel, loves Maggie more than he can admit, but he also finds her meddling in other people's lives aggravating. A realist, he has settled in his life for an underachieving, shiftless son and has given up on his dream of a medical career to run his father's frameshop. Not Maggie. For her life is one constant breathing lesson. And just as the breathing lessons for natural childbirth ease a woman's pain during labor, so too does Maggie's eternal optimism, naive though it may be, allow her to make her way through life, despite its pain and disappointments.

Two important scenes in the novel illustrate the level of emotion necessary to maintain this struggle for life. In a scene in the kitchen, Maggie realizes that she is not alone in her worries about her family. When she breaks down crying, she looks up to find Ira sitting there with his head in his hands. Suddenly Maggie realizes that Ira is just as worried as she is and that he is experiencing the same disappointments and worries that she is. This knowledge lifts her spirits and binds her to Ira as never before. For Ira the pivotal moment comes after he realizes the significance of his family's disastrous trip to Harborplace in downtown Baltimore. Reflecting back upon the event, Ira realizes that, instead of being a burden to him, his family has been a blessing and that "the true waste was . . . not his having to support these people but his failure to notice how he loved them" (BL 175). This realization, by both Maggie and Ira, of the importance of the people in their lives, despite the dependency, despite the responsibility, is what gives their lives meaning.

For Further Reading

Croft, Robert W. *Anne Tyler: A Bio-Bibliography.* Westport, CT: Greenwood Press, 1995. 81–86.

Evans, Elizabeth. *Anne Tyler*. New York: Twayne, 1993.

Petry, Alice Hall. *Understanding Anne Tyler*. Columbia: University of South Carolina Press, 1990. 233–53.

Voelker, Joseph C. *Art and the Accidental in Anne Tyler*. Columbia: University of Missouri Press, 1989. 165–77.

Wagner-Martin, Linda. "*Breathing Lessons*: A Domestic Success Story." *Anne Tyler as Novelist*. Ed. Dale Salwak. Iowa City: University of Iowa Press, 1994: 162–74.

Selected Book Reviews

Eder, Richard. "Crazy for Sighing and Crazy for Loving You." *Los Angeles Times Book Review* 11 Sept. 1988: 3.

Hoagland, Edward. "About Maggie, Who Tried Too Hard." *New York Times Book Review* 11 Sept. 1988: 1+. [Reprinted in *Critical Essays on Anne Tyler*. Ed. Alice Hall Petry. New York: G. K. Hall, 1992: 140–44.]

Klinghoffer, David. "Ordinary People." *National Review* 30 Dec. 1988: 48–49. [Reprinted in *Critical Essays on Anne Tyler*. Ed. Alice Hall Petry. New York: G. K. Hall, 1992: 137–39.]

McPhillips, Robert. "The Baltimore Chop." *Nation* 7 Nov. 1988: 464–66. [Reprinted in *Critical Essays on Anne Tyler*. Ed. Alice Hall Petry. New York: G. K. Hall, 1992: 150–54.]

New Yorker 28 Nov. 1988: 121.

Olson, Clarence E. "Odd Ties That Bind." *St. Louis Post-Dispatch* 11 Sept. 1988: F5.

Stegner, Wallace. "The Meddler's Progress." *Washington Post Book World* 4 Sept. 1988: 1+. [Reprinted in *Critical Essays on Anne Tyler*. Ed. Alice Hall Petry. New York: G. K. Hall, 1992: 148–49.]

Towers, Robert. "Roughing It." *New York Review of Books* 10 Nov. 1988: 40–41. [Reprinted in *Critical Essays on Anne Tyler*. Ed. Alice Hall Petry. New York: G. K. Hall, 1992: 145–47.]

Wolitzer, Hilma. " 'Breathing Lessons': Anne Tyler's Tender Ode to Married Life." *Chicago Tribune Books* 28 Aug. 1988: 1+.

"The Bride in the Boatyard." *McCall's* June 1972: 92–93+. This story confronts the problem of maintaining a separate identity in the midst of the most claustrophobic relationship known to man—marriage. It is also interesting to note that Sarah's response to Martin's marriage proposal, "Oh, well. Why not?" (93), is the same response that Tyler gave to her husband Taghi's marriage proposal.

When she is first married, Sarah feels that she still possesses her own identity, but when she and Martin move to Baltimore their two identities seem to merge into one. Yet inside Sarah remains distinctly separate. Preferring Venetia's imaginary world, Sarah chooses to believe Venetia's version of the truth because it gives Venetia a power that Sarah feels she has lost—the power to shape her own reality. Sarah dislikes Martin's pragmatism and rebels against his appropriation of her life.

Synopsis: A few months after meeting each other at a party, Sarah and Martin Schmidt marry. After living briefly in Martin's one-room apartment where Sarah's belongings remain "as separate as a guest's" (93), they move to Baltimore, where Martin has found an instructor's job. There Sarah's life is no longer separate from Martin's. Her possessions (and her life) mingle with his, so none of their new "joint friends" know "that she had once been Sarah Mellor and had had a whole life of her own" prior to her marriage to Martin (126).

While Martin teaches summer school, Sarah goes to the boatyard two or three days a week to fix up an old sailboat they have purchased. One day, while she is varnishing the boat's mast, Sarah meets Venetia Oliver, who lives in an old shack near the boatyard. When Venetia discovers that Sarah is a newlywed, she starts questioning Sarah about how she met Martin. Venetia is particularly interested in the couple's wedding, which, to her disappointment, was only a small affair in a registry office with two witnesses.

Then Venetia begins to discuss in detail her own big wedding and romantic courtship with her husband Teddy. Soon Venetia is coming by almost every day, each time describing something new about her wedding or Teddy, who she says works with motorcycles. Sarah never sees Teddy though. Sensing that Venetia's life seems to have ended with her wedding, Sarah tells Martin that she wants to invite Venetia and Teddy to go sailing with them one weekend. When Sarah invites Venetia, however, Venetia admits that she and Teddy are separated. Nevertheless, Venetia accompanies them and seems cheerful, although she never talks about her wedding.

Now Venetia shifts from talking about her wedding to talking about her separation, which resulted from Teddy's unreasonable behavior. When Sarah suggests that Venetia might try to be more conciliatory, however, Venetia becomes upset, so Sarah doesn't mention the separation to Martin.

Then one morning in August, Mr. Clarkson, an old man who lives next door to Venetia, informs Sarah that Venetia has never been married. When Sarah confronts her with the truth, Venetia readily admits that she has simply invented Teddy. Since she enjoys making things up and since Sarah was "leading just an ordinary life," Venetia explains that "*somebody* had to have things worth talking about" (128).

That night Sarah tells Martin the truth. Yet when he claims to have been suspicious all along because the description of Venetia's husband had been so flimsy compared to the descriptions of the wedding itself, Sarah disagrees. In her mind, the lie had come to seem more real than this "second version" of the truth. To Sarah, even the imaginary husband had become real: "There *was* such a person; having been called up in her mind, he protested his nonexistence" (128). Martin, however, does not understand his wife's feelings. Instead he gets defensive, "confident of claiming forever Sarah's only, only life" (128).

"The Bridge." *Archive* Mar. 1960: 10–15. One of the five stories Tyler published in Duke University's literary magazine, the *Archive*, "The Bridge" uses the symbol of a bridge to reveal the inability of people to make connections with each other. Thus, the story's chief theme is isolation and alienation. What is most interesting in this early story of Tyler's is the way that she transfers that theme to the world of the artist. Harriet Landing's detached, observant stance as an artist created her style. But it has also condemned her to live a life separated irrevocably from the world that she attempts to capture in her paintings.

Tyler herself had once dreamed of becoming a book illustrator. This story reveals her early understanding of the cost of living an artistic life—whether as a painter or as a writer.

Synopsis: Aging artist Harriet Landing walks along thinking to herself. When she crosses a bridge, she notices a 10-year-old girl staring at the river. The girl intrigues Harriet, so she sits on a stone bench in the middle of the bridge and watches the girl. Then Harriet starts recalling her first paintings, abstract works that the critics had called "weird pieces of introspection . . . cold, and lacking all emotion" (11). Back then Harriet had wanted to paint everything and to capture "some one emotion, one action, that was the summation of all the emotions and actions that had ever been" (11).

Rising, Harriet says hello as she passes the child. Although the girl responds, Harriet can see that she wants to be alone. Harriet understands how the girl feels. Sometimes she dreams of a procession of people passing by her, as if in a parade, who seem to want to tell her something. She realizes, however, that the only way to break through this communication barrier is to speak to other people. Although she considers returning to the bridge to speak to the little girl, Harriet wonders which little girl she would be talking to: "a separate silent entity [or] the other, an animated conversationalist gesturing in the wind" (11). Additionally, Harriet wonders which person she would paint if she painted a picture of the girl and what the critics would think of a Harriet Landing painting that contained some emotion.

Thinking back to 1934, Harriet recalls how she had been attempting to identify her painting style. Having just declined the marriage proposal of a small blond man who collected folksongs whose name she has since forgotten, she felt at loose ends. A green wheelbarrow in the garden behind her house stirred something in her memory, causing her to want to paint it, "as if the empty wheelbarrow were a caricature of herself" (12). Strangely, this abstract painting of the wheelbarrow had defined her style. Critics loved the painting, calling it a "study in detachment" (12).

Returning to her apartment, Harriet finds her brother Edward, who is visiting from his home in Grover. To him she reveals her plan to paint a picture of a child, a drastic departure in both her style and subject matter. The painting will be her last attempt to find "the nameless emotion" that might turn out to be love (12). As she starts painting, however, she becomes annoyed with her brother's probing questions. Chastising herself for letting him know too much about her, Harriet yearns for privacy, as if there was "a certain shamefulness in letting a person know too much about you" (12).

Continuing in this isolated vein, Harriet recalls how she has always thought how bad it would be to love someone. Although Harriet had loved her mother, she had died when Harriet was only 10. Unable to attend the funeral because of her age, Harriet had sat in a green wheelbarrow in the yard instead. The most important thing that her mother had told her was to keep her dignity.

During the next three weeks Harriet works on the painting of the little girl. She begins to eat only tea and grape-nuts, sleeping little because she is always thinking about the painting. It is as if "she would be proved wrong on something" (13) if she can get the painting to turn out right. But she cannot paint the child's face because she cannot decide which face to paint: the "loving" face or the "dignified" one (13).

During the evenings Harriet takes walks to clear her mind. With her artist's eye, she notices people and sometimes experiences a little of the old feeling she had felt when she first started to paint. The only person she discusses these emotions with is Bernard, a young poet who lives in the apartment below hers. He identifies her feelings as a "basic emotional need" (14) and asks whether she has ever contemplated marriage. Harriet remembers when her brother Edward had asked her the same question when they were at the beach with their parents. Harriet had replied that marriage was the "longest and most final thing you could do" (14). Then Bernard asks her if she loves someone she knows, someone other than people on street corners. Harriet doesn't reply. She simply wishes that he would stop talking and let them "be two separate people thinking their own separate thoughts" (14).

Three weeks later, with the paint dry on the canvas and the face still missing, Harriet returns to the bridge. Although she waits all day for the girl to walk by, she never does. The next afternoon, however, when Harriet returns to the bridge, the little girl shows up, but this time she is not alone; she has two friends with her and seems much livelier than before. Harriet turns away for a minute. When she looks again, the little girl is alone, much as she had been the first time Harriet had seen her. Then Harriet walks over to her. The child remembers her and says hello. Harriet replies and adds a comment about the cold weather. The child agrees with her and seems to be waiting for Harriet to say something more. Harriet, however, can think of nothing else to say and leaves.

On the way home, Harriet decides not to paint the face in the picture after all. Instead, she will simply enter it into an exhibition with the blank space intact. Having made this decision, she feels an immediate sense of relief and begins to think about finishing up another painting, the still life she had put aside to work on the girl's painting. This thought makes her smile, and she walks faster, her face now calm and her shoulders "straight and firm" (15).

Joe Bright. (LY) realtor who rents an apartment to Susie Grinstead and Driscoll Avery.

Mrs. Brimm. (AT) an older patient Muriel Pritchett met while she was working at the hospital; she let Muriel and Alexander come live with her after Muriel's husband, Norman, left them.

Ann-Campbell Britt. (SC) Dorcas and Joe Pete Britt's 9-year-old daughter.

Dorcas Britt. (SC) a neighbor of Justine and Duncan Peck's in Caro Mill who has married and divorced her husband, Joe Pete Britt, three times.

Joe Pete Britt. (SC) Dorcas Britt's ex-husband, who owns the Texaco station in Caro Mill.

Mrs. Britt. (BL) older choir member who mistakenly tells Maggie that Ira Moran had been killed in a training accident.

Will Britt. (LY) Delia Grinstead's only boyfriend before she married Sam Grinstead.

Brook. ("Laps") Sue Ellen's youngest child.

Miss Brook. (TCT) the woman Lou Pike was sewing a dress for when her daughter, Janie Rose, was killed.

Arle Brooks. ("Laura") former Presbyterian minister, now an atheist, who brings the news of Laura's death and officiates at her funeral.

Cicely Brown. (SM) Ian Bedloe's pretty girlfriend, who goes to college and eventually breaks up with Ian; she winds up living in California with a folk guitarist.

Stevie Brown. (SM) Cicely Brown's little brother, whom she must babysit.

Bruce. ("Two People") Melinda's oldest brother.

David Brustein. (MP) Kate Gower's Jewish boyfriend, whom she eventually marries.

Kathleen (Kate) Gower Brustein. (MP) See KATHLEEN (KATE) GOWER.

Buddy. (CN) medical student boarding with the Paulings in 1968.

Mr. Bunch. (BL) Jesse Moran's sixth grade teacher.

Mrs. Daniel Bunn. (AT) Macon Leary's seatmate on the flight from Winnipeg to Edmonton.

Billy Burnham. (DHR) one of Jenny Tull's pediatric patients.

Don Burnham. (BL) friend of Jesse Moran's, who had transferred to Jesse's school in eleventh grade and told Jesse that he had talent, thus ruining Jesse's life (according to his father, Ira Moran).

Mrs. Burnham. (DHR) Billy Burnham's mother.

Billy Burns. ("Who Would Want") Mary Burns' 5-year-old brother.

Mary Burns. ("Who Would Want") 8-year-old girl who is the focal point of the story; she grows to love her foster brother, Jason Schmidt.

Mr. Burns. ("Who Would Want") Mary and Billy Burns' father.

Mrs. Burns. ("Who Would Want") Mary and Billy Burns' mother, who takes in a foster child, Jason Schmidt.

buses. ("Outside," SC, TCT) See TRAVEL.

Butkins. (MP) the efficient clerk who works for Morgan Gower at Cullen Hardware; his wife is an invalid with a degenerative muscle disease; their only child had been killed by a hit-and-run driver.

Debbie and Dorrie Butler. (AT) 16-year-old twins who live next door to Muriel Pritchett and sometimes babysit for Alexander.

C

Cade. (EP) one of the men who helps Jake Simms get his stolen car unstuck.

Darnell Callender. (EP) Mindy Callender's father; the owner of a feed store who always wears a Panama hat.

Mindy Callender. (EP) Jake Simms' pregnant 17-year-old girlfriend.

Laurel Canfield. (AT) Scott Canfield's mother, whom Macon Leary runs into while shopping for clothes for Alexander Pritchett.

Scott Canfield. (AT) an old classmate of Ethan Leary's.

Zack Caraway. (SDL) proprietor of the Unicorn, the roadhouse where Drumstrings Casey sings.

cards. (BL, MP, SC) See GAMES.

caretakers. (AT, BL, CW, EP, LY, SM, TCT) Caretakers of all different types inhabit most of Anne Tyler's novels. The most common type of care-taker is a mother, such as Maggie Moran in *Breathing Lessons*, Charlotte Emory in *Earthly Possessions*, and Delia Grinstead in *Ladder of Years*. As early as *The Tin Can Tree*, however, other women have stepped into the role of caretaker. Joan Pike, in *The Tin Can Tree*, helps her family through a crisis, and Rose Leary looks after her brothers in *The Accidental Tourist*.

The most important caretaker in all of Tyler's fiction, though, is Elizabeth Abbott in *The Clock Winder*. She happens upon the Emerson family one day and stays first as handyman and then as priest, psychologist, and chief cook and bottle washer for the entire family, finally marrying Matthew Emerson.

Carl. (CW) Polly's husband; Elizabeth Abbott's brother-in-law.

Mr. Carleton. (TCT) Larksville taxi driver.

Bob Carney. (AT) Sue Carney's husband.

Delilah Carney. (AT) Bob and Sue Carney's 3-year-old daughter.

Sue Carney. (AT) Macon Leary's neighbor who invites him to dinner with her family twice: first, after Sarah leaves him, and once again after Macon and Sarah reconcile.

carnivals. (MP, SC) Many of Tyler's characters do not want to remain within the constraints of an ordinary life. Therefore, a carnival offers an attractive alternative to an otherwise mundane existence. In the case of Morgan Gower and Emily Meredith in *Morgan's Passing*, their life is one long puppet show as they move from one fair, carnival, or church bazaar to the next, living out their fairy tales in real life just as they do on the stage. In *Searching for Caleb*, however, the carnival becomes Justine and Duncan Peck's life at the end of the novel. After traveling around for nearly twenty years from job to job, house to house, and town to town, Justine and Duncan accept Alonzo Divich's offer to become the fortuneteller and mechanic for his traveling show. This lifestyle offers the perfect combination of constant travel and change, while still supplying the necessary stability that even the peripatetic Justine and Duncan need.

Carol. ("Artificial") teenaged babysitter who keeps Mary Glover's daughter, Samantha, even after Toby Scott volunteers to.

Carol (or Karen). (DHR) a social worker; the only one of Cody Tull's girlfriends who doesn't like Ezra; she feels he is too nurturing.

Caroline. (AT) the girl who works with Muriel Pritchett at the Meow-Bow Animal Hospital.

Della Carpenter. (SC) neighbor of Justine and Duncan Peck's in Semple, Virginia; she has a mentally handicapped daughter.

Mr. Carpenter. ("With All Flags") 82-year-old farmer and father of five daughters, who goes to live in a nursing home on his own initiative.

Neely Carpenter. (SC) doctor's son whom Justine Peck dates in high school.

Carrie. (CN) Miss Vinton's sister.

Jamie Cartwright. ("I'm Not Going") one of Noona Long's violin students, whose ambition is to be a square-dance fiddler.

Bertram "Drumstrings" (Drum) Casey. (SDL) cool, intense 19-year-old rock singer with black hair, who marries Evie Decker; a high school dropout, he works part-time at the A & P and sometimes helps his father at the filling station.

Evie Decker Casey. (SDL) See EVIE DECKER.

Obed E. Casey. (SDL) Drum Casey's father, who works in a gas station.

Mrs. Ora Casey. (SDL) Drum Casey's mother.

catalogues. (BL, CN, LY, "Two People") Anne Tyler loves catalogues. Whenever she discovers one in her mailbox, she pours through it, fascinated with the variety of offerings, as well as the ingenuity of the inventors. In her works her characters display a similar fascination with catalogues, for these wonderful books take them out of their quotidian lives and transport them to other worlds. Aunt Sony, sitting on her front porch in "Two People and a Clock on the Wall," flipping through the Sears catalogue, provides an early example of this phenomenon. But so, too, does Jeremy Pauling in *Celestial Navigation*, whose restricted world requires some outlet. These catalogues allow him a peek into the world outside. For Tyler's characters, catalogues truly are wish books.

Paul Cates. (LY) a dorky boy Courtney met at her Christian Fellowship group and intentionally gave a wrong phone number.

cats. (AT, EP, LY, MP, SC, SM) See PETS.

Celestial Navigation. Jeremy Pauling, the agoraphobic sculptor of *Celestial Navigation*, is the character that Tyler considers most like herself, although she is not as isolated as Jeremy. Jeremy's way of viewing life "from a distance" and even "[living] at a distance" (CN 145) parallels Tyler's own narrative objectivity and habit of observing the world from a distance.

During the course of the novel, Jeremy attempts to find his way off the island of isolation upon which he is "marooned" (CN 100) in the boardinghouse of his overprotective mother, who has just died at the beginning of the novel. In addition, his fragmented artistic sensibility that allows him to view life as a series of photographic flashes "imprinted . . . upon his eyelids" (CN 49) further isolates him from the world around him. Ironically, at the same time, this artistic vision grows deeper and richer throughout the course of the novel, thus setting him further apart from other people.

Into Jeremy's isolated life walks Mary Tell, a young mother with a child, who has left her husband and run off to Baltimore with a married man. At first Mary's realness almost overwhelms Jeremy, but after her boyfriend returns to his wife, Jeremy gathers the courage to ask Mary to marry him, an act of Herculean courage for him, especially since it takes place outside his home. Although Mary cannot accept Jeremy's proposal because her first husband won't grant her a divorce, Mary and Jeremy pretend to be married. Almost immediately, they start on a family of their own, producing five children over the next ten years.

Over these ten years, however, Jeremy and Mary begin to grow apart. Jeremy feels increasingly "baffled" (CN 157) by the growing number and size of his children, whom he considers "visitors from the outside world" (CN 158). Worse yet, he begins to view Mary as a mother substitute, "supplier, feeder, caretaker" (CN 160). From her perspective, Mary feels isolated from Jeremy as he buries himself ever deeper into his sculptures. Growing tired of always being "the interrupter, the overwhelmer" (CN 202), she finally leaves after Jeremy forgets their wedding date, her husband finally having agreed to a divorce after ten years.

Left alone, Jeremy at first thinks that he can finally concentrate on his art, allowing his celestial navigation to guide him. What he discovers, however, is that he needs the connection to Mary and the children to enrich his art. Unfortunately, when he finally gathers the courage to go after Mary, who has taken the children to live in a boathouse, Jeremy cannot communicate his feelings to Mary. Instead he makes an ineffectual attempt to prove his competence by weatherproofing the windows of the boathouse and by airing out the sails of a sailboat for her. In the end, though, he only manages to sail around in circles, symbolic of his artistic and personal isolation. Thus, the novel ends in failure. Although this ending gives *Celestial Navigation* one of the rare "unhappy" endings in Tyler's fiction, it was, as Tyler explained in a 1981 interview with Wendy Lamb, the only ending possible because Jeremy and Mary are "two absolutely separate people . . . [who] couldn't possibly have stayed together."

For Further Reading

Carson, Barbara Harrell. "Art's Internal Necessity: Anne Tyler's *Celestial Navigation*." *The Fiction of Anne Tyler*. Ed. C. Ralph Stephens. Jackson: University Press of Mississippi, 1990: 47–54.

Croft, Robert W. *Anne Tyler: A Bio-Bibliography.* Westport, CT: Greenwood Press, 1995. 45–49.

Evans, Elizabeth. *Anne Tyler.* New York: Twayne, 1993.

Farrell, Grace. "Killing Off Mother: Failed Matricide in *Celestial Navigation.*" *Critical Essays on Anne Tyler.* Ed. Alice Hall Petry. New York: G. K. Hall, 1992: 221–32.

Inman, Sue Lile. "The Effects of the Artistic Process: A Study of Three Artist Figures in Anne Tyler's Fiction." *The Fiction of Anne Tyler.* Ed. C. Ralph Stephens. Jackson: University Press of Mississippi, 1990: 55–63.

Linton, Karin. *The Temporal Horizon: A Study of the Theme of Time in Anne Tyler's Major Novels.* Uppsala, Sweden: Acta Universitatis Upsaliensis, 1989.

Petry, Alice Hall. *Understanding Anne Tyler.* Columbia: University of South Carolina Press, 1990. 98–127.

Voelker, Joseph C. *Art and the Accidental in Anne Tyler.* Columbia: University of Missouri Press, 1989. 67–87.

Selected Book Reviews:

Bell, Pearl K. "The Artist as Hero." *New Leader* 4 Mar. 1974: 17–18.

Clapp, Susannah. "In the Abstract." *Times Literary Supplement* 23 May 1975: 577. [Reprinted in *Critical Essays on Anne Tyler.* Ed. Alice Hall Petry. New York: G. K. Hall, 1992: 69–70.]

Godwin, Gail. "Two Novels." *New York Times Book Review* 28 Apr. 1974: 34–35. [Reprinted in *Critical Essays on Anne Tyler.* Ed. Alice Hall Petry. New York: G. K. Hall, 1992: 71–72.]

Pryce-Jones, Alan. "Five Easy Pieces: One Work of Art." *Washington Post Book World* 24 Mar. 1974: 2. [Reprinted in *Critical Essays on Anne Tyler.* Ed. Alice Hall Petry. New York: G. K. Hall, 1992: 73–74.]

Ridley, Clifford A. "Novels: A Hit Man, a Clown, a Genius." *National Observer* 4 May 1974: 23.

change. ("As the Earth," AT, BL, "Bridge," CN, CW, DHR, EP, "Feather," IMEC, "Laura," MP, SC, SDL, SM) Anne Tyler herself does not much believe in the possibility of change. Therefore many of her characters seem stuck in lives that stagnate. The Pecks with their black Fords, the Learys with their ritually prepared baked potatoes—all of these characters seem incapable of stepping out of their suspended lives. At the end of *If Morning Ever Comes*, Ben Joe Hawkes seems reassured when the train conductor informs him that he "won't have to change" (IMEC 266) as Ben Joe and Shelley Domer make their way back to New York. Yet, as in the case of Ben Joe, whether Tyler's characters like it or not, they are all caught up in the process of change merely by being in the flow of time. In *The Accidental Tourist*, Macon Leary, who hates to travel, nevertheless travels almost constantly, updating his Accidental Tourist guidebook. As his editor Julian Edge tells him, "Change! It's what keeps us in the black" (AT 90). In *Searching for Caleb*, change is constant for Justine and Duncan Peck, who move around constantly. Even in Justine's fortunetelling, she invariably advises her clients to "take the change. Always change" (SC 29). Ultimately, change is an integral part of Tyler's fictional landscape.

Charleen. (TCT) another tobacco hander to Mrs. Hall; she suggests that Joan Pike act as Mrs. Lou Pike's receptionist until Mrs. Pike recovers.

Dan Charles. (DHR) one of Jenny Tull's medical partners; his wife is mentally ill.

Charlotte. ("Feather") Charles and Lucy Hopper's only daughter; she is Joshua's mother.

Great-Aunt Charlotte. (EP) the relative after whom Charlotte Emory is named.

Cherie. ("Geologist") several of Maroon's nieces with the same name; one of them is the first in the family to graduate from high school.

Chester. (BL) one of the Morans' cats over the years.

child abuse. (DHR) Pearl Tull's frustration with the responsibilities of raising three children alone leads to her verbal and even physical abuse of Cody, Ezra, and especially Jenny. Unfortunately, this cycle of abuse is repeated when Jenny, overburdened by the pressures of medical school, strained finances, and single motherhood, inflicts similar abuse on her daughter, Becky.

childbirth. (BL, CN, MP) Birth is generally a happy event in Tyler's fiction, yet births often lead to potential conflicts. In *Celestial Navigation*, Mary Tell and Jeremy Pauling's marriage suffers one of its greatest crises when Mary goes to the hospital without him. In *Morgan's Passing*, Emily Meredith's pregnancy precipitates Morgan's removal from his old life and his entry into a new one. In *Breathing Lessons*, Leroy's birth does not solve the problems between Jesse and Fiona Moran. Instead, Maggie Moran becomes more involved than ever and ultimately lonelier than ever after Fiona leaves with Leroy.

childhood. (BL, "Laps," "Lights," "Neutral," SC, SM, "Two People," "Who Would Want," "Your Place") Childhood is a difficult time for Anne Tyler's characters, a time of uncertainty and fear, fear of growing up, fear of change, fear of loss. Therefore, many of Tyler's characters struggle during their early years. Her earliest short stories, as well as her later novels, include such portraits of childhood.

children's perspective. ("Laura," "Lights," "Neutral," SM, TCT, "Who Would Want") Anne Tyler is very sensitive to the feelings and insights of children. Perhaps this rare ability to empathize with children and to view the world from their perspective stems from her own childhood during which she developed a sense of being both an outsider and an observer. Two of her earliest stories, "Laura" and "The Lights on the River," attempt to present events from a child's perspective. Later stories, such as "Neutral Ground" and "Who Would Want a Little Boy," explore a child's reaction to life-altering events such as divorce and separation from family.

Chuckie. (SM) young soldier who dies in Vietnam when he jumps out of his plane without a parachute; Sister Lula's son.

circles. (BL, CN, LY, SM) In Anne Tyler's fiction, everything usually winds up where it started. Subsequently, the circle serves as a major motif in many of her stories and novels. Jeremy Pauling, in *Celestial Navigation*, sails around in circles at the end of the novel, unable to break out of the pattern of his life. In almost every other novel the circular pattern asserts itself as well. At the end of *Ladder of Years*, Delia Grinstead returns home. At the end of *Saint Maybe*, Ian Bedloe goes upstairs to retrieve his new child and bring him downstairs to present to his family in much the same way that his brother Danny had presented his daughter Daphne more than twenty years earlier. Thus, the circle becomes both an enclosure circumscribing the limits of Tyler's characters' lives and, at the same time, a comforting symbol of the unity and cohesiveness of the life cycle.

Claire. ("Linguistics") an American college student who meets and marries a foreigner.

Claire. (MP) Emily Meredith's second cousin.

Clara. (SM) a member of the Church of the Second Chance, whom the children think Ian Bedloe is interested in until he announces that he is marrying Rita diCarlo.

Clara. ("With All Flags") Mr. Carpenter's daughter (almost 50), who reminds him of her mother; although Clara has six children, she tries to convince her father to stay with her family rather than go into a nursing home.

Mr. Clarkson. ("Bride") an old man who lives next to Venetia Oliver.

Claude. (MP) Claire's husband, a dentist.

Claudette. (DHR) Beck Tull's lady friend, whom he is considering marrying after his first wife Pearl Tull's death.

Claudia. (SC) the Mayhews' maid in Philadelphia.

Claudine. (BL) character on a soap opera that Maggie and Fiona Moran used to watch together; Claudine was in love with Peter.

claustrophobia. (BL, EP) See RESTRICTIVENESS.

Durwood Clegg. (BL) classmate of Maggie Moran and Serena Gill's, whom Maggie had not liked during high school, but who had settled in the neighborhood; in high school Maggie had turned down a date with him because he was "too soft" (BL 70), too much like her father.

Peg Clegg. (BL) Durwood Clegg's wife.

Clement. (DHR) truck driver who gives Luke Tull a ride as far as Richmond, Virginia.

clocks. (BL, CW) See TIME.

The Clock Winder. Significant as the first Tyler novel set in Baltimore, *The Clock Winder* is set in Roland Park, an upscale north Baltimore neighborhood, although she does allow her caretaker heroine, Elizabeth Abbott, to return home to North Carolina in the middle of the novel, setting up another of Tyler's escape/return paradigms.

Despite claiming not to "like people you can have so much effect on" (CW 14), Elizabeth Abbott becomes a caretaker to the monumentally unself-reliant Emerson family. Over the course of the ten-year timeframe of the novel, the Emerson family grows increasingly dependent upon Elizabeth. Although when Elizabeth first joins the Emerson household she works only as a handyman, she soon becomes indispensable to Mrs. Pamela Emerson, the recently widowed matriarch of the family, and, for various reasons, to her seven grown children. In fact, Elizabeth's influence is so great that Timothy Emerson commits suicide because of her, Andrew Emerson shoots her in the arm, and Matthew Emerson eventually marries her.

Before all this assimilation can take place, however, Elizabeth must work through her own feelings of identity and dependency. Following the crisis of Timothy's suicide, Elizabeth returns to her home in North Carolina, where, under pressure from her parents, she almost marries her old boyfriend, Dommie Whitehall. With the aid of Margaret Emerson, who has driven down for the wedding, however, Elizabeth leaves Dommie at the altar and moves on with her life.

Not returning to Baltimore immediately, Elizabeth works for a while teaching crafts at a reform school. When an Emerson family crisis develops (Mrs. Emerson's stroke), however, Elizabeth is drawn back into the family web and settles once again back into the fold. This return prompts Andrew's attack on her, Mrs. Emerson's calling her "Gillespie," and ultimately her name changing to Emerson officially with her marriage to Matthew. Thus, at the end of the novel, Elizabeth is once again acting as caretaker to the entire Emerson clan, which has grown by this time to include two children of her own, one of whom she nurses "like a broad golden madonna" (CW 309). Such a conventional ending, however, did not really suit Tyler, who noted in a 1972 interview with Clifford Ridley that Elizabeth's choice to return to the Emerson home does her "irreparable damage" yet provides what is "the best and happiest thing for her."

For Further Reading

Croft, Robert W. *Anne Tyler: A Bio-Bibliography.* Westport, CT: Greenwood Press, 1995. 44–45.

Evans, Elizabeth. *Anne Tyler.* New York: Twayne, 1993.

Marovitz, Sanford. "Anne Tyler's Emersonian Balance." *Critical Essays on Anne Tyler.* Ed. Alice Hall Petry. New York: G. K. Hall, 1992. 207–20.

Petry, Alice Hall. *Understanding Anne Tyler.* Columbia: University of South Carolina Press, 1990. 73–97.

Voelker, Joseph C. *Art and the Accidental in Anne Tyler.* Columbia: University of Missouri Press, 1989. 48–66.

Selected Book Reviews

Easton, Elizabeth. *Saturday Review* 17 June 1972: 77.

Levin, Martin. "New & Novel." *New York Times Book Review* 21 May 1972: 31. [Reprinted in *Critical Essays on Anne Tyler.* Ed. Alice Hall Petry. New York: G. K. Hall, 1992: 67.]

Smith, Catharine Mack. "Indian File." *New Statesman* 16 Feb. 1973: 240–41.

Clotelia. (SDL) African American maid who has worked for the Deckers for the past four years and yet still remains an outsider; nevertheless, she acts as a surrogate mother to Evie Decker.

clothes. ("Base-Metal," CN, MP, TCT, "Under Tree") See ESSENTIALS.

clutter. (CN, SM, "With All Flags") See ORDER.

Sarah Cobbett. ("I'm Not Going") Noona Long's thin, 38-year-old friend; a history teacher.

Amanda Coble. ("Teenage") Daisy and Matt Coble's daughter, who gets less attention from her mother because of the time Daisy spends with their troubled son, Donny.

Daisy Coble. ("Teenage") Matt Coble's wife; Donny and Daisy's mother; a former fourth grade teacher.

Donny Coble. ("Teenage") Daisy and Matt Coble's troubled 15-year-old son, who eventually runs away from home.

Matt Coble. ("Teenage") Daisy Coble's husband; Donny and Daisy's father; an insurance agent.

Miss Cohen. (CN) neighbor of the Paulings who lives with her widowed mother.

college. (BL, CW, DHR, IMEC, SM, "Street") Jenny Tull's experience in college and medical school in *Dinner at the Homesick Restaurant* and Ian Bedloe's single semester at Sumner College in *Saint Maybe* are the only Tyler novels that treat college life in any great detail. Instead, most of Tyler's characters have not attended college or have had to sacrifice their dreams of college (as Ian ultimately does) in order to care for family members, for example, Sammy in "A Street of Bugles," Elizabeth Abbott in *The Clock Winder*, and Ira Moran in *Breathing Lessons*.

coming of age. ("Base-Metal," "Foot-Footing," "Laura," SM) Growing up is not easy, as many of Anne Tyler's characters learn. Perhaps the hardest phase of life for anyone to navigate is the transitional section between childhood and adulthood. Most of her characters eventually realize that adulthood does not offer all of the answers to life's questions. Instead, adulthood brings only more ambiguity and more responsibility. In "The Base-Metal Egg," Mary Beth Polk realizes that she cannot maintain her own identity. Later, in "Foot-Footing On," she comes to understand that she will move on to the next stage of her life—marriage—despite her reservations. In *Saint Maybe*, Ian Bedloe is forced to grow up quickly as he assumes responsibility for three children. In the same novel, Daphne Bedloe, however, struggles with her new adulthood, drifting from job to job as she searches for her identity and her place in the world.

"The Common Courtesies." *McCall's* June 1968: 62–63+. With its anachronistic Southern setting and situation, this story seems a bit outdated today. Yet the compassion with which Tyler invests each of her characters and the consideration that each exhibits to the other are central to Tyler's view of life. Such a consideration for individual differences and an understanding of others' feelings would make the world a better place. In this story everyone seems to exhibit that compassion to Miss Lorna, a woman who obviously loves her daughter but fears losing her. The question, of course, is how long can this concentration of concern on one person be maintained without exacting a debilitating toll on the other characters. *Synopsis:* Despite the May heat, Miss Lorna Johnson, a rather large woman, has been sitting out on her front porch, eating Sunshine biscuits for three weeks because she is angry at her daughter Melissa for having a baby. Miss Lorna is waited on by Ida Donner, her loyal black maid, whom Lorna describes as "colored, but her heart was in the right place" (121). Miss Lorna always sits in the same wicker chair, even though her husband, Mr. Billy, had bought her a Strato-Lounger for her birthday.

When the chair begins to give way from Miss Lorna's weight and all the sitting she's doing this May, Ida reinforces the chair's seat with a piece of plywood. Miss Lorna is very grateful to Ida and tells her, with an ache in her chest, that fixing the chair is "the kindest thing anyone has ever done for [her]" (123).

Despite Mr. Billy's repeated pleas over the past weeks, Miss Lorna has refused to come in out of the heat. She tells him that she's "having to watch over [her] heart" (123). This heart trouble had begun last October when Melissa had announced that she was expecting a baby in April. For months Miss Lorna has worried about her daughter because she had been such a sickly child. Miss Lorna had also specifically warned Melissa to take care not to become pregnant after she married Joel, an insurance man whom no one knew. Toward the end of the pregnancy, Miss Lorna had stopped seeing her daughter at all. So on April 30, when the baby was born, Miss Lorna had taken to her chair out on the porch and begun her vigil.

Three weeks later, on May 21, Ida tells Miss Lorna that the baby is being christened and that he has been named William after his grandfather. Miss Lorna acts as if she does not care, but she really does. She begins to think back to her courtship with "Mr. Billy," a formal name that she has always insisted on because, according to her, "the little things are the ones that count in the end. The little graces, the common courtesies" (126). She also remembers how her father had admired her and spent a fortune on voice lessons for her. Ida, who's heard these stories many times before, sits listening to Miss Lorna reminisce about her fame as a singer.

Time seems to run together as Miss Lorna thinks about the christening. For a moment she even forgets whose christening it is. She also confuses her present porch-sitting protest with a previous incident last August. In that episode she had sat outside for twenty-nine days because she had mistakenly thought that Mr. Billy was having an affair with his secretary. Thinking about that incident upsets Miss Lorna and she cries. Ida comforts her.

After William's christening, Mr. Billy, Melissa, and Joel come by to show the baby to his grandmother. Melissa apologizes for "the concern" (129) she's caused her mother. Although Miss Lorna looks at the baby, she declines Melissa's offer to hold him. Instead she criticizes the way William is bundled up on such a hot day and begins talking about her singing career while she munches her Sunshine biscuits. As they have many times before, the others just sit and listen to Miss Lorna.

communication. (CW, DHR, "Flaw," "Linguistics," LY, "Nobody," "Some Sign," TCT) Anne Tyler's characters usually don't communicate well. In *Dinner at the Homesick Restaurant*, Pearl Tull, after being deserted by her husband, asserts: "There ought to be a whole separate language . . . for . . . perfect, absolute truth" (DHR 10). Without this other language no human being can fully communicate with any other; therefore, Tyler's characters are faced with the dilemma of reconciling their desire to communicate with those around them, especially those they love and care about, with the limitations of language and their own fears of making such connections. Usually, they either fail to make the effort to communicate, or more often, make the attempt only to be misunderstood. For example, in "Some Sign That I Ever Made You Happy," Sam Simmons' attempt to convey his love to his busy wife only results in an argument with her. In the end, Sam is relegated to the isolation of his own living room. Sometimes, however, Tyler's characters do manage to triumph over communication barriers. In the story "Linguistics," an American woman marries a foreigner and experiences some language difficulties. Over the years, however, the couple develops their own language that allows them to communicate their personal feelings quite effectively. Thus, communication for Tyler's characters, though usually difficult, is not impossible.

computers. (LY) See GADGETS.

Miss Cone. (SDL) teacher at Pulqua High School; Evie Decker's father takes over her class.

connections. (BL, CW, EP, MP) E. M. Forster's famous admonition, "Only connect," is certainly applicable to most of Tyler's characters. They all attempt, more or less successfully, to establish, maintain, and/or strengthen connections to other people in their lives. In *Breathing Lessons*, Maggie Moran endeavors to reestablish a connection to her granddaughter, Leroy. Mrs. Emerson, in *The Clock Winder*, tries to maintain connections to her children as they grow up and away from her even as she attempts to overcome the loss of her husband. In *Earthly Possessions*, Charlotte Emory strives to break away from her family connections only to discover that they are an intrinsic part of her life; thus, in the end, she returns home. Although connections are necessary in Tyler's world, they are double-edged swords, cutting and comforting her characters at the same time.

Miss Connolly. (SDL) nurse at the hospital where Evie Decker gets stitches.

Rev. Connors. (BL) minister at Max and Serena Gill's wedding.

contests. (AT, CN, SDL, TCT) See GAMES.

control. (AT, BL, "Holding," "Teenage") All of Tyler's characters, whether it be the anal retentive Learys of *The Accidental Tourist* or the manipulative Maggie Moran of *Breathing Lessons*, yearn to achieve some measure of control over their chaotic lives. Despite their best efforts, however, absolute control remains impossible. As Mrs. Coble discovers in "A Teenage Wasteland" after attempting to protect her son and alter his lifestyle, control is ultimately only an illusion.

Mrs. Herbert Lee Cooke. (CN) wealthy Baltimore woman who buys one of Jeremy Pauling's statues and lends it for Jeremy's one-man show.

Coquette. (MP) fifth grade classmate of Kate Gower's, who also likes Jackson Eps.

Coralette. (SC) woman who works in the concession stand in Alonzo Divich's carnival.

Corey. ("Woman") a housewife married to Ben; her life follows stages much like the cicadas' seventeen-year cycles.

"The Country Cook." *Harper's* Mar. 1982: 54–62. This story is an abridged version of chapter five of *Dinner at the Homesick Restaurant*. It concentrates on how Cody Tull and Ruth Spivey fall in love. Sections not related to Cody's campaign to steal Ruth away from his brother, Ezra Tull, are deleted.

Courtney. (LY) beautiful young blonde who gives Paul Cates the wrong number, thus setting up the argument between Susie Grinstead and Driscoll Avery that causes them to postpone their wedding.

courtship. (BL, DHR) See ROMANCE.

cradles. (BL, SM) See FURNITURE.

Florence Crisawn. ("I Never Saw") high school classmate of Pearl Domer's, who now lives in Carroll, Georgia; she and her husband pay Pearl a visit.

John Crisawn. ("I Never Saw") Florence Crisawn's husband; a photographer.

Billy Cullen. (MP) Bonny Gower's baby brother, who has been married three times.

Ollie Cullen. (MP) Bonny Gower's uncle who supervises Morgan Gower's work at the hardware store.

Priscilla Cullen. (MP) Billy Cullen's new wife.

Mr. Cunningham. (CW) the dying 86-year-old man Elizabeth Abbott looks after in North Carolina.

Curt. (SM) Daphne Bedloe's inventor boyfriend who drives Rita diCarlo to the emergency room.

Natalie Czernov. (MP) neighbor of Louisa Gower's who had brought her a fruitcake one Christmas when Morgan Gower was a child; Natalie's husband had suffered a stroke.

D

Abby Daley. (SM) Claudia and Macy Daley's oldest child.

Barney Daley. (SM) Claudia and Macy Daley's second child.

Cindy Daley. (SM) Claudia and Macy Daley's third child.

Claudia Bedloe Daley. (SM) Ian Bedloe's older sister, who has eight children whom she and her husband, Macy, name alphabetically: Abby, Barney, Cindy, Davey, Ellen, Frances, George, and Henry.

Davey Daley. (SM) Claudia and Macy Daley's fourth child.

Ellen Daley. (SM) Claudia and Macy Daley's fifth child.

Elmer Daley. (BL) Maggie Moran's brother.

Frances Daley. (SM) Claudia and Macy Daley's sixth child.

George Daley. (SM) Claudia and Macy Daley's seventh child.

Henry Daley. (SM) Claudia and Macy Daley's eighth and youngest child.

Josh Daley. (BL) Maggie Moran's brother, who is the same age as Maggie's husband, Ira.

Macy Daley. (SM) Claudia's husband, who gets a promotion and moves his family to Pittsburgh.

Mrs. Daley. (BL) Maggie Moran's mother, a former English teacher who always corrected her children's grammar; Mrs. Daley's father had been a lawyer, so she disapproved of the way the generations in her family had gone downhill.

Natalie Daley. (BL) Maggie Moran's brother Josh's ex-wife, to whom Maggie had given her favorite green dress.

Danny. ("Woman") Corey and Ben's older son.

Mr. Darcy. (CN) Mary Tell's father; a high school principal and a Baptist.

Mrs. Darcy. (CN) Mary Tell's mother; an English teacher and a Baptist.

Darwin Two. ("Base-Metal") Mary Beth Polk's present boyfriend, the handsomest boy in her senior class.

dating. (AT, IMEC, "I Never Saw," SDL) Two of Tyler's early novels deal with dating in a significant way. Ben Joe Hawkes and Shelley Domer date in *If Morning Ever Comes*, and Evie Decker and Drumstrings Casey go out in *A Slipping-Down Life*. Later novels, produced after Tyler was married for many years herself, concentrate more on married couples.

Dave. (BL) member of Jesse Moran's band, who offers Jesse and Fiona an apartment his mother has in Waverly.

Mr. Davies. (DHR) assistant principal who suggests that Slevin St. Ambrose might need counseling during a parent conference with his stepmother, Jenny Tull.

Rev. Davitt. (EP) pastor of Holy Basis Church who performs Charlotte and Saul Emory's marriage ceremony.

Tucker Dawcett. (SC) policeman in Caro Mill who comes to check on Caleb Peck.

Mrs. Tucker Dawcett. (SC) a neighbor of Justine and Duncan Peck's in Caro Mill, who fears that her husband is being unfaithful.

Lucy Dean. (SM) See LUCY DEAN DULSIMORE BEDLOE.

death. ("As the Earth," AT, BL, CN, DHR, EP, "Feather," "Half-Truths," IMEC, "Laura," "Lights," LY, MP, SC, SDL, SM, TCT, "Under Tree," "With All Flags") From the very beginning of her work, Anne Tyler's novels have incorporated death. Her first short story, "Laura," deals with a young girl's growing knowledge of the world through the death of an old woman in the community that she lives in. Later Tyler's characters have just as much trouble assimilating the knowledge of the death of someone they care about and overcoming the effects of that death. In *The Accidental Tourist*, Macon Leary struggles to overcome the death of his son Ethan. In *Saint Maybe*, Ian Bedloe strives to overcome the guilt in helping to cause his brother Danny's death. Some characters even go so far as to run away, as Ben Meagan does in "Half-Truths and Semi-Miracles" after the death of his son. Others retreat into themselves like Mrs. Pike in *The Tin Can Tree*. Ultimately, however, the most successful of Tyler's characters grieve and then move on with their lives, having come to accept death as a natural part of the cycle of life.

death of parents. ("Bridge," EP, "Knack," "Lights," MP, SC, SDL, SM, "Some Sign") A surprising number of Tyler's characters have experienced the death of one or both of their parents. In *Earthly Possessions*, Charlotte Emory loses her ineffectual father and then later her mother. Charlotte's struggle to cope with these losses is actually a struggle to find her own identity, which for so many years she has felt has been separate from her parents'. Her mother's death, however, teaches her that she is her mother's child. In *Searching for Caleb*, Justine Peck loses her father and her mother. Then she must deal with the guilt that her marriage to her first cousin Duncan had precipitated their deaths. A character with a similar problem is Morgan Gower in *Morgan's Passing*, whose attempts to understand the reasons for his father's suicide prove unsuccessful.

Aster Debney. (EP) Gerard Debney's wife, who doesn't like her husband's family.

Clarence Debney. (EP) Gerard and Aster Debney's fat son, who has adenoid problems.

Gerard Debney. (EP) Lacey Ames' short, fat brother.

Eve Abbott Decker. (SDL) Evie Decker's mother, who died of childbed fever after Evie's birth.

Evie Decker. (SDL) overweight 17-year-old girl who cuts the name of rock singer Drum Casey on her forehead; later she marries him but then leaves him after she becomes pregnant.

Sam Decker. (SDL) Evie Decker's quiet father; a high school math teacher and a widower who does not meddle in Evie's affairs; he dies of a heart attack.

Glorietta de Merino. (SC) Duncan's high school girlfriend who always wore red.

demolition derby. (EP) Tyler got the idea for Jake Simms' unusual profession as a demolition derby driver from an article in the *Baltimore Sun*.

Denise. ("Woman") Dudley's college girlfriend who attends Towson State; on a bet she eats a cicada's wing.

Lillian Denneson. ("Knack") Susan Sebastiani's mother, who committed suicide.

Mr. Denneson. ("Knack") Susan Sebastiani's father; a farmer.

dependency. (BL, CN, CW, DHR, "Holding," SM) In "Holding Things Together," the young wife laments her husband's inability to maintain either his car or their home. As a result, the young woman begins to feel that all the responsibility falls on her shoulders and that her husband depends entirely on her. In *Dinner at the Homesick Restaurant*, Pearl Tull feels a similar burden after her husband Beck deserts her, leaving her with three young children to raise. This feeling of dependency irks Tyler's characters, yet at the same time, as Ian Bedloe comes to understand in *Saint Maybe*, the dependency of others on a person creates a bond and builds a relationship of trust. So, too, as time passes, the dependency may shift as it does from Ian's parents to Ian. Ultimately, however, when Thomas, Agatha, and Daphne grow up, they begin to take on responsibility for Ian. Dependency thus becomes a cycle that, when it works best, becomes a mutually beneficial process. Only when one person feels overburdened or completely restricted does the dependency become destructive.

depression. (DHR, "Outside," TCT) See MENTAL ILLNESS.

Mark Derby. (BL) the guy Fiona Moran dated for three months, who got mad when she wrecked his car.

desertion. ("Average," CN, DHR, "Half-Truths," "Street") Many of Tyler's women and children suffer from the effects of a husband or father who has deserted his family. In "Average Waves in Unprotected Waters," Bett must deal with the care of a mentally handicapped son after her husband abandons her following their son's birth. In *Celestial Navigation*, Mr. Pauling left his family, leaving Jeremy Pauling in his mother's smothering care. In *Saint Maybe*, Lucy Dean is abandoned, pregnant and alone, by Mr. Belling. In "Half-Truths and Semi-Miracles," Ben Meagan leaves his wife Susanna after she is unable to save their dying son. Most significantly, in *Dinner at the Homesick Restaurant*, Pearl Tull's life is completely altered by Beck's desertion one night in 1944 after he decided that he didn't want to be married anymore.

Diana. ("Half-Truths") one of Susanna Spright Meagan's sisters who worked in their father's pharmacy but soon married.

diaries. (DHR, "Some Sign," "Under Tree") Seemingly instruments for recording one's most intimate thoughts, in Tyler's work diaries more often serve to obscure a person's real thoughts. Just as, in *Dinner at the Homesick Restaurant*, Pearl Tull would scribble "Apple Apple" over parts of her diary that she wanted no one to read, no one reading another person's diary really gets an accurate picture of the person's true thoughts. As Sam Simmons learns in "Some Sign That I Ever Made You Happy," his father remains as much a mystery to him after he reads his diary as before. Most of his father's diary entries merely record the weather and the mundane aspects of life, not his inner feelings.

Bobbeen diCarlo. (SM) Rita diCarlo's loud mother.

Rita diCarlo. (SM) See RITA DICARLO BEDLOE.

Reverend Didicott. (SC) minister who performs Justine and Duncan Peck's marriage ceremony.

diets. (BL, EP) Maggie Moran in *Breathing Lessons* is continually dieting while still eating whatever she wants. Her diet, like many of Tyler's responses to food, is merely an attempt to control some aspect of her otherwise uncontrollable life.

Mr. Dillard. (SC) youngest son of the headmaster of Salter Academy, Caleb Peck's school.

Mrs. Dillard. (SC) Mr. Dillard's wife, who makes homemade butter mints.

Dinner at the Homesick Restaurant. In *Dinner at the Homesick Restaurant*, Tyler focuses on her major theme: family and the conflicting feelings of an individual toward his or her family, as well as the strange phenomenon of how family members, as she admitted in a 1979 interview with George Dorner in a local Baltimore periodical, *The Rambler*, manage to "endure together—adapt, adjust, grate against each other, give up, and then start over again in the morning." In *Dinner at the Homesick Restaurant*, the members of the Tull family manage, despite many obstacles during their childhoods, to endure. As Jenny Tull tells her brother Ezra years later: "Why, the three of us turned out fine, just fine!" (DHR 200).

Before reaching that point in their lives, however, the three Tull children—Cody, Ezra, and Jenny—must endure quite a bit. Most of their problems stem from their traveling salesman father Beck Tull's desertion one Sunday night in 1944 when they are 14, 11, and 9, respectively. Beck's desertion leaves them at the mercy of their mother, Pearl, who becomes "an angry sort of mother" (DHR 19), overwhelmed by the tremendous responsibilities associated with raising children. Worse yet, without Beck's support, Pearl feels that the "whole, entire house . . . [rests] on [her] shoulders" (DHR 16). Therefore, Pearl turns most of her attention to her work and to the upkeep of the Baltimore rowhouse that she rents, rather than on her children. The perfect metaphor for this lack of maternal nurturing in a novel with a title related to food is the exhausted Pearl's habit of merely half-warming up canned food for her family's hasty meals and the store-bought pies she serves even on holidays.

The effect of this emotional starvation shows up in each of Pearl's children in different ways. Cody, who feels guilty for his father's desertion, plays practical jokes on Ezra, Pearl's obvious favorite, in a futile attempt to gain his mother's attention. Nothing works, however, for Pearl always sees right through Cody's ruses. Later, as an adult, Cody struggles to achieve business success to rival and surpass his father's in order to gain more love from his mother. Although Cody moves up the corporate ladder of material success, switching from Pontiac to Cadillac to Mercedes and finally buying the rowhouse for Pearl, he finds little peace or satisfaction in his personal life. He doubts the faithfulness of Ruth Spivey, the wife he stole from his brother Ezra, and neglects their son, Luke. Ironically, Cody's neglect of Luke parallels Cody's own father's neglect of him as a boy. There is a difference, however. Cody never deserts his family. In fact, he even makes them move around the country with him from job to job, although that means that they never get to put down roots or build a home of their own. This insistence of Cody's to maintain his familial ties offers the one hope that Cody might be able to overcome the pain of his childhood and break the cycle of emotional immaturity that stunted his youth.

Jenny Tull suffers the most because of her mother. Although Jenny grows up to be a beautiful, intelligent young woman, Pearl's emotional abuse causes her to feel unwanted and isolated. Ultimately, she develops a mild case of anorexia. More problematic, she seems unable to sustain a relationship with a man, resulting in two failed marriages. Worst of all, the cycle of abuse that Jenny endured as a child repeats itself when, under the mental, emotional, and financial strain of medical school and single motherhood, Jenny begins to inflict a similar abuse on her own daughter, Becky. Luckily, with some financial help from Cody and a hand from Pearl caring for Becky, Jenny is able to ride out the crisis, finish medical school, and establish a successful life for herself. Ironically, her chosen profession, pediatrics, turns her into a surrogate mother for hundreds of children. Even more important, she finds a ready-made family of six stepchildren with her third husband, Joe St. Ambrose. These connections, which Jenny learns not to take too seriously, perhaps because neither her patients nor her stepchildren are her sole responsibility, allow her to develop a habit of taking "life on a slant" (DHR 212).

For Ezra, the effect of his mother's control is the deepest and longest lasting. After Cody steals Ruth away from him, Ezra spends the rest of his life living with Pearl. His one escape is the restaurant that he inherits from another mother figure, Mrs. Scarlatti. Ezra transforms Scarlatti's into the Homesick Restaurant, a place where people come for the home-cooked food made with love. The restaurant's name is a dual metaphor for Tyler's view of the family. On the one hand, absence or alienation from one's family can produce a nostalgic homesickness in the conventional sense of the term. On the other hand, problems in a home can be the source of many of the emotional and/or psychological weaknesses of a family member, as evidenced in different ways by Cody, Jenny, and Ezra. Outside the restaurant, Ezra's life becomes emptier and more circumscribed with each passing year. He never marries or has children. Emotionally, he remains arrested in a perpetual state of adolescence, never really achieving complete psychological maturity.

Throughout the novel, Ezra's only goal is to pull off one complete family dinner to make up for the closeness his family never had while he and his siblings were growing up. For various reasons, however, the first four dinners never make it past the first few courses. At the end of the novel, though, in the final dinner scene, ironically held after Pearl's funeral, there is some hope that the family may make it through dessert. With their father, Beck, finally back together with his family, the opportunity for reconciliation is present. Unfortunately, a crisis develops. During a distraction, Beck disappears, a development that threatens to ruin yet another dinner. When Cody, the one most hurt by Beck's desertion, turns out to be the one who finds the old man, however, Ezra's plan to reunite the family and to heal their emotional wounds with his food may finally have some chance of success.

For Further Reading

Bond, Adrienne. "From Addie Bundren to Pearl Tull: The Secularization of the South." *Southern Quarterly* 24 (Spring 1986): 64–73.

Croft, Robert W. *Anne Tyler: A Bio-Bibliography*. Westport, CT: Greenwood Press, 1995. 69–75.

Eckard, Paula Gallant. "Family and Community in Anne Tyler's *Dinner at the Homesick Restaurant*." *Southern Literary Journal* 22 (Spring 1990): 33–44.

Elkins, Mary J. "*Dinner at the Homesick Restaurant*: The Faulkner Connection." *Atlantis: A Women's Studies Journal* 10 (Spring 1986): 93–105. [Reprinted in *The Fiction of Anne Tyler*. Ed. C. Ralph Stephens. Jackson: University Press of Mississippi, 1990: 119–35.]

Evans, Elizabeth. *Anne Tyler*. New York: Twayne, 1993.

Petry, Alice Hall. *Understanding Anne Tyler*. Columbia: University of South Carolina Press, 1990. 186–209.

Robertson, Mary F. "Anne Tyler: Medusa Points and Contact Points." *Contemporary American Women Writers: Narrative Strategies*. Ed. Catherine Rainwater and William J. Scheik. Lexington: University of Kentucky Press, 1985: 119–42. [Reprinted in *Critical Essays on Anne Tyler*. Ed. Alice Hall Petry. New York: G. K. Hall, 1992: 184–204.]

Town, Caren J. "Rewriting the Family During *Dinner at the Homesick Restaurant*." *Southern Quarterly* 31 (Fall 1992): 14–23.

Voelker, Joseph C. *Art and the Accidental in Anne Tyler*. Columbia: University of Missouri Press, 1989. 125–46.

Wagner, Joseph B. "Beck Tull: 'The absent presence' in *Dinner at the Homesick Restaurant*." *The Fiction of Anne Tyler*. Ed. C. Ralph Stephens. Jackson: University Press of Mississippi, 1990: 73–83.

Selected Book Reviews

de Mott, Benjamin. "Funny, Wise and True." *New York Times Book Review* 14 Mar. 1982: 1+. [Reprinted in *Critical Essays on Anne Tyler*. Ed. Alice Hall Petry. New York: G. K. Hall, 1992: 111–14.]

Gornick, Vivian. "Anne Tyler's Arrested Development." *Village Voice* 30 Mar. 1982: 40–41.

Mars-Jones, Adam. "Family Mealtimes." *Times Literary Supplement* 29 Oct. 1982: 1188.

McMurtry, Larry. "Tyler Artfully Mixes Domestic Fare, Tragedy." *Chicago Tribune BookWorld* 21 Mar. 1982: 3.

See, Carolyn. "The Family's Hold—A Caress or Grip?" *Los Angeles Times* 30 Mar. 1982, sec. VI: 6.

Seton, Cynthia Propper. "Generations at Table." *Washington Post Book World* 4 Apr. 1982: 7.

Sheppard, R. Z. "Eat and Run." *Time* 5 Apr. 1982: 77–78.

Updike, John. "On Such a Beautiful Green Little Planet." *New Yorker* 5 Apr. 1982: 189+. [Reprinted in *Critical Essays on Anne Tyler*. Ed. Alice Hall Petry. New York: G. K. Hall, 1992: 107–10; and in his *Hugging the Shore: Essays and Criticism*. New York: Knopf, 1983: 292–99.]

Wolcott, James. "Strange New World." *Esquire* Apr. 1982: 123–24. [Reprinted in

Critical Essays on Anne Tyler. Ed. Alice Hall Petry. New York: G. K. Hall, 1992: 115–16.]

dinners. (AT, DHR, LY, SC, SM) Meals provide Tyler's families opportunities to gather. In some cases the gatherings only serve to reinforce old habits, as the Learys' potato eating ritual illustrates in *The Accidental Tourist*. In other instances, these family dinners provide opportunities for conflict. In *Ladder of Years*, one dinner is interrupted by an irate mother-in-law and another family dinner is suspended after Nat Moffat's heartrending breakdown upon realizing the significance of the passage of time. The most significant use of the dinner motif occurs in *Dinner at the Homesick Restaurant*, where a series of family dinners that never quite come off, orchestrated by Ezra Tull, chart the course of Ezra's attempt to bring his family together. At the end of the novel the family that was broken apart when Beck Tull deserted it in 1944 is finally reunited when Beck attends his wife Pearl's funeral in 1979 and joins the family for dinner afterwards. Ironically, Pearl is not at this final dinner. Nevertheless, this last dinner survives more courses than any of the previous dinners and promises to reach its conclusion, despite Beck's running away and being caught by his son Cody Tull.

disguises. (BL, CW, MP) See IMPOSTORS.

Alonzo Divich. (SC) 52-year-old owner of a traveling carnival show; he has been married seven times; at the end of the novel he hires Justine Peck as the carnival's fortuneteller and Duncan Peck as its mechanic.

divorce. (AT, BL, CN, DHR, LY, "Neutral") Divorce is uncommon in Anne Tyler's fiction. When it does occur, however, Tyler's interest is concentrated on the aftereffects of the divorce, rather than its causes. Fiona and Jessie Moran's breakup in *Breathing Lessons* creates unsettling effects in Maggie Moran's life. The Leary brothers all move back home after their breakups. The most poignant effects of divorce, however, fall on the children, as seen in "Neutral Ground."

doctors. (CW, DHR, LY, MP, SM) As the wife of a physician, Anne Tyler certainly has firsthand knowledge of the long hours and constant demands on members of the medical profession. Until *Ladder of Years*, however, with her portrait of Sam Grinstead, she uses doctors only in secondary roles when other characters are hurt or sick.

Dodie. ("Knack") Susan Sebastiani's ex-roommate.

dogs. (AT, MP, SM) See PETS.

For Further Reading

Cuningham, Henry. "An Accidental Tourist's Best Friend: Edward as Four-Legged Literary Device." *Notes on Contemporary Literature* 23.4 (1993): 10–12.

Jesse Dole. (SC) Caleb Peck's only friend at the nursing home; a horn player who dies in August 1972.

dolls. (EP, SM) Dolls are more than playthings in Anne Tyler. For her characters they are clues to identity. In *Earthly Possessions*, the doll houses that Linus Emory makes mirror the furniture and lives of the Emory family. In *Saint Maybe*, Thomas Bedloe's doll, Dulcimer, provides the clue to the children's true name—Dulsimore.

Mr. Domer. ("I Never Saw") Shelley Domer's father.

Mrs. Pearl Domer. ("I Never Saw") Shelley Domer's mother.

Phoebe Domer. (IMEC, "I Never Saw") Shelley Domer's little sister who watches Ben Joe Hawkes and Shelley come home from their date in "I Never Saw Morning"; later in the novel, she dies in a car wreck, along with her parents.

Shelley Domer. (IMEC, "I Never Saw," "Nobody") Ben Joe Hawkes' first girlfriend in Sandhill, North Carolina; she elopes to New York with him at the end of the novel.

Don. ("Spending") Lindy's husband, whose mother's legacy provides the money for the check Lindy gives to her parents, Joe and Dory Bell.

Donna. (LY) one of Nat Moffat's four daughters; she refuses to attend his wedding to Binky.

Ida Donner. ("Common") Miss Lorna Love Johnson's African American maid, who brings her cookies while she sits out on the porch.

Hattie Doone. ("Half-Truths") a healer who advises Susanna Spright Meagan to accept her gift of healing for what it is.

Dorothy. (CW) Mrs. Emerson's sister, who attends her nephew Timothy Emerson's funeral.

Aunt Dorrie. (CN) Lisa McCauley's aunt, who is taking her on an art tour of Europe.

Dot. (SM) Lucy Dean Bedloe's friend and fellow worker at the Fill 'Er Up Cafe; she is out with Lucy the night Danny dies.

Dotty. (DHR) Clement's wife, whose first daughter, Lisa Michelle, died of crib death.

Billy Douglas. ("Outside") Brandon and Melanie Douglas' fat, lonely, 10–year-old son, whom Jason McKenna tutors.

Brandon Douglas. ("Outside") Billy Douglas' alcoholic father; a wealthy factory owner.

Melanie Douglas. ("Outside") Brandon Douglas' depressed wife.

Mrs. Dowd. (CN) owner of neighborhood grocery store near the Paulings' boardinghouse.

Jamie Dower. (IMEC) 84-year-old man who returns to Sandhill to die after being away since he was 18; Gram, who used to have a crush on him, remembers his whole name: Algernon Hector James Dower III.

Samuel Dower. (IMEC) Jamie Dower's only son, whose mother died when he was born; he married and now has six children.

Sandra Dower. (IMEC) Samuel's daughter; Jamie's granddaughter, who went to Europe and saw the Pope.

dreams. (AT, BL, "Bridge," CN, CW, DHR, EP, IMEC, "Laps," LY, "Misstep," MP, SC, SDL, SM, "Some Sign," "Spending," "Street," TCT) Tyler uses dreams to reveal the emotional state of her characters. In *The Accidental Tourist*, Macon Leary's dreams show his grief over his son Ethan's death, as well as his growing interest in Muriel Pritchett. In *Ladder of Years*, Delia Grinstead's dreams express her loneliness after she leaves her family. In *Saint Maybe*, the children's dreams expose their feelings of abandonment and loss after their parents' deaths, while Ian experiences a series of dreams that chronicle his recovery from guilt over causing his brother Danny's death.

drugs. (BL, MP, SC, SDL) A few of Anne Tyler's characters do smoke marijuana, such as Duncan Peck in *Searching for Caleb* and Morgan Gower's daughter Kate in *Morgan's Passing*. But these instances don't create serious problems.

Boris Drumm. (BL) Maggie Moran's determined, solid boyfriend in high school, who taught her to drive and planned to marry her as soon as he graduated from college.

"Dry Water." *Southern Review* NS 1 (Spring 1965): 259–91. One of Tyler's longest short stories, "Dry Water" is set in North Carolina and faithfully recreates the language and customs of its place and time. The story is told from the perspective of a child, young 13-year-old Jonas Anders, whose coming to grips with his favorite uncle's death causes him to grow up. Uncle Wurssen's suicide shatters the boy's innocent world view and forces him to accept a dry, sterile, and very confusing world. Many of Tyler's other early stories, such as "The Lights on the River," "Laura," and "The Tea-Machine," adopt a similar youthful perspective.

Significantly, at the end of "Dry Water," Jonas manages to ameliorate the bleakness of life's sterile existence by reaching out to his younger brother, Arn, seemingly accepting the responsibility of caring for the boy. Walking like the other Anders family members, Jonas has discovered the one viable means of breaking though the world's isolation: reaching out to another human being.

Synopsis: Arn Anders wakes up to find his brother Jonas gone. At breakfast his mother (Liz), Uncle Abbott, and older brother Samuel discuss Jonas' past episodes of running away, as well as his latest. Last night Jonas just up and left when he was supposed to have been watching Arn. Liz blames Jonas' wanderlust on her husband's family: "pure Anders . . . nothing but his plain old *duty*" (262).

Admonishing Arn and Samuel not to think about running off, Liz recalls how, even at the age of 4, Jonas had once ridden off on his tricycle. She says he's like a wind-up car whose wheels keep going when you pick it up and races off again the minute you put it down.

A package for Liz arrives from Asheville. Just then, Jonas walks up the street whistling "Waltzing Matilda." Jonas takes the package from Arn, despite the little boy's protests, and gives it to Liz, who chides him for leaving when he should have been watching Arn.

Liz is about to go off to work when Arn reminds her about the package. First she opens the accompanying letter from Lucille Anders, Liz's now dead husband's brother Walston's ex-wife. Walston, nicknamed "Wurssun" because he was the worst one of the lot, was a ne'er-do-well. Lucille's letter explains that the package contains Wurssun's ashes sent to her from Norfolk by Pearl Joe (a friend of Wurssun's), who had had him cremated (at Walston's request) after he killed himself on a date. She also adds that Wurssun had requested that his ashes be spread over Penobscot Bay.

Jonas, who was close to Wurssun, refuses to believe he's dead. Unlike the others, he knows that Penobscot Bay is in Maine because Wurssun had told the boy that he went there once by accident and wanted to go back one day. Jonas insists on opening the package to prove that Wurssun's ashes are in it. Inside they find a red vase.

Jonas becomes angry that they don't plan to go to Maine to fulfill Wurssun's request. Uncle Abbott tells him, "Water's water" (272), and asks Liz facetiously if they should take off work since there's been a death in the family. This comment really angers Jonas, who stomps out of the room and then the house, banging the screen door behind him. When Arn asks his mother what they're going to do with Uncle Wurssun, she tells him she doesn't know yet. Then she instructs him to finish dressing and go outside. Liz and Abbott go to work, leaving Arn with Jonas.

Once he's dressed, Arn goes outside, where he finds Jonas sitting in an apple tree. Jonas confides in Arn, telling him where he was last night: pitching coins and drinking cheap wine (muscadoodle) with the tramps down by the railroad tracks. When Arn threatens to tell their mother, Jonas acts as if he doesn't care. Instead he begins to recall Uncle Wurssun, who had led an adventurous life as a sailor, a logger, and a gandy dancer, concluding that "what he don't know I wouldn't care to know" (275).

Getting down from the tree, Jonas heads off to his friend Joe Murphy's house, with Arn tagging along behind him. Sandy Ballew and an older boy named Al are there, too, helping Joe make jigsaw puzzles for charity (at Mrs. Murphy's insistence). With little trouble, Jonas convinces them to come outside to their clubhouse to smoke cigarettes, informs them of Uncle Wurssun's demise, and asks them to participate in his plan to spread his uncle's ashes on the river next to the factory.

While Joe goes to get the key to unlock his father's boat, the other boys walk back to the Anders' house to get the vase with Uncle Wurssun's ashes and some of the wine, which Jonas puts in a washed-out Clorox bottle. When Arn asks what their mother will think of his taking the ashes, Jonas speaks resentfully about how little his mother cared about Wurssun because he was too much like their father. Bitterly, he recalls that when their dad was accidentally run over while loafing in front of the feed store, his mother had not grieved; instead she had baked four pies.

The boys meet Joe back at the shed and start off for the river. They take back streets and skirt a field so as not to attract attention. Arn gets caught by some brambles and falls behind the others. By the time he extricates himself they are almost out of sight. He has to run to catch up to them, finally rejoining them just as they make it to the factory beside the polluted river.

Joe locates his father's boat and unchains it. Although Jonas tries to get Arn to stay on the shore, the younger boy insists on coming with them. Joe and Sandy row out to the middle of the river. Jonas recalls Uncle Wurssun reading an article in the paper once about "wetter water" (286) and calls the water in the river "bone-dry" (287). When Jonas throws the vase in the river, it doesn't sink. The others suggest that he hit it with the oar, but he tells them to leave it because this way it will hopefully make it to the sea all in one piece.

Then Jonas tells them it is time for the second part of the ritual: drinking "muscadoodle" from the washed-out Clorox bottle. Back on the bank, Sandy asks Jonas why he didn't run away to the sea himself to make sure that Uncle Wurssun's ashes would really get there. Taking a drink of the wine, Jonas explains that he can't understand why his idol killed himself: "Wurssun knew everything I ever hoped to know. . . . Then he went and killed himself, like either he knew there wasn't no point living or else he didn't know as much as I thought he did" (288). Then Jonas urges the wine on the others, even Arn. They all take a sip. Although Jonas wants them to finish the bottle, they are ready to go home.

Arn starts crying and develops a case of the hiccups. Jonas walks him home and scares him by saying that a bird is following them. This trick cures Arn's hiccups, and they both laugh. Arn notices that Jonas, who used to walk like Uncle Wurssun, now walks like the rest of the family.

Todd Duckett. (DHR) worker at Scarlatti's Restaurant and later Ezra's Homesick Restaurant.

Dudi. (LY) Nat Moffat's daughter who cuts off her hair when she learns of his engagement to Binky.

Dudley. ("Woman") Ben and Corey's younger son; he marries Laura and moves to California.

Boyd Dugan. (AT) Muriel Pritchett's father; a used car salesman.

Claire Dugan. (AT) Muriel Pritchett's 17-year-old sister, whose blonde looks and slightly plump figure contrast Muriel's appearance completely; she eventually moves in at Muriel's.

Lillian Dugan. (AT) Muriel Pritchett's mother.

Great-Aunt Mercer Dulaney. (MP) Emily Meredith's great-aunt, who lives in Taney, Virginia, Emily's hometown; she keeps Leon Meredith's mother up to date on his current address; Emily attends Aunt Mercer's funeral in 1976.

Dulcimer. (SM) Thomas Bedloe's doll; it provides a clue to the children's real name: Dulsimore.

Thomas Robert Dulsimore. (SM) Lucy Dean Bedloe's first husband; Agatha and Thomas Bedloe's real father; Eli Everjohn finds out that Tom Dulsimore had been killed in a motorcycle wreck in 1967.

Lawrence Dunn. (BL) patient at Silver Threads Nursing Home confined to a wheelchair.

John Dupree. (DHR) Pearl Tull's old boyfriend; a casualty of World War I.

E

Earthly Possessions. Perhaps the closest that Tyler has ever come to writing a feminist novel, *Earthly Possessions* chronicles the escape and return of Charlotte Emory, a 35-year-old housewife who is kidnapped during a bungled bank robbery while she is withdrawing funds to make her own getaway from a repressive marriage.

Stylistically, *Earthly Possessions* also has one of Tyler's most intricate plots. Alternating between chapters set in the present and the past, Tyler charts Charlotte's "kidnapping" while she examines both Charlotte's childhood and marriage.

As a child Charlotte had wondered if she had been switched at birth with her parents' real daughter. This fear had been double-edged, for while Charlotte feared that she would be discovered as a fraud and sent away, she also worried that she might actually turn out to be her eccentric parents' real daughter and "never, ever manage to escape to the outside world" (EP 15). Consequently, Charlotte has struggled all her life to achieve a sense of her true identity. Ironically, when she was 7, Charlotte had been kidnapped by a war refugee who had mistaken Charlotte for a daughter she had lost during the war. Although Charlotte had been found and returned to her parents the very same day, since then she has viewed her life as "a history of casting off encumbrances, paring down to the bare essentials, stripping for the journey" (EP 37).

Charlotte's marriage to her next-door neighbor, Saul Emory, whose character had been inspired by an article Tyler read about storefront ministers, had not freed Charlotte from her own family as she expected. In fact, the opposite occurs; her family (as well as her encumbrances) merely grows. Soon after their marriage, Saul had surprised her by becoming a "hellfire preacher," "the only person odder than [Charlotte's] mother" (EP 84), thus tying her down to his Holy Basis Church, the only place Charlotte can think of as being more restrictive than her home.

To make matters worse, Charlotte's world begins to close in on her even more as Saul brings all the furniture from his mother's house into Charlotte's parents' house where they are living, Charlotte having taken over her father's photography business after his untimely death. Then along come Saul's four brothers, returning home each in turn in various broken states in need of care, not to mention the motley assortment of church members who come and go.

Following her mother's slow death from cancer, Charlotte's feelings of repression and her need to find her place in life reach a crisis point. Overwhelmed by the "web, criss-crossed by strings of love and need and worry" (EP 182) that she lives in, she begins to discard her possessions one by one and to stop taking people's pictures. What she wants she says is to take a "wilderness course" (EP 187), which would teach her to survive without any equipment or encumbrances. When she finds a "Keep on truckin'" badge in a cereal box, she takes it as a sign that it is time for her to leave and goes to the bank to withdraw money for her journey.

In her encounter and the pursuant getaway with Jake Simms, whose demolition derby background had also been inspired by an article Tyler read in the *Baltimore Sun*, Charlotte's and Jake's roles are soon reversed. Before long it is quite evident that Charlotte is in no danger from the inept Jake and that she stays with him only because it suits her. In fact, one could argue that Charlotte remains because she sees how much Jake needs her. First he needs her to help his pregnant girlfriend, Mindy Callender, to escape from a home for wayward girls. More important, Jake needs Charlotte to convince him that he can make a commitment to Mindy and their soon-to-be-born child. That feat accomplished, Charlotte feels free to leave Jake and return to her own family by her own choice.

Back home, Charlotte finds that little has changed in her absence. Yet she has changed. She resumes her photography and continues taking care of her family, now content with the life that she once fled. When Saul suggests that they take a trip, Charlotte rejects the idea, asserting that they "have been traveling . . . all [their] lives" (EP 200).

For Further Reading

Croft, Robert W. *Anne Tyler: A Bio-Bibliography.* Westport, CT: Greenwood Press, 1995. 52–55.

Evans, Elizabeth. *Anne Tyler.* New York: Twayne, 1993.

Johnston, Sue Ann. "The Daughter as Escape Artist." *Atlantis: A Women's Studies Journal* 9 (Spring 1984): 10–22.

Nesanovich, Stella. "The Individual in the Family: Anne Tyler's *Searching for Caleb* and *Earthly Possessions.*" *Southern Review* 14 (Winter 1978): 170–76. [Reprinted in *Critical Essays on Anne Tyler.* Ed. Alice Hall Petry. New York: G. K. Hall, 1992. 159–64.]

Petry, Alice Hall. *Understanding Anne Tyler.* Columbia: University of South Carolina Press, 1990. 154–85.

Voelker, Joseph C. *Art and the Accidental in Anne Tyler.* Columbia: University of Missouri Press, 1989. 106–24.

Selected Book Reviews

Delbanco, Nicholas. *New Republic* 28 May 1977: 35–36. [Reprinted in *Critical Essays on Anne Tyler.* Ed. Alice Hall Petry. New York: G. K. Hall, 1992: 85–87.]

Johnson, Diane. "Your Money or Your Life." *Washington Post Book World* 29 May 1977: F1+.

Leonard, John. "A Loosening of Roots." *New York Times* 3 May 1977: 39.

Reed, Nancy Gail. "Novel Follows Unpredictable Escape Routes." *Christian Science Monitor* 22 June 1977: 23.

Updike, John. "Loosened Roots." *New Yorker* 6 June 1977: 130+. [Reprinted in *Critical Essays on Anne Tyler.* Ed. Alice Hall Petry. New York: G. K. Hall, 1992: 88–91; and in his *Hugging the Shore: Essays and Criticism.* New York: Knopf, 1983: 278–83.]

Buddy and Sissy Ebbetts. (AT) older neighborhood children who walk to school with Alexander Pritchett.

Mr. Ebsen. (SC) customer who likes Caleb Peck's home-baked bread at Bess Pickett's cafe in Box Hill, Louisiana.

economy. (AT, MP) See ESSENTIALS.

Eddie. (DHR) co-owner of the body shop where Josiah Payson works.

Julian Edge. (AT) Macon Leary's 36-year-old editor and the owner of the Businessman's Press; he is a nattily dressed, divorced playboy who settles down and marries Macon's sister, Rose Leary.

Mrs. Edge. (SC) coordinator of the Polk Valley Church bazaar, where Justine Peck tells fortunes.

Rose Leary Edge. (AT) See ROSE LEARY.

education. (AT, LY, MP, "Teenage") Strangely enough for a writer whose educational background includes a degree from Duke and graduate work at Columbia, many of Tyler's characters possess little formal education beyond high school. The exceptions, of course, are a few doctors, such as Agatha

Bedloe-Simms in *Saint Maybe* and Sam Grinstead in *Ladder of Years*, as well as a few teachers, such as Doug and Bee Bedloe in *Saint Maybe* and Sarah Leary in *The Accidental Tourist*. As for the educational system itself, Tyler expresses concern for the state of public schools in *The Accidental Tourist*, where Macon Leary offers to pay for Alexander Pritchett's tuition to a private school. Similarly, in *Morgan's Passing*, Gina Meredith eventually attends a private school due to the inadequacies of her public school. In *Ladder of Years*, Delia Grinstead, who works for a school principal, actually tries to help a few troubled students by tutoring them after school.

Edward. (AT) Ethan Leary's four-and-a-half-year-old Welsh corgi, who begins to misbehave after Ethan's death.

efficiency. (AT, DHR, LY) Many of Tyler's characters are obsessed with efficiency, getting the most work done with the least amount of effort in an attempt to impose order on their otherwise chaotic worlds. In *The Accidental Tourist*, Macon Leary's elaborate systems for everything from washing his clothes to fixing his breakfast illustrate his own misguided attempt to make sense out of a world of which his son Ethan is no longer a part. In *Dinner at the Homesick Restaurant*, Cody Tull actually works as a time efficiency expert. His job is to help factories cut down on the time and manpower needed to produce their products. Unfortunately, Cody translates this mindset to his personal life and fails to expend the necessary emotional effort on his own family. Saving time thus serves no purpose unless a person has something to do with the time saved.

Francis Elburn. (DHR) boy Edith Taber likes instead of Cody Tull.

electronic gadgets. (LY, SM) See GADGETS.

Elise. ("Woman") Virginia's youngest child; Corey's favorite grandchild; she is 13 in 1987.

David Elliott. (SDL) Drum Casey's energetic, blond drummer/manager; during the day he works as an insurance salesman.

Aunt Sony Elliott. ("Two People") the aunt Melinda has been sent to stay with in hopes of curing her sleepwalking; Sony sits on her porch reading the Sears catalogue; Melinda makes her nervous.

elopement. (CN, SC, SDL) See WEDDINGS.

Cousin Elsa. (DHR) relative of Pearl Tull's who might be the woman in the blouse at the picnic in the photograph Ezra Tull describes for his blind mother.

Andrew Carter Emerson. (CW) Mrs. Emerson's mentally unstable son; Timothy's twin; he shoots Elizabeth Abbott in the arm.

Billy Emerson. (CW) Mrs. Emerson's dead husband, who had made a fortune in real estate.

Elizabeth Priscilla Abbott Emerson. (CW) See ELIZABETH ABBOTT.

George Emerson. (CW) Elizabeth and Matthew Emerson's son.

Henry Emerson. (CW) Billy Emerson's brother, who never talks.

Jenny Emerson. (CW) Elizabeth and Matthew Emerson's daughter.

Margaret Carter Emerson. (CW) Mrs. Emerson's daughter who runs away with a delivery boy and later marries Brady Summers.

Mary Carter Emerson. (CW) Mrs. Emerson's daughter who marries Morris and has two children.

Matthew Carter Emerson. (CW) Mrs. Emerson's oldest son, who marries Elizabeth Abbott.

Melissa Carter Emerson. (CW) Mrs. Emerson's high-strung daughter, who works as a model.

Mrs. (Pamela) Carter Emerson. (CW) matronly matriarch of the Emerson clan; recently widowed at the start of the novel.

Paula Jean (P. J.) Grindstaff Emerson. (CW) girl from Georgia who marries Peter Emerson.

Peter Carter Emerson. (CW) Mrs. Emerson's youngest child, who is five years younger than Melissa; he serves in Vietnam and then becomes a chemistry teacher.

Timothy Carter Emerson. (CW) Mrs. Emerson's son; a medical student; Andrew's twin brother; he commits suicide.

Emily. ("Outside") Brandon and Melanie Douglas' maid; despite being a bad cook, she doesn't get fired because she is the only one who will put up with the dysfunctional Douglas family.

Emma. (SDL) Drum Casey's cousin who had her rehearsal dinner at the Parisian night club.

Emmaline. (DHR) Pearl Tull's friend who takes her to Charity Baptist Church, where she meets Beck Tull.

Reverend Emmett. (SM) a former Episcopalian seminarian who founds the Church of the Second Chance.

Alberta Emory. (EP) Saul Emory's mother, who runs away with her father-in-law.

Amos Emory. (EP) Saul Emory's oldest brother, who has a tendency to run away; he becomes a musician.

Catherine (Selinda) Emory. (EP) Charlotte and Saul Emory's daughter, Catherine, who switches names with her imaginary playmate when she is a little girl.

Charlotte Ames Emory. (EP) 35-year-old housewife who is kidnapped by Jake Simms during a foiled bank robbery; she is married to Saul Emory.

Edwin Emory. (EP) Saul Emory's father; a radio repairman who drinks too much.

Julian Emory. (EP) Saul Emory's youngest brother, who has a gambling problem.

Linus Emory. (EP) Saul Emory's brother who has a nervous breakdown; he builds dollhouse furniture.

Saul Emory. (EP) Charlotte Emory's 39-year-old husband; a preacher at Holy Basis Church.

endurance. (AT, "Average," BL, EP, LY) At the end of Faulkner's famous Nobel Prize Acceptance Speech, he asserted his hope that mankind would not only "endure but prevail." In her work Anne Tyler modifies even Faulkner's guarded optimism. For many of her characters one of their main goals is simply to endure. In *The Accidental Tourist*, Macon Leary struggles to endure the death of his son; in *Breathing Lessons*, Maggie Moran attempts to endure the loss of her idea of family; in *Ladder of Years*, Delia Grinstead tries to come to grips with her children growing up and leaving home; and in *Earthly Possessions*, Charlotte Emory must realize that she cannot run away from her own life. Endurance, therefore, is a virtue for Tyler's characters. The best of them, however, learn to do more than merely endure, in the process achieving a greater and deeper understanding and appreciation of life and of themselves.

entrapment. (BL, "Genuine," "Respect," SM) See RESTRICTIVENESS.

epistolary sections. (CW, DHR, SC) Borrowing an eighteenth-century literary convention, Tyler often uses letters to carry forward her plot as a means of condensing action. Jenny Tull's vacillation over accepting Harley Baines' perfunctory (written) marriage proposal in *Dinner at the Homesick Restaurant* is rendered in a succinct written response. Like the obligatory Peck bread-and-butter thank you notes, composed on the way home from a visit, both Daniel and Caleb Peck write letters in *Searching for Caleb*. In fact, in his letter, Daniel Peck reveals a depth of feeling that his granddaughter Justine never knew he had. Tyler's epistolary tour de force, however, is chapter seven of *The Clock Winder*, in which Elizabeth Abbott writes and receives a series of letters to and from several characters, most notably death threats from Andrew Emerson. Finally, Elizabeth responds to his threats with a threat of her own, yet even this letter reveals how deeply and irrevocably her life has become intertwined with the Emersons' lives.

Jackson Eps. (MP) a fifth grade boy Kate Gower and Coquette both like.

Ernest. (EP) Selinda Emory's nearly deaf dog.

escape. ("Artificial," "I Play," "Respect") See RESTRICTIVENESS.

escape/return. (BL, CW, EP, IMEC, LY, "Outside," SC, "Street," TCT) The title of Anne Tyler's short story excerpt from *Ladder of Years* is "The Runaway Wife." But Anne Tyler's characters have been running away from their restrictive lives from the very beginning of her work. In *If Morning Ever Comes*, Ben Joe Hawkes returns home to North Carolina, thinking that his family needs him only to discover that his family is running just fine without him. His solution to the dilemma is to take a piece of home, in the form of his old girlfriend Shelley Domer, back to New York with him. In *The Tin Can Tree*, both Joan and Simon Pike run away from home, Joan because she cannot convince James Green to marry her and Simon because he feels neglected by his mother. Ironically, the search for Simon keeps everyone so occupied that almost no one even notices Joan's absence. In *The Clock Winder*, Elizabeth Abbott is first drawn into the Emerson family, becomes overburdened by them, and escapes briefly back to her home in North Carolina, but eventually returns to become their mainstay. In *Earthly Possessions*, Charlotte Emory plans her escape only to be kidnapped by Jake Simms. By the end of their journey, however, Charlotte learns that she does not really want to escape from her family and returns. In *Searching for Caleb*, Caleb Peck pulls off a sixty-three year escape from the restrictive Peck family. At the end of the novel, Caleb does return home briefly. But even as he leaves once more the stamp of the Pecks is indelibly upon him, for he writes the obligatory Peck thank you note. Escaping from family, therefore, is not really possible. Families stamp their members with lifelong marks that neither time nor distance can completely erase.

essentials. ("Artificial," AT, BL, EP, MP, "With All Flags") For many of Tyler's characters, less is definitely more. They love to travel light, packing, as Macon Leary does in *The Accidental Tourist*, only travel size packets of any absolute necessities. For most of her characters these necessities are few in number. What is essential is not nearly as much as most people think. At the end of "The Artificial Family," Mary Scott leaves with just her daughter and their nightgowns. In *Earthly Possessions*, Charlotte Emory spends her life casting off excess encumbrances, "stripping for the journey" (EP 37) that she senses is coming. In *Morgan's Passing*, Emily Meredith's three leotards and wrap-around skirts appeal to Morgan Gower's sense of simplicity. And at the end of *Breathing Lessons*, Fiona Moran cuts short her impromptu visit to her in-laws, leaving behind everything except the essentials: her purse, her daughter Leroy, and Leroy's baseball glove.

etiquette. (BL, CW, MP) Characters like Maggie Moran's mother in *Breathing Lessons* who are overly concerned with matters of propriety do not fare well in Tyler's fiction. These characters' ineffectual attempts to impose order on an inherently chaotic world invariably end in disappointment and frustration.

Aunt Eunice. ("Half-Truths") Susanna Spright Meagan's paternal aunt who lived with the Spright family during the Depression; she is the first person Susanna heals.

Miss Evans. ("Teenage") Donny Coble's history teacher.

Eli Everjohn. (SC, SM) private detective who locates Caleb Peck in *Searching for Caleb*. In *Saint Maybe*, he is Sister Bertha King's son-in-law, who finds out about Agatha and Thomas Bedloe's father, Thomas Dulsimore.

F

---

fairy tales. (CN, CW, DHR, LY, MP, SM) In her 1976 review of Bruno Bettelheim's book, *The Uses of Enchantment: The Meaning and Importance of Fairy Tales*, Tyler admits that the story of Beauty and the Beast seems to have become a part of her life in many ways. So, too, in her stories, do fairy tales come to life. In *Dinner at the Homesick Restaurant* Jenny Tull imagines her mother raising her to eat her like the witch in Hansel and Gretel. In *Saint Maybe*, Agatha Bedloe dreams of wandering through a dark forest like Hansel and Gretel. In the most fairy-tale like novel, *Morgan's Passing*, Emily Meredith and Morgan Gower ultimately live out the tale of Beauty and the Beast until, in the end, through their puppet shows, they literally become the participants in various fairy tales. Yet, as Tyler points out in her review of Bettelheim's book, the true value of fairy tales is not the "happily ever after ending." Instead, the most important lesson is "the value in growing, in struggling, and persisting." Ultimately, that is what all of her characters do: struggle and endure.

For Further Reading

Davis, Davie Susanne. "An Examination of Fairy-Tale Motifs in Anne Tyler's *Dinner at the Homesick Restaurant*." *Publications of the Arkansas Philological Association* 16.2 (1990): 31–40.

Shafer, Aileen Chris. "Beauty and the Transformed Beast: Fairy Tales and Myths in *Morgan's Passing*." *Anne Tyler as Novelist*. Ed. Dale Salwak. Iowa City: University of Iowa Press, 1994. 125–37.

faith healers. ("Half-Truths," SC) Like ministers, faith healers provoke some suspicion in Tyler's fiction. In *Searching for Caleb*, Arthur Milsom's mother, a self-proclaimed faith healer, wears white, acts condescendingly, and obviously preys on the gullibility of those who attend her meetings. In "Half-Truths and Semi-Miracles," however, the less self-assured faith healer, Susanna Meagan, elicits more sympathy because she realizes that it is not she who works the miracles; instead the faith of the people who come to her for help makes her "semi-miracles" possible.

family. (AT, BL, CW, DHR, EP, IMEC, LY, MP, SC, SM, "Street," TCT, "Tea-Machine") Tyler's greatest theme, her constant interest, is the family. For Tyler, however, family is a contradictory force in any individual's life. On the one hand, family exerts a very positive and essential influence. Family nurtures individuals, giving them comfort, sustenance, security, a sense of belonging, and, most important of all, love. It is from the family that an individual also gets his or her most basic sense of identity.

Because of its closed-in nature, though, family can also be a destructive force in an individual's life, stripping an individual of his or her freedom and restricting the person's outlook, opportunities, and personality to the point of stagnation. That is why, in many of Tyler's novels, individuals often escape from their families, if only briefly. Nevertheless, most of these same characters eventually return to their families. Despite the scars that family life inflicts, for the most part, even these individuals recognize their need for their families and return.

For Further Reading

Carroll, Virginia Schaefer. "The Nature of Kinship in the Novels of Anne Tyler." *The Fiction of Anne Tyler*. Ed. C. Ralph Stephens. Jackson: University Press of Mississippi, 1990: 16–27.

Eckard, Paula Gallant. "Family and Community in Anne Tyler's *Dinner at the Homesick Restaurant*." *Southern Literary Journal* 22 (Spring 1990): 33–44.

Evans, Elizabeth. *Anne Tyler*. New York: Twayne, 1993. 127–50.

Gibson, Mary Ellis. "Family as Fate: The Novels of Anne Tyler." *Southern Literary Journal* 16 (Fall 1983): 47–58. [Reprinted in *Critical Essays on Anne Tyler*. Ed. Alice Hall Petry. New York: G. K. Hall, 1992: 165–74.]

Nesanovich, Stella. "The Individual in the Family: Anne Tyler's *Searching for Caleb* and *Earthly Possessions*." *Southern Review* 14 (Winter 1978): 170–76. [Reprinted in *Critical Essays on Anne Tyler*. Ed. Alice Hall Petry. New York: G. K. Hall, 1992: 159–64].

family trees. (SC) The Pecks' diamond-shaped family tree serves as a metaphor for the insularity of their family, closing back in upon itself after a generation of expansion. Still, Tyler suggests that the possibility of another expansion exists, starting with Meg Peck, Duncan and Justine's daughter.

farming. (IMEC, "Knack," SC, "Some Sign," TCT, "With Flags") The tobacco farming in *The Tin Can Tree*, the story of a trip to a Farmers' Market in *If Morning Ever Comes*, and Duncan Peck's attempt to raise goats in *Searching for Caleb* provide agricultural settings in Tyler's novels. Here Tyler is using her own personal experience as background for her fiction, for she worked in tobacco when she was a teenager in North Carolina and her father once raised goats. She also utilizes farmers as characters in some of her short stories: Mr. Denneson in "A Knack for Languages," Mr. Carpenter in "With All Flags Flying," and Mr. Simmons in "Some Sign That I Ever Made You Happy." The fact that all these farmer characters are old men who are at or near retirement, or even dead, reflects the unfortunate decline of farming as a profession in contemporary society.

"The Feather Behind the Rock." *New Yorker* 12 Aug. 1967: 26–30. This story employs a familiar Tyler motif, a journey, as a metaphor for life. Interestingly, both old and young generations are represented on this journey, giving the reader perspectives from the beginning and end of life's journey. Time itself is also telescoped through Tyler's technique of using her characters' memories. Thus, a day in 1913, more than fifty years earlier, seems as recent as last week. Finally, Tyler uses the motif of the nightly movies to reinforce her concept of the cyclical nature of time. Consequently, no night seems that different from any other. Instead of creating a sense of despair at life's sameness, however, that knowledge seems somehow comforting in this story.

Synopsis: Charles and Lucy Hopper, a couple in their seventies, have asked their grandson Joshua to accompany them on their cross-country drive. They plan to drive from Wilmington, North Carolina, to San Francisco, California. Each day they follow the same routine, never stopping to sightsee during the day, but always going to the movies at night. During the movie, Lucy discusses the movie out loud, much to Joshua's embarrassment.

One night in Kansas, they are watching a movie and Lucy starts talking about one of the actors. Joshua gets mad, tells them how any fool could tell who the villain is, and walks out. The next day their journey continues as always. Mr. Hopper relates the story of how a boy he knew in college (Harvey Stample) wished that a load of beer would be delivered in front of their dorm and it was. This day, he says, was perhaps the happiest day of his life. Lucy asserts that the happiest day of one's life is the day a person gets married. The old couple start to reminisce about their marriage and how they broke up for two years before they finally got married.

Because of the heat, they stop at a drive-in where Lucy collapses. A doctor who happens to be there examines her and advises Charles to seek further medical attention. Joshua also urges them to turn back or even fly home. But Lucy insists on continuing, so Charles relents.

They continue on down the curving roads, and that night they go to a movie as usual. During the movie, Lucy talks about the Indian's "feather behind the rock" being a sign of imminent danger. The feather represents her own coming death, which she realizes she can't avoid.

Miss Feather. (EP) old woman from Holy Basis Church, who lives with the Emorys after being evicted from her apartment in the spring of 1963.

feeders/nonfeeders. (CN, CW, DHR, SC) Tyler's characters often fall into two categories: those who care for and nurture others and those who do not. In *Dinner at the Homesick Restaurant*, these people are categorized as feeders and nonfeeders based on their attitudes toward food. Cody Tull, whose work takes up so much of his time that he has little time or interest in eating, is a nonfeeder. His brother Ezra, on the other hand, is a feeder who runs a restaurant that serves homemade food made with love. In addition, he steadfastly attempts to pull off a series of family dinners throughout the course of the novel in an ill-fated attempt to bring his family together emotionally. Cody and Ezra's sister, Jenny, is a combination of the two types. Emotionally abused as a child, she is so starved that she becomes physically anorexic and emotionally unable to sustain a relationship, as evidenced by her first two failed marriages. In her choice of a profession and her third marriage, however, she becomes a surrogate mother to hundreds of children in her pediatric practice and a stepmother to Joe St. Ambrose's six children.

Cynthia Ramsay Felson. (LY) Delia Grinstead's grandmother; Isaiah Felson's wife who had married him because he was a doctor and promised that, unlike the rest of her family, she would not die of tuberculosis.

Dr. Felson. (CW, LY) Delia Grinstead's physician father who dies the winter before the novel opens; he had hired Sam Grinstead as an assistant more than twenty years ago. Dr. Felson appears first in Tyler's work as the old Roland Park physician who tends Elizabeth Abbott's wounds when she cuts her wrist and later when Andrew Emerson shoots her in *The Clock Winder*.

Eliza Felson. (LY) Delia Grinstead's old-maidish eldest sister, 52; she works at the Pratt Library; she still lives at home with Delia and Sam until the end of the novel when she rents an apartment on Calvert Street.

Isaiah Felson. (LY) Delia Grinstead's grandfather, a doctor, who founded his medical practice in 1902.

Linda Felson. (LY) Delia Grinstead's older sister and the mother of Thérèse and Marie-Claire; a Francophile, she is divorced from a French literature professor and now lives in Michigan.

female viewpoint. ("Artificial," BL, "Bride," CN, CW, EP, "I Play") Although Tyler is not considered a feminist writer, in her works she does sometimes present situations from an exclusively feminine viewpoint. In "The Artificial Family," Mary Scott bemoans the difference between maternal and paternal responsibilities in childrearing. In *Breathing Lessons*, two-thirds of the book is related from Maggie Moran's viewpoint as a wife and mother. In *Celestial Navigation*, the highlight of Mary Tell's short marriage to Guy Tell is the female bonding that she shares with her mother-in-law, Gloria Tell. Most tellingly, in "I Play Kings," Francie Shuford laments the loss of dramatic possibilities that would be hers if only she had been a man.

Bootsy Fisher. (LY) Delia Grinstead's only friend in Baltimore; they used to carpool together.

"A Flaw in the Crust of the Earth." *Reporter* 2 Nov. 1967: 43–46. Tyler lived in Montreal from 1963–67. She, too, worked in a library (the McGill University Law Library), a job that, like Peter, she enjoyed because she could leave her work there during the day and not have to carry anything home. Thus, she could spend her evenings writing.

In the story, Peter's sense of isolation and the lack of communication the characters experience are perennial Tylerian themes. The motif of the bridge, linking Peter to the woman in the next apartment, ultimately proves untenable, as well as untranslatable to his friend, Joe. Most interesting, however, is the story's ending in which, despite the woman's warning about the "flaw in the crust of the earth," Peter apparently chooses to brave the world and overcome his fear. This ultimate endurance despite the odds almost always shines through in a Tyler work.

Synopsis: At about midnight Peter walks into his Montreal apartment, not realizing that he has been robbed until he reaches out to turn on his radio. Peter calls the police, but he can't really help the investigating officer (Graves) because he doesn't know the brand names of the appliances that have been stolen. As they attempt to make a list of the stolen objects, Peter notices that a photograph of himself at his typewriter has also been taken from its place on the kitchen wall. Unable to imagine why the thief would want his picture, Peter feels that the burglary has become "something personal, something plotted and carried out by a human-faced being who had stolen [his] likeness" (44). Not giving Peter much hope for the recovery of his property, Graves leaves.

The next day Peter arrives half an hour late for his job in the copy room of the university library. His supervisor only clicks her tongue when Peter tells her that he was burglarized, and he assiduously avoids the eyes of the other workers. Peter actually likes having a job he can leave at the end of the day. After work he goes home to find the apartment just as he had left it. Instead of cleaning up, he lies down on his daybed and falls asleep.

By the time Peter wakes up, it is dark. Through his window, he watches a woman in the next apartment building. Wondering if she saw the burglar, Peter imagines building a bridge with an ironing board over to her window in case there is a fire. Yet she never looks at him.

Feeling suffocated, Peter does not want to stay in his apartment, so he spends the night on the couch at his friend Joe Salter's place. Joe sympathizes with Peter about the burglary, but when Peter tries to explain about the woman and the fire, Joe doesn't understand. As he listens to Joe's snoring, Peter thinks about people, who are "so fragile . . . that they could be cut down by . . . the direct, dark intent of any chance intruder who wanted someone else's possessions" (45). Finally, he falls asleep.

When Peter wakes in the morning, he discovers that he has acquired trench mouth from sleeping with his mouth open. On his lunch hour, he goes to the dentist, making a joke about what could happen next to him. After lunch the copy machine breaks. Although he calls the copier repair company three times, each time a deaf old man answers, so Peter gives up and leaves work.

Heading to the train station, Peter decides to take the next train to anywhere. As he looks at the train schedules, he imagines a train crashing and realizes that he's afraid of trains. An old lady asks if he's OK. Peter responds, "I'm just grounded. I'm stuck here" (46). Then she tells him her reason for leaving: The city is built on a flaw in the crust of the earth. From her remarks, Peter realizes that there's danger everywhere and gets up feeling "lighter" (46).

Belle Flint. (LY) Delia Grinstead's outlandish landlady, and eventual best friend, in Bay Borough; she sells real estate.

Mr. Flint. ("Street") the owner of the *Odessa*, who can't even sail himself.

Mrs. Flint. ("Street") Mr. Flint's inappropriately dressed wife, who christens the *Odessa*.

Florence. (BL) Mr. Daniel Otis' sister.

fog. (BL, LY) Life often obscures meaning, making it difficult for characters to figure out where they are and what they are doing. In *Ladder of Years*, this metaphor of life's uncertainty is portrayed perfectly by the town baseball game played in the fog. As people step in and out of the fog, it seems to Delia that they are appearing and disappearing just as her new friends have appeared in her life and as her family has disappeared from it.

Dr. Fogarty. (MP) Bonny Gower's obstetrician, whose office is on St. Paul Street; Morgan Gower takes Emily Meredith to him when she gets pregnant.

Fong. ("Tea-Machine") Chinese man who lives in a shed by the Bartletts' house; he helps at the auction.

food. (AT, BL, CN, CW, DHR, IMEC, LY, MP, "Outside," SC, SDL, SM, TCT) Food plays a very important role in almost every Tyler novel, most especially in the form of family dinners that bring families together, such as in the case of *Saint Maybe* and *Ladder of Years*. Food portrays the stability of these families. In other novels, however, food reveals the quirkiness and/or conflict inherent in a family. In *The Accidental Tourist*, the Learys' traditional eating habits amount almost to obsession, symbolizing the family's insularity. In *Dinner at the Homesick Restaurant*, it is the absence of food that most closely resembles the family's emotional state. When the Tull children are young, Pearl never cooks for them; instead she simply half-warms up canned foods. The result is a group of children who are emotionally starved for her attention. When he grows up, Ezra opens his own restaurant and attempts to pull off a series of family dinners to heal the family's emotional wounds. Ironically, the only dinner that comes close to completion is the final one, which is held after Pearl's funeral.

"Foot-Footing On." *Mademoiselle* Nov. 1977: 82+. Tyler's mixed feelings about marriage and the possibility for change are explored in this story. Feeling trapped in the roles that society has thrust upon her—fiancée, wife, and, ultimately, mother—Mary Beth feels powerless to step off the path life has thrust her upon. When she does make an attempt to stop the relentless countdown to her wedding day, however, her method is most improbable— a letter to a circus. Apparently, she does not really want to change that much, or she would take more definite steps to stop her impending nuptials. Mary Beth seems caught in a state of limbo between the fear of change and an intense desire for it. Tyler wisely leaves the young woman's conflicting feelings unresolved.

Synopsis. Mary Beth Polk is having second thoughts about her approaching marriage to Tucker Randolph. She exasperates her parents, who are caught up in the elaborate wedding plans, by suggesting that she might become a nun, even though she is not Catholic. Despite Mary Beth's doubts, the days keep counting down.

At her mother's suggestion, Mary Beth and Tucker go shopping for a blue hat for Mary Beth to wear to go away in. Although Mrs. Polk has warned him not to let her daughter choose the hat because she has terrible taste, Tucker does not protest when Mary Beth chooses an awful purple felt hat with flowers encircling the crown.

The next day, four days before the big event, Mary Beth and her mother are opening some of the young couple's many wedding gifts. Although they seem to have received every gift imaginable, there are no duplicates because Mrs. Polk has given every store in town a gift list. The phone rings and

Mrs. Polk answers it, taking care of one of the many details for the wedding. This call prompts Mary Beth to ask her mother what she would do if some boy, "someone unsuitable, some bad *influence*" (82) called and asked to speak to Mary Beth, pleading that it "means more to [him] than anything" (82). Mrs. Polk responds that, of course, she would hang up on the boy, just as Mary Beth thought she would.

Three days before the wedding, Mary Beth goes to her gynecologist, who is distressed that she has waited so late to make an appointment with him. Mary Beth shocks the doctor further by announcing that she does not plan to use any birth control, insisting that she will probably just have a baby right off since that is what she is supposed to do: "First you're engaged, then you're married, then you have a baby" (82).

The following day, just two days before the wedding, Mary Beth is talking to Tucker on the phone and watching television at the same time. Tucker wants to know if she really loves him, but, even though she really does love him deeply, she does not feel like being asked the question so directly. So Mary Beth simply asks him why he is questioning her feelings for him. Then Tucker asks her to tell him what she is thinking "exactly at this moment" (86). Mary Beth replies that she thinks that their lives are being "written by someone else" and that they have to keep "foot-footing on" (86) down the path others have set for them.

After she hangs up, Mary Beth writes a letter to the circus on her best stationery to apply for a job. She says that she will work at any job regardless of the danger or just work as a seamstress sewing costumes. She leaves the letter face up on the table. Later she notices that the letter is gone. Her mother never says a word about the letter, and the wedding goes on as planned.

foreigners. (DHR, "Knack," "Linguistics," SM, "Uncle Ahmad," "Who Would Want," "Your Place") As the wife of an Iranian-born psychiatrist, Tyler has had firsthand contact with foreign relatives over the course of her more than thirty-year marriage. Some of these experiences she has converted into fiction. In every case, it seems that the foreigners have a rough time negotiating the cultural differences between their native country and the United States. In particular they struggle, often with comic results, with the language barrier. Thus, they, like most of Tyler's characters, experience a sense of isolation in the foreign country of America. Nevertheless, as Tyler almost always manages to bring out in her stories, most of them persist and ultimately adapt so that some form of communication, however limited, is established.

the foreigners. (SM) a changing group of Middle Eastern graduate students who live on Waverly Street; they take American names such as Joe, Jim, Jack, Ray, Fred, John, John Two, Ollie, Manny, Buck, and Mike. They attend many of the Bedloe family's holiday dinners and special occasions; they also provide some of the novel's comic relief. Tyler has said that she based these characters on a few of her husband's Iranian relatives, who have a fascination with Western technology.

For Further Reading

Caesar, Judith. "The Foreigners in Anne Tyler's *Saint Maybe.*" *Critique: Studies in Contemporary Fiction* 37.1 (1995): 71–79.

Mrs. Lelia Fortney. ("Half-Truths") Aunt Eunice's best friend, who has arthritis; she is the second person Susanna Spright Meagan heals.

fortunetellers. (DHR, "Nobody," SC) Life is uncertain and it is impossible to see the future. Nevertheless, Tyler's fortunetellers advise others to remain open to the future and the possibilities for change that it offers. In *Dinner at the Homesick Restaurant*, Emma Parkins advises the uncertain Jenny Tull to marry her first husband rather than be "destroyed by love" (DHR 96). In *Searching for Caleb*, Justine Peck visits a series of fortunetellers in her search for answers following her parents' untimely deaths. Unlike the others, the last fortuneteller she consults, Madame Olita, assures Justine that she has the power to change not only the future but the past as well, or at least "what hold it has on you" (129). This knowledge prompts Justine to become a fortuneteller herself and to dispense the same advice to her clients: "Take the change. Always change" (SC 29).

Francie. ("With Flags") Clara's only daughter, 13; Mr. Carpenter's favorite grandchild.

June Frank. (SC) neighbor of Justine and Duncan Peck's in Semple, Virginia; she gives Justine a begonia as a going away present.

Mary Jo Frankel. ("I'm Not Going") poor piano student Noona Long gives a lesson to at the end of the story.

Bill Frick. (LY) mayor of Bay Borough.

funerals. (BL, CN, CW, DHR, TCT) Three Tyler novels open in the wake of or preparation for a funeral. In *The Tin Can Tree*, the Pike family is returning from Janie Rose's funeral; in *Breathing Lessons*, Maggie and Ira Moran are preparing to go to the funeral of Max Gill; and in *Celestial Navigation*, Laura Pauling is returning home for her mother's funeral. Different characters respond differently to funerals. Some see the conflict that death presents and must incorporate it into their mindsets before they can move forward with their lives. Yet with Tyler's characters, despite these sobering thoughts, there is always room for life. In addition to the grief characters often exhibit, conflict and even humor abound as the reenactment of Max and Serena Gill's wedding ceremony during Max's memorial service illustrates. In the midst of death, Tyler's characters still celebrate life.

furniture. (AT, EP, SM) Objects that take up space, furniture in Anne Tyler's fiction sometimes only gets in the way. In *Earthly Possessions*, the dollhouse furniture that Linus Emory makes doubles the clutter of two housefuls of furniture that Charlotte Emory attempts, unsuccessfully, to rid her life of. As such, furniture symbolizes responsibility. In *Saint Maybe*, however, furniture provides first an escape for Ian Bedloe, who finds his work at a cabinetmaking shop a necessary outlet from the responsibilities of his home life. At the end of the novel, though, his attitude toward furniture changes. With a new son of his own on the way, he launches into building a cradle with curved lines, symbolic of his acceptance of responsibility and his reentry into the flow of time.

G

Ben Gabriel. (BL) childless widower in his seventies who lives at the Silver Threads Nursing Home, whom Maggie Moran used to have a crush on; he is deathly afraid of fire and once owned a power-tool company.

gadgets. (AT, "Knack," LY, MP, SC, SM) Tyler's characters are often fascinated with tools and various gadgets. From Macon Leary's systems in *The Accidental Tourist* to Morgan Gower's hardware store contraptions in *Morgan's Passing* to the electronic wonders of the foreigners in *Saint Maybe*, Tyler's characters attempt to install more order and control into their lives. But, more often than not, that attempt to bring order and control leads to disaster, as evidenced by Macon's systems and the foreigners' dangerous exploits. In the end, no machine or appliance can bring order or absolute control to life.

games. ("As the Earth," AT, BL, CN, DHR, IMEC, LY, SC, SM, TCT) Life is a game for many of Tyler's characters, who attempt to discover its rules and establish an orderly pattern in their lives. All too often, however, they soon learn that life's rules do not resemble those of any board game's, for they are always changing. In *Dinner at the Homesick Restaurant*, Cody Tull cheats at Monopoly in order to win, but what he discovers later in his own personal life is that cheating ultimately robs him of his own happiness. In *Breathing Lessons*, Ira Moran's isolation is portrayed by the game that he plays throughout the novel: solitaire. In *The Accidental Tourist*, the insular Leary family invents a card game called Vaccination, with rules so arcane that no one outside the immediate family can learn how to play. Thus, the game insulates them from outside intrusions much the same way that vaccinations protect people from diseases. In *Saint Maybe*, the dice that Ian and the children throw while playing Parcheesi become, in Agatha's dream, the dice of fate, rattling to determine the children's fate.

For Further Reading

Koppel, Gene. "Maggie Moran, Anne Tyler's Madcap Heroine: A Game Approach to *Breathing Lessons*." *Essays in Literature* 18 (Fall 1991): 276–87.
Sweeney, Susan Elizabeth. "Anne Tyler's Invented Games: *The Accidental Tourist* and *Breathing Lessons*." *The Southern Quarterly* 34.1 (1995): 81–97.

gardening. (BL, CW, DHR) Gardening provides an outlet for several women in Tyler's fiction. Most notably, in *The Clock Winder*, Mrs. Emerson's gardening parallels her futile attempts to maintain control over her family.

Michael Garter. (LY) the boy Courtney hoped would ask her to the dance.

Jennifer Gates. ("Saints") Laura Gates' sister, whose clothes Laura puts in the garbage to get her to stay and talk to her.

Laura Gates. ("Saints") Mary Robinson's best friend throughout school; she suffers a nervous breakdown.

Gavin. ("Some Sign") one of the pharmacists who works for Sam Simmons.

"The Genuine Fur Eyelashes." *Mademoiselle* Jan. 1967: 102–3+. One of Tyler's funniest stories, "The Genuine Fur Eyelashes" presents a cast of characters straight out of *L'il Abner* or *God's Little Acre*, the Bennett family of lower-class tenant farmers. Their outlandish behavior, however, is humanized by Bridget Muggins' feelings for Eugene. Despite her mother's disapproval of the whole Bennett clan, Bridget cannot seem to discount her feelings for Eugene. This human connection, once established, seems to know no boundaries of class. Nor can it be severed. Although Bridget leaves the auditorium, Eugene finds her and leads her back inside. As the little black girl sitting on the steps points out to Bridget, change (or escape, depending on how one looks at it) seems impossible.

Synopsis: Bridget Muggins, a young school teacher, is waiting out by the mailbox for her boyfriend, Eugene Bennett, to pick her up because her mother does not approve of Eugene. When Eugene arrives, with several of his rowdy younger siblings in the car, Bridget gets in to accompany the family to Sunderburg for the graduation of Maggie, the first Bennett to graduate from ninth grade (albeit from a reform school, where she was sent for stealing). Eugene drives fast because he is trying to catch up with his father and mother, who have set out ahead of them in the family's pickup truck.

As they drive along the country roads, Pansy, one of Eugene's sisters, shows Bridget the graduation gift that the family has bought for Maggie: a set of fake fur eyelashes. Maggie had requested these because the school's supervisor had taken away her mascara.

Outside Sunderburg, they catch up with the Bennetts' pickup and follow it the rest of the way to the school. Bridget thinks back to seventh grade, when she had been in the same class as Eugene, before he quit school and joined the army. She used to watch him and the other boys play pranks. Then when he came back from the army this past year they had started dating.

At the school, Eugene pulls in beside the pickup. Mrs. Bennett, nine months pregnant, speaks briefly to Bridget. The family members walk into the assembly hall and sit all in a row. When Maggie and the other girls file in, Mr. Bennett calls out to Maggie. Eugene takes the family's camera up to take a picture, and the minister has to wait to pray until Eugene gets his shot. Everyone laughs, but Bridget is completely embarrassed.

During the commencement speech, Maggie signals that she wants the eyelashes she requested, so Eugene sneaks by the commencement speaker (a senator's wife) by crawling in front of the raised stage on all fours. Therefore, everyone in the audience can see him, but not the speaker, who continues talking, oblivious to the drama unfolding beneath her. Once by the speaker, Eugene slides the package across the stage floor to a triumphant Maggie, who immediately puts on the eyelashes, much to the disapproval of the school supervisor. Eugene returns to his seat and puts his arm around Bridget.

Completely embarrassed by Eugene's actions, Bridget walks out of the auditorium. On her way out of the building, she passes a "colored" girl who is crying and asks the girl about transportation out of town. The girl responds, "Ain't *no* way out of here" (138). Temporarily stuck, Bridget walks around the building and sits down under a dogwood tree. A few minutes later Eugene finds her there and asks her to come back inside to see Maggie receive her diploma. At first Bridget refuses, but then when Eugene says that he'll stay outside with her if she doesn't come in, she relents.

As she goes back inside, led by Eugene, Bridget once again passes the crying girl and contemplates asking why she's crying: "But then she remembered she was crying because there was no way out of here" (138).

"The Geologist's Maid." *New Yorker* 28 July 1975: 29–33. Tyler has sometimes been criticized for not including more African American characters in her fiction, especially since Baltimore has such a large black population. In Tyler's defense, however, she has explained that she feels inadequate to portray characters that she doesn't know intimately, and thus would feel presumptuous even to attempt to convey the African American experience. Therefore, when African American characters do appear in her fiction, it is always in connection to a white character. While this compromise may seem inadequate to some critics, it actually provides a more interesting perspective because, instead of limiting herself to one perspective, she attempts to portray the nexus at which the two perspectives come together. And, for a writer, that place of contact between cultures and perspectives is much more interesting.

In "The Geologist's Maid," Tyler presents just such an interracial connection. In his isolation, Professor Bennett Johnson looks longingly at his maid Maroon's seemingly rich, busy life. Even though her life soon becomes more real than his own, however, he does not manage to break through her isolation to learn about her problems.

From Maroon's perspective, as Tyler reveals, her isolation is just as deep as her employer's. Thus, the two, although of different races, share far more similarities than differences. Ironically, they don't see the similarity. But that is the exact point and the irony of the human situation, in which everyone struggles along alone and yet somehow manages to endure. The story is thus a story of a failure to communicate among people in general, not races in particular.

Synopsis. Looking in the picture window of Dr. Bennett Johnson's living room, one might see Maroon, his middle-aged black maid, taking care of her employer, a geology professor recuperating from a massive heart attack six weeks ago. Maroon is no stranger to sickness. Most of her family has slowly died off from cancer. She spent last night in the emergency room with her sister Violet, who has asthma. As Maroon brings Bennett his breakfast and changes the sheets on his bed, she talks about her family and her problems. She lives in a crime-ridden neighborhood in downtown Baltimore.

Bennett spends his days looking out the picture window of his living room, sometimes feeling as if he were already dead and simply hanging on in purgatory. He likes hearing about Maroon's colorful life. Maroon is saving up ten dollars to send off for a miracle prayer parchment embedded in a plastic paperweight from a revivalist preacher on the radio. She is determined to save a dollar a week until she can get the parchment because, according to the preacher, this prayer will solve all her problems. Although Bennett has asked Maroon what problems she needs help with, she keeps that information a secret.

At 11:00, Bennett gets up to go to the bathroom, "the major event of his morning" (30). Although he wishes that Maroon would assist him, she just keeps listening to the preacher on the radio. For lunch, Maroon gives Bennett bland food (unsalted chicken soup), but she eats good, rich food herself. When Bennett asks for a cup of tea, she takes what seems to him a very long time getting it. Even though he resents her actions, he accepts the tea without comment.

After lunch, during what is supposed to be Bennett's naptime, Maroon tidies the room and talks about her former employer, Mrs. Jeffrey Simpson-Jones of Roland Park, who had let her go after seventeen years with hardly any notice when she divorced and sold her big house. Then Maroon notices how tired Bennett looks and stops talking. But it does not matter. Bennett has heard it all many times before. All about Mrs. Simpson-Jones, the exploits of Maroon's many nieces—all seemingly named Cherie, and the fancy chandelier in Maroon's dining room purchased by her husband who died alone on a trip to North Carolina, which he was forced to take by the unfeeling white woman he worked for as a chauffeur too soon after he had just suffered a minor stroke. Somehow Maroon's life has become intertwined with Bennett's memories until it seems that Bennett has led two lives. And, by comparison, his own life—from his sickly childhood with an overprotective mother to his present lonely bachelorhood—seems less real to him than Maroon's.

After his nap, Bennett tries to grade a few papers. Later two old colleagues of his from the college drop by with his mail and the latest news from school. Both of them are basically alone, too—one widowed and the other divorced—so they have plenty of spare time. But Maroon interrupts their visit, much to Bennett's annoyance, by bringing in his afternoon snack, which he does not really want. Worse yet, she eats an even heartier meal herself, which he resents but again says nothing about. His friends leave.

As she closes the curtains in the room, Maroon talks some more about getting that prayer parchment. Although still angry with her, Bennett wants to ask her what she will ask for when she gets the parchment. Yet he keeps silent. Bennett thinks of how unsatisfactory everything Maroon does is, but he also feels sorry for her. He remembers how she had talked about going to group therapy once, but had stopped going because the other members of the group were mostly white people who could not relate to her problems.

At 5:30, the doctor, an old friend of Bennett's, drops by to check on him, but he does not examine Bennett. Instead, he just asks a few questions and makes small talk. Again Maroon interrupts when she slams the kitchen door. Before she leaves for the day, Maroon brings Bennett his meager supper. She always seems in a hurry, with her hat already on, but today she waits. It is pay day. Bennett gives her an envelope containing her pay. Maroon takes out one dollar and holds it up asking, "How come things goes so wrong for me and so right for the wicked?" (33). Bennett wonders if this dollar is the one for her prayer parchment and how close she is to reaching her goal, but he does not ask. As Maroon leaves, she lays her hand on Bennett's pillow, "unanswered questions echoing on and on long after she has departed" (33).

For Further Reading

Shafer, Aileen Chris. "Anne Tyler's 'The Geologist's Maid': 'till human voices wake us and we drown.' " *Studies in Short Fiction* 27 (Winter 1990): 65–71.

George. (LY) the stray cat Pete Murphy gives Delia Grinstead.

Gideon. (SM) Daphne Bedloe's two-timing high school boyfriend.

George Gill. (BL) Max Gill's brother.

Max Gill. (BL) Serena Gill's husband, who dies of cancer.

Serena Palermo Gill. (BL) Maggie Moran's friend since first grade, who made a point of being different but "coveted everydayness" (63).

Giulia. ("Knack") Mark Sebastiani's younger sister.

Gloria. ("Nobody") an old friend of Ben Joe Hawkes'; she had once worn knee-socks to a formal dance.

Samantha Glover. ("Artificial") Mary Glover Scott's 5-year-old daughter.

Amy Gower. (MP) Morgan and Bonny Gower's oldest daughter; she marries Jim Murphy and remains in Baltimore.

Bonny Jean Cullen Gower. (MP) Morgan Gower's wealthy wife, a couple of years older than he; she is the mother of their seven daughters.

Carol Gower. (MP) one of Morgan and Bonny Gower's twin daughters; she divorces after only one week of marriage; she eventually moves to Charlottesville, Virginia, where her twin sister Susan lives.

Elizabeth (Liz) Gower. (MP) Morgan and Bonny Gower's sixth daughter, who moves back home in 1976 during a difficult pregnancy; she and her husband, Chester Wing, live in Nashville.

Jean Gower. (MP) Morgan and Bonny Gower's second daughter; she marries and stays in Baltimore.

Joshua (Josh) Gower. (MP) Morgan Gower and Emily Meredith's son.

Kathleen (Kate) Gower. (MP) Morgan and Bonny Gower's youngest daughter, who gets arrested for possession of marijuana when she is 18; she marries David Brustein and moves to Chicago.

Louisa Gower. (MP) Morgan Gower's widowed mother, who lives with him.

Molly Gower. (MP) Morgan and Bonny Gower's third daughter; she stammers as a child; she later marries and moves to Buffalo.

Morgan Gower. (MP) 42-year-old (in 1967) inveterate impostor who moves from one identity to another; he is married to Bonny Gower but later moves in with Emily Meredith.

Samuel Gower. (MP) Morgan Gower's father, a former high school English teacher who committed suicide when Morgan was a senior in high school.

Susan Gower. (MP) one of Morgan and Bonny Gower's twin daughters, who has nightmares; she plays the piccolo; she never marries but moves to Charlottesville, Virginia.

Gram (Bethany Jane Chrisawn Hawkes). (IMEC) Ben Joe Hawkes' 78-year-old grandmother; she is Phillip Hawkes' mother and now lives with her daughter-in-law Ellen Hawkes and her grandchildren.

grammar. (AT, BL, CN, DHR, IMEC, LY, TCT) Many of Tyler's stuffier characters, such as Maggie Moran's mother in *Breathing Lessons*, all the Learys in *The Accidental Tourist*, and Joel Miller in *Ladder of Years*, obsess over proper grammar and judge others based on their ability or inability to use proper English. In their pursuit of perfect language, these characters see a chance to restore some of the order that their world is missing. Needless to say, their quest is frustrating and, ultimately, fruitless.

grandchildren. (BL, "Under Tree," "Woman") In Tyler's work, grandchildren represent connections to the future that some grandparents, such as Maggie Moran in *Breathing Lessons*, actively seek to maintain. Others, usually older grandparents, such as Dolly Tilghman in "Under the Bosom Tree," however, seem less connected to their grandchildren.

grandparents. (AT, IMEC, LY, SC) Tyler's grandparents played a very influential role in her early life. In *Searching for Caleb*, she paid tribute to her grandfather by modeling the character of Daniel Peck, who is like a father figure to Justine Peck, after her own grandfather. Other significant grandparent figures include the Learys' grandparents in *The Accidental Tourist*, who took over the task of raising the Leary children after their father's death and their mother's de facto desertion and who turned them into their Leary selves; Gram in *If Morning Ever Comes;* and Nat Moffat, Noah Miller's spry grandfather, in *Ladder of Years.*

Dr. Grauer. (AT) Rose Leary's minister; he performs Rose and Julian Edge's marriage ceremony.

Graves. ("Flaw") 18-year veteran of the Montreal police department who investigates the burglary of Peter's apartment.

Ansel Green. (TCT) James Green's 26-year-old brother; a hypochondriacal alcoholic.

Clara Green. (TCT) James and Ansel Green's sister who still lives at home.

Claude Green. (TCT) James and Ansel Green's brother, who still lives at home.

James Green. (TCT) a tall, quiet 28-year-old photographer who likes Joan Pike.

Madge Green. (TCT) James and Ansel Green's sister who is now a missionary in China.

Mr. Green. (TCT) James and Ansel Green's strict, religious father.

Delilah Greening. (DHR) full-time babysitter Cody Tull hires to look after his niece, Becky, while his sister, Jenny Tull, is in medical school.

grief. (AT, "Half-Truths," LY, SC, SM, TCT) Tyler's characters struggle to overcome grief in various ways. Mrs. Pike in *The Tin Can Tree* shuts herself off from the world following the death of her daughter Janie Rose until her son Simon's running away draws her back into her role as mother. In "Half-Truths and Semi-Miracles," Ben and Susanna Meagan respond quite differently to their son's death. Ben runs away; Susanna hangs on. In *The Accidental Tourist*, Macon Leary strives to cope with his son Ethan's death. Eventually Muriel Pritchett manages to pull him out of his insular Leary world into the wider world. In *Saint Maybe*, Ian Bedloe's struggle to overcome his grief is tinged with guilt over causing his brother Danny's death. In *Ladder of Years*, Delia Grinstead's escape from her own family is triggered in part by her feelings of grief over her father's death.

Mr. Grindstaff. (CW) P. J. Grindstaff Emerson's father; a Georgia tobacco farmer.

Mrs. Grindstaff. (CW) P. J. Grindstaff Emerson's mother.

Carroll Grinstead. (LY) Delia and Sam Grinstead's growing 15-year-old son.

Cordelia (Delia) Felson Grinstead. (LY) 40-year-old woman who has lived in the same house in Roland Park all her life; she leaves her family for sixteen months.

Eleanor Grinstead. (LY) Sam Grinstead's very independent mother, who reared her son all by herself; she lives in a rowhouse on Calvert Street; Delia Grinstead calls her "the Iron Mama" (LY 31).

Ramsay Grinstead. (LY) Delia and Sam Grinstead's 19-year-old son; a freshman at Johns Hopkins; he has a 28-year-old girlfriend named Velma.

Dr. Samuel (Sam) Grinstead. (LY) Delia Grinstead's 55-year-old husband; he came to work as her father's assistant twenty-two years ago and then married her.

Susan (Susie) Grinstead. (LY) Delia and Sam Grinstead's 21-year-old daughter; a junior at Goucher; she is engaged to Driscoll Avery.

grocery stores. (BL, CN, CW, LY) Grocery stores provide the setting for significant scenes in three Tyler novels. In *Breathing Lessons*, Maggie Moran shops with her grandchild and ex-daughter-in-law. In *Celestial Navigation*, Jeremy Pauling's futile effort to follow Mary Tell out of his isolation falters outside a grocery store. In *Ladder of Years*, Delia Grinstead and Adrian Bly-Brice meet for the first time in a grocery store. Grocery stores, thus, are very public places for essentially private events in Tyler's characters' lives, another example of her ability to transcend the mundane and to charge the ordinary events of life with heightened import.

guilt. (DHR, MP, SM) Guilt is a powerful emotion that can eat away at a person. In *Dinner at the Homesick Restaurant*, Cody Tull builds up a life-long guilt for having, somehow, caused his father, Beck Tull, to desert his family. Not until the end of the novel does Beck return and explain that his reasons for leaving had nothing to do with Cody. By that time, however, the damage of carrying so much guilt for so long has been done. Even so, some hope remains that Cody might recover from the harmful effects of his guilt. In *Morgan's Passing*, both Morgan Gower and Emily Meredith feel tremendous guilt because of their affair. Neither wants to hurt their respective spouses; nevertheless, in the end they break off from them and establish their own life together. And in *Saint Maybe*, Tyler's most fully developed exploration of guilt, Ian Bedloe pays penance for more than twenty years for the mistake that led to his brother Danny's death. Only through his religious faith, his family connections, and, ultimately, the establishment of his own family does Ian finally overcome the ravages of this guilt. Ironically, in the end, he realizes that his greatest obstacle to overcoming his guilt is forgiving himself and moving on with his life.

H

Carol Gower Haines. (MP) See CAROL GOWER.

"Half-Truths and Semi-Miracles." *Cosmopolitan* Dec. 1974: 264–65+.
Tyler's view of religion has sometimes been harsh, especially when she depicts revivalist preachers or dogmatic, fanatical sectarians. Yet in this story, Tyler presents what is probably the closest view to her own faith. Like Tyler's, Susanna's faith is not absolute; she always maintains a healthy skepticism about her healing powers. That faith is sorely tested when her son Benny dies and then her husband Ben deserts her. Susanna's faith, it seems, has ultimately served only to isolate her further—this time more completely than in all the rest of her life. Even so, Susanna endures. Her conversation with Hattie Doone gives her renewed courage and a sense of balance. Accepting what burdens she can, Susanna continues her life's mission in the best way she knows how. What more can anyone do?

Synopsis: The narrator, Susanna Spright Meagan, now 60, starts the story by saying that she always tells people that she's "just an ordinary woman" (264). Yet people do not believe her because they all harbor so many hopes that she will heal them. Her hands have always been unusual, with very wrinkled knuckles. She used to ask her father, who owned a pharmacy, for creams to put on them.

Susanna first learned of her healing power when she was 17, while she was caring for her Aunt Eunice, who had terrible migraines. On an impulse, Susanna put her hand on her aunt's forehead, and the migraine disappeared. A few days later Aunt Eunice brought her friend, Mrs. Leila Fortney, to see

Susanna. Although Susanna was reluctant to try again because she didn't understand what had happened with Aunt Eunice, the two women prevailed upon her to make the attempt. When Aunt Eunice placed Susanna's hands on Mrs. Forney's arthritic joints, the suffering woman looked at Susanna with the same "sudden, startled, *recognizing* look that Aunt Eunice had had when her headache left" (265). This time Susanna felt the power, too.

More people began to come for Susanna to "lay hands on" (265). She was especially fond of the children whose parents brought them for her to heal. Even though people offered, Susanna never took money. Although she felt no different, Susanna's father, mother, and sisters began to treat her differently. When Susanna finished school, she started working full-time in the pharmacy and healing many of those who sought her help. Yet she became increasingly isolated and introspective, often wondering "why God had singled [her] out, what He knew about [her]" (269). At times the healing wouldn't work, but Susanna just considered these failures as God's way of keeping her humble.

The Depression ended, times improved, and Susanna's sisters married, leaving Susanna alone with her parents and Aunt Eunice. Susanna, who was 28, began to wonder if anything was ever going to happen to her. Then one night at a tent revival, she met Ben Meagan, who, when she asked him what was wrong with him, told her, "*You* are my sickness" (269). He declared his love and, on the last night of the revival, asked permission to call on her. Susanna assented, and Ben began to visit her almost every night, even though he lived in Murryville—forty miles away.

In September they married, and Susanna moved to Murryville. There she continued healing. People seemed drawn to her. Once she even cured Ben of a backache, although he just said that he thought the pain was gone.

For many years Susanna and Ben lived happily together with only one regret—they had no children. Then at age 37, Susanna finally became pregnant and had a son, Benny (Benjamin Jr.), who was Ben's pride and joy. Susanna worshipped the boy, too, but, above all else, she wanted him to be ordinary. When Benny was 6, however, he was struck by a car. Although Ben begged Susanna to heal their son, despite her best efforts, Benny died.

After the funeral, Ben could not forgive Susanna for failing to save Benny and left her. Nevertheless, Susanna eventually resumed her ministry. After Benny's death, though, the healing was different: It became a battle with God to heal "God's victims" (271). Susanna developed a new intensity.

Sensing the change in her, Susanna's pastor suggested that she go see Hattie Doone, another healer who lived across the state line. Susanna told Hattie how lonely she felt and about her healing turning into "a bitter war" (271). When Susanna had finished unburdening her soul, Hattie just took her in her arms as if to say that it had been the other people's faith in her, not God, that had made her a healer: "You witnessed their miracles and their semi-miracles and their utter failures. When they said you were responsible, you accepted the burden. What more can anyone do? Now rest awhile. Lean on me. Believe my half-truths, they are all we have" (302).

Apparently, Hattie's advice had been exactly what Susanna needed. The story ends with Susanna, now 60, living alone but still working at the church and performing such semi-miracles.

Mrs. Hall. (TCT) the fastest tobacco stringer in the county.

Hamid. ("Uncle") Hassan Ardavi's second cousin by marriage, whom Uncle Ahmad forgets to uninvite to a party.

Mrs. Connie Hammond. (TCT) a friend of Mrs. Lou Pike's; at the Hammond family reunion she asks James Green to take a picture of Great-Aunt Hattie; later she comes over to try to raise Lou's spirits.

Danny Hammond. (TCT) Connie Hammond's 7-year-old son, who made a salt shaker shaped like Great-Aunt Hattie's head.

Great-Aunt Hattie (Hammond). (TCT) a former Latin teacher whose picture James takes at the Hammond family reunion.

Maisie Hammond. (TCT) young woman who likes Ansel Green.

Willie Hammond. (SDL) young man Brother Hope uses as an example of the evils of dancing; Willie had crashed into an ice cream truck and died driving home from a nightclub with marijuana in his glove compartment.

Jean Gower Hanley. (MP) See JEAN GOWER.

Mr. Harberg. ("I'm Not Going") Paul Harberg's father.

Mrs. Harberg. ("I'm Not Going") Paul Harberg's red-haired mother.

Paul Harberg. ("I'm Not Going") Noona Long's prize cello student.

Captain Harding. ("Street") a man who assists in launching the *Odessa*.

Mr. Harding. (TCT) the Potter sisters' insurance agent.

hardware stores. (MP, "Spending") See GADGETS.

Mrs. Harper. (LY) 92-year-old patient of Sam Grinstead's.

Sister Harriet. (SM) a large, plain looking woman who recently moved to Baltimore and is a member at the Church of the Second Chance; she used to be a teacher but now works for Northeastern Life Insurance Co. She comes to dinner when the children are trying to fix Ian Bedloe up with Miss Pennington.

Carol Harris. (CN) John Harris' wife; a model.

John Harris. (CN) a married photographer who brings Mary Tell to Baltimore, but then reconciles with his wife; to Jeremy Pauling he looks like a man in a cigarette ad.

Mr. Bill Harrison. (SDL) principal of Pulqua's high school.

Mrs. Martha Harrison. (SDL) Mr. Harrison's wife.

Harry. (MP) Louisa Gower's black Labrador.

Uncle Harry. (SC) Red Emma Borden's uncle, who owns the Caro Mill Diner.

hats. (DHR, "Foot-Footing," MP, SC) See IMPOSTORS.

Benjamin Josiah (Ben Joe) Hawkes. (IMEC, "Nobody") a 25-year-old law student at Columbia who returns home to Sandhill, North Carolina, to see about his family; a few years earlier in "Nobody Answers the Door," he is working at the bank to support his mother and six sisters after his father's death. Cf. entry for "I Never Saw Morning," where he is called Ben Joe *Hayes.*

Bethany Jane Chrisawn Hawkes. (IMEC) See GRAM.

Ellen Hawkes. (IMEC, "Nobody") Ben Joe Hawkes' independent mother; she works in a bookstore.

Jane Hawkes. (IMEC, "Nobody") one of Ben Joe Hawkes' twin sisters; she and Lisa are next in age to Susannah; they both work at the bank; identified only as one of "the twins" in "Nobody Answers the Door."

Jenny Hawkes. (IMEC, "Nobody") Ben Joe Hawkes' next-to-the-youngest sister, who graduated high school last spring; she now works as a secretary; the most practical of the six sisters, she writes him letters and takes care of the family's finances.

Joanne Hawkes. ("Nobody") Ben Joe Hawkes' oldest sister, who calls to say that she has gotten married. See JOANNE HAWKES BENTLEY.

Lemuel Hawkes. (IMEC) Ben Joe Hawkes' paternal grandfather; Gram's husband; he died of influenza after their four daughters and one son (Phillip) were grown.

Lisa Hawkes. (IMEC, "Nobody") one of Ben Joe Hawkes' twin sisters; she and Jane are next in age to Susannah; they both work at the bank; identified only as one of "the twins" in "Nobody Answers the Door."

Dr. Phillip Hawkes. (IMEC) Ben Joe Hawkes' father, a doctor who left his mother; he has been dead six years.

Susannah Hawkes. (IMEC, "Nobody") Ben Joe Hawkes' sister; next to Ben Joe in age; she works at the school library; in "Nobody Answers the Door," she is called Susan and receives many phone calls.

Tessie Hawkes. (IMEC, "Nobody") Ben Joe Hawkes' youngest sister (10); like Ben Joe, she has blond hair and their father's narrow eyes.

Donald Hawser. (LY) an executive at the furniture plant in Bay Borough; he and his wife have just bought a house through Belle Flint; they attend Belle's Thanksgiving dinner.

Melinda Hawser. (LY) Donald Hawser's wife, who doesn't think marriage is all it's cracked up to be.

Ben Joe Hayes. ("I Never Saw") Shelley Domer's boyfriend, who is two weeks older than she is. See BEN JOE HAWKES.

Brandon Hayes. (IMEC) African American man on the train who knows Ben Joe Hawkes because Dr. Hawkes set his broken leg; he gets drunk on the train ride to Sandhill, North Carolina.

Matilda Hayes. (IMEC) Brandon Hayes' wife; she yells at him to be quiet, but she really cares for him; they have a baby daughter named Clara Sue.

Violet Hayes. (SDL) Evie Decker's only friend; she is also overweight.

heaven. (DHR, SC) In her 1976 article, "Because I Want More Than One Life," Tyler described her fantasy of meeting all her characters in a small town where she retired and is catching up on what they have been doing. Daniel Peck's version of heaven in *Searching for Caleb* is quite similar. Instead of pearly gates and streets paved with gold, he envisions "a small town with a bandstand in the park and a great many trees . . . [where he] would know everybody . . . and none of them would ever die or move away or age or alter" (SC 190).

Helen. (AT) Macon Leary's cat, whose foray into the clothes dryer serves as the catalyst for Macon's accident.

Danny Hendrix. (MP) lifeguard who saves Robert Roberts from drowning himself.

Herbert. (SDL) disc jockey of "Sweetheart Time," the radio program on which Evie Decker first hears Drum Casey.

heredity. (AT, "Average," CW, DHR, "Dry," IMEC, SC) The impact of heredity on the members of a family is very strong in Anne Tyler's work. In *The Clock Winder*, Mrs. Emerson laments that all her children turn out like their father, despite her having given every single one of them her maiden name, Carter, as a middle name. In *The Accidental Tourist*, Macon Leary wonders in amazement at how similar he and his other fair-haired siblings are. While they sit around playing cards, he looks at a childhood portrait in which they occupy almost the exact same positions that they do now. In *Searching for Caleb*, the "Peckishness" of the Peck family is transmitted even to the family's rebels—Justine, Duncan, and Caleb Peck—for they too possess certain Peck qualities.

Mrs. Hewitt. (SC) a neighbor of Justine and Duncan Peck's in Caro Mill; she owns a poodle.

Mrs. Hewlett. (CW) friend of Mrs. Emerson's who catches Elizabeth Abbott and Timothy Emerson buying a turkey at the grocery store.

Ashley Higham. (SC) old classmate of Caleb Peck's who writes an article about Salter Academy in the Honora *Herald*.

Hilary. (CW) the Abbotts' dog.

Hillary. ("Woman") Corey and Ben's first grandchild; Virginia and Ted's daughter.

hitchhiking. (DHR, "With Flags") Hitchhiking provides a means of escape and adventure. In *Dinner at the Homesick Restaurant*, Luke Tull runs away from his parents to visit his uncle and grandmother in Baltimore by hitching a series of rides. In "With All Flags Flying," 82-year-old Mr. Carpenter celebrates his final day of freedom before moving into a nursing home by hitchhiking on a motorcycle from his farm to his daughter's house in Baltimore.

Marvel Hodge. (EP) Jake Simms' brother-in-law; owner of Marvelous Chevrolet.

Sally Hodge. (EP) Jake Simms' sister; Marvel Hodge's wife.

Ed Hodges. (SC) Lucy Hodges Peck's brother, who hires Duncan Peck to work in his cabinetmaking shop in Virginia.

Marybelle Hodges. (SC) Ed Hodges' wife, whom Justine Peck gives a massive walnut breakfront.

"Holding Things Together." *New Yorker* 24 Jan. 1977: 30–35. Lucy Simmons' control problem is a metaphor for Tyler's view of life. On the one hand, Lucy, like many of Tyler's other characters, wants to maintain herself in a comfortable state, weathering life's problems with socket wrench and caulking gun in hand. Yet life is not that simple. Problems that cannot be fixed may, and seemingly always do, arise. Thus, Lucy develops insomnia worrying about potential problems while ignoring the joys of her present life. Worse still, her marriage suffers because, by taking all of the responsibility on herself, she is stripping her husband Alfred of his sense of worth and, in the process, alienating her most valuable ally in life's struggle—her spouse. This dilemma between sharing control and trusting one's life into another's hands is played out time and time again by Tyler's characters, the wisest of whom, unlike Lucy, learn to accept the contradiction, share the load, and endure.

Synopsis: Lucy (Mrs. Simmons) has been married to Alfred for two years. During that time she has learned that Alfred, a school principal, does not talk much about himself. Alfred's father had died when Alfred was only nine, so Alfred had been raised in a house full of women. Consequently, he never learned how to fix things. Lucy has had to make the household repairs herself. When she complains that she does not know "where he'd be without [her] to hold things together" (30), he responds by walking away sad.

Lucy is very concerned about keeping her car, a 5-year-old Ford, running right. Her greatest fear is "being stranded on the roadside, hood raised and white handkerchief fluttering, no one to stop for [her] but a couple of escaping convicts" (30). So at the slightest sign of a problem, Lucy brings her car in to the neighborhood Exxon station. As a result, she knows the station's mechanics, Victor and Joel, by their first names. In April, Lucy takes her car in because the brakes are squeaking, but Victor assures her that nothing is wrong.

By contrast, Alfred completely ignores the mechanical upkeep of his car, an old battered Plymouth. The car is a disgrace both inside and out. But its condition does not bother Alfred. Although Lucy nags him about proper maintenance, he does not pay attention, contending that his car is "fine" (31).

In June, Lucy is going out to lunch with her old college roommate, Bee, when her car starts stalling out. Forgetting about lunch completely, Lucy immediately drives to the Exxon station, where the car shuts off "like a desert wanderer staggering into an oasis" (31). Lucy, who has learned "auto parts the hard way, the same way soldiers learn geography" (31), questions Joel about which part he thinks might be causing the problem.

While Joel checks the car, Lucy and Bee go inside the station to wait in the office. Bee suggests that perhaps Lucy should consider taking an auto mechanics course: "Be adventurous. There aren't any *roles* anymore" (32), she urges Lucy. Bee says that she once took a course in landscape architecture when she did not know what to do with her lawn. But Lucy wants to know if Bee took the course because she wanted to or because she realized that no one else was going to take the responsibility for her lawn. Bee does not answer her question though. Joel comes in and assures Lucy that the problem—a minor one involving a filter—will be fixed by 5. Bee's sister-in-law comes to pick up Lucy and Bee and gives them a ride home. Later when Alfred gets home, he drives Lucy to pick up her car.

Lucy remembers meeting Alfred while she was student-teaching at his school. At the time she had thought he was "so authoritative" (32), but the two years since have taught her that he is not responsible. He knows nothing about running a house or keeping up their finances. So Lucy has started taking care of everything. She has even developed insomnia, lying awake at night, worrying and feeling that "everything depended on [her]" (33).

In August, Lucy takes her car in to have the transmission checked. But when she and Joel test drive the car, he finds nothing wrong. Lucy tells him that she has stopped driving on freeways because she does not want to be too far away from a service station. Joel assures her that the car is fine. Lucy worries, however, that soon she will just stay home all day, afraid to go anywhere. Joel says that he wishes his wife would take that attitude and stay closer to home. He says that his wife is always going out and that she is constantly changing. Lucy agrees with him that marriage is hard to figure out and adds, "No one told us it would be so permanent" (34).

In September, Lucy visits her family for a week, but she feels out of place there now. On her return, Alfred has missed her, but he has also torn up the mower trying to mow the lawn to impress her. Exasperated by his incompetence, Lucy castigates him, "Can't you do something right? Will I always have to be the one?" (35). Alfred replies, "You just have to be in control; it's always you that holds the power" (35). Lucy responds by saying she does not want the power and holds out her hands as if offering him to take it, but he walks away. Since this incident, Lucy has continued to care for everything. And her car has been running well. It only needs gas.

holidays. (AT, CW, LY, SM) Holidays provide opportunities for families to get together, as well as exhibiting the changes that time has brought about. In *Saint Maybe*, the first Christmas celebration in which the newly married Danny Bedloe and his wife are so happy contrasts sharply with the subdued Christmas celebration the following year. Even so, Ian notices that most of the family's traditions remain intact. In *The Accidental Tourist*, the Learys' Thanksgiving celebration hints at the changes that are coming in the family. Only Julian Edge, Rose's future husband, will dare to eat Rose's undercooked turkey. Because of her relationship with Julian, Rose's life changes, but in the end both Rose and Julian ultimately return to the Leary home, where they will celebrate the rest of their holidays. And in *Ladder of Years*, Delia Grinstead's lonely Christmas away from her family makes her reevaluate her feelings for them, as well as her feelings about her surrogate family, the Millers.

Marilyn Holmes. ("Woman") Corey's beautician friend; she makes up dance steps to avoid stepping on the locusts.

Honeybunch. (SM) a stray cat the Bedloe family takes in.

Brother Evan Hope. (SDL) traveling evangelist who preaches a two-week revival at the Pulqua Tabernacle of God; he condemns Evie Decker from the pulpit.

Dr. Hope. ("Two People") Melinda's doctor.

Joanna Hope. ("As the Earth") 16-year-old neighbor of Mrs. Brauw.

Mrs. Hope. ("As the Earth") Joanna Hope's mother.

Charles Hopper. ("Feather") a small round man in his seventies who decides to take a cross-country trip.

Lucy Hopper. ("Feather") Charles Hopper's small, round wife, who talks during movies.

John Horner. (IMEC) the man who is dating Shelley Domer and later Joanne Hawkes Bentley; he is starting a construction company.

Mr. Houck. (CN) boarder at Jeremy Pauling's boardinghouse at the end of the book.

houses. (AT, CN, CW, DHR, EP, IMEC, LY, MP, SC, SDL, SM, TCT) Anne Tyler's families live in a variety of houses. From large, stately homes in Roland Park (Mrs. Emerson's house in *The Clock Winder*, the Peck homes in *Searching for Caleb*, the Gowers' house in *Morgan's Passing*, and the Grinsteads' house in *Ladder of Years*) to rowhouses in downtown Baltimore (the Tulls' house in *Dinner at the Homesick Restaurant* and Muriel Pritchett's place in *The Accidental Tourist*), all these houses hold families whose emotional and physical conditions are reflected in the houses in which they live.

The solidity of the Pecks in *Searching for Caleb* and their stagnation are mirrored in the large, nearly identical brick edifices that they inhabit in the Peck compound. By contrast, the two Peck family rebels, Justine and Duncan Peck, live in a series of sometimes ramshackle domiciles and eventually wind up living in a trailer in a traveling carnival. In *The Accidental Tourist*, the Leary home is an inheritance from their grandparents that ultimately comes to house, at one time, all four siblings, from which only Macon Leary, with Muriel Pritchett's help, manages to escape. In *Saint Maybe*, the Bedloe family home almost bursts at the seams when a new set of children grows up in it, yet it survives. By the time of Bee's death, however, the house is showing its age and the effects of this constant wear and tear. The roof leaks and the lawn is dying. Rita diCarlo, the Clutter Counselor, arrives to put everything into its proper place and to organize the contents of the house. In the process she also brings order to Ian Bedloe's life by marrying him and bearing his son.

Other houses of significance include the three-family triplex that the Pikes share with the Greens and the Potters in *The Tin Can Tree*, expressing the concept of extended family; the house that Evie Decker inherits from her father that provides a place for her and her coming child in *A Slipping-Down Life*; the Emerson house in *The Clock Winder*, which Elizabeth Abbott takes care of first as handyman and then as caretaker for the entire family; the boardinghouse in *Celestial Navigation*, which is Jeremy Pauling's entire world with its changing cast of boarders and its growing number of children; the Emory house in *Earthly Possessions*, which combines two households into one; and Delia Grinstead's home where she has lived all her life in *Ladder of Years*.

For Further Reading

Shelton, Frank W. "Anne Tyler's Houses." *The Fiction of Anne Tyler*. Ed. C. Ralph Stephens. Jackson: University Press of Mississippi, 1990: 40–46.

Howard. (CN) medical student who boards at the Paulings' boardinghouse during 1960–61.

Mrs. Howard. (CW) organist at Elizabeth Abbott's near wedding in North Carolina.

Buddy Howland. (SDL) the only boy Evie Decker had ever dated before Drum Casey; Buddy's voice had not changed.

Leah Hume. (DHR) Jenny Tull's neighbor who doesn't let her repeated business failures get her down.

humor. (AT, BL, CN, CW, "Dry," "Genuine," IMEC, "I'm Not Going," "Linguistics," LY, MP, SC, SM, "Woman") Anne Tyler is noted for the humor in her novels. She has a knack for laughing amid the tears of life, which allows her characters to endure their troubles. Her humor, whether it comes from verbal mistakes (Muriel Pritchett's mispronunciations in *The Accidental Tourist*) or implausible situations (Maggie Moran's hitting a Pepsi truck as she drives out of a body shop where she has just had her car repaired in *Breathing Lessons*), Tyler creates humor that has two sides to it. One could classify her humor as tragi-comic, for no matter what the situation, the humor could produce serious consequences if things had turned out differently. The foreigners' exploits in *Saint Maybe*, while funny, exhibit quite apparent danger. In *Morgan's Passing*, Morgan Gower's exploits, while amusing, don't always lead to happiness for his wife Bonny, and ultimately result in the destruction of his marriage. Yet, despite these negative aspects of Tyler's humor, these episodes add spice to her characters' lives and allow them to endure the bad times.

For Further Reading

Bennett, Barbara A. "Attempting to Connect: Verbal Humor in the Novels of Anne Tyler." *South Atlantic Review* 60.1 (1995): 57–75.

"I Never Saw Morning." *Archive* Apr. 1961: 11–14. A prequel to *If Morning Ever Comes*, "I Never Saw Morning" illustrates the ravages of time upon relationships. To Shelley Domer, Mrs. Crisawn's old friendship with Shelley's mother and the woman's boring marriage appear ridiculous in the face of Shelley's blossoming (and seemingly timeless) love for Ben Joe Hayes. Yet what Shelley has been confronted with on this night is a picture of the future that she has never contemplated—a world in which change is inevitable and where not even her love for Ben Joe can remain unaltered. This realization sobers Shelley and forces her to grow up.

Synopsis: Returning home from a date, Shelley Domer and Ben Joe Hayes linger on Shelley's front porch steps, reluctant to say good night. Shelley's younger sister Phoebe calls down to her from her window and asks where they've been and urges her sister to come inside. As Shelley searches for the key in the mailbox, she asks Ben Joe if they'll see each other the next day.

Just then Mrs. Crisawn, an old friend of Shelley's mother's, swings open the door, hugs Shelley, and remarks how she has grown up. Mrs. Crisawn announces that she and her husband John are spending the night. Shelley's mother tells Shelley to introduce Ben Joe to Mrs. Crisawn and invites the reluctant couple inside for something to eat.

John Crisawn and Shelley's father are in the den working on the stereo, so Shelley talks to Mrs. Crisawn until the men come back into the living room. Then Mrs. Crisawn begins to talk about her husband's shirts, so Shelley is free to daydream about Ben Joe. Looking at his hands and his blond hair, she wonders if Ben Joe somehow knew when she was born, since he is two weeks older than she is.

Mrs. Crisawn continues to talk and starts discussing the two young girls who work in her husband's photography studio. To break the boredom, Shelley and Ben Joe play with their cookies. Mrs. Domer frowns at them. Then Mrs. Crisawn notes she doesn't mind the two young girls working alone with her husband because she knows they don't find him attractive at his age—50.

Shelley and Ben Joe look at Mr. Crisawn to see how he is responding to his wife's comments, but he just sits there, apparently used to her garrulous insensitivity. Something in Shelley snaps, though, and to everyone's horror, she blurts out, "Damn." Flush with thoughts of her own idealized love for Ben Joe, she challenges Mrs. Crisawn: "When you think about poor old John lying in his crib, maybe waking up suddenly or just smiling, the moment you were born, and when you think, I never saw morning but that he saw it too, even when I didn't even know him, and then you go and say a damn thing like that" (13).

With everyone else now speechless, Shelley runs upstairs and begins undressing for bed. Lying down in bed beside Phoebe, Shelley tries to ignore the young girl's questions. Downstairs Shelley hears Mr. and Mrs. Crisawn talking amiably about a trip they took in the early days of their marriage. Shelley cannot believe that she had taken up for the man, who is now acting as if nothing has happened. She feels "as if she had wasted something, not just a night but something real like money" (14). Questioning Shelley about her date with Ben Joe, Phoebe asks, "Does it just come to you *naturally*, to climb [the steps] that slowly?" (14). But Shelley doesn't answer her. Instead she thinks about Ben Joe.

"I Play Kings." *Seventeen* Aug. 1963: 338–41. In this early story, Tyler tackles the changes that time produces in everyone. Through memory, the narrator recalls her visit to New York, where she learned of Francie Shuford's pregnancy—a change that would move her friend irrevocably out of childhood and into adulthood. This change is hard for the narrator to comprehend because Francie seems to imply that the same changes will soon capture the narrator and because it seems like such a short time ago that Francie and the narrator were young girls playing in the leaves.

Francie's comment that she would have had a better chance as an actor if she had been male is one of Tyler's rare overtly feminist statements.

Synopsis. Sometimes when she is lonely, the narrator's mother complains that none of her four children ever tell her anything about their lives. On this day she turns to them and asks her 12-year-old son Seth, who sits reading an encyclopedia, what happened when he and his 19-year-old sister (the narrator) went to New York a year ago to buy his cello. Seth doesn't reply, but the narrator responds that nothing unusual happened. The mother is especially troubled because the two of them were supposed to look up Francie Shuford, the daughter of a neighbor, Mrs. Shuford, and tell her how Francie was getting along in New York. But when they returned home to Raleigh, the narrator had not gone to see Mrs. Shuford. The mother had had to go in her place and make up a story about Francie being fine. Seth just keeps reading his encyclopedia and soon the mother starts asking about other matters. The narrator and Seth don't look at each other, much less talk about what happened in New York.

Then the narrator begins to remember the trip. It was important because it was their first time being on their own. As they were leaving, Mrs. Shuford had come over with an envelope with Francie's address on it. Francie was in New York studying acting. Mrs. Shuford had asked many people from Raleigh to check on her daughter in the past year, and Francie had always sent them away. Therefore the narrator was not eager to go see her.

Nevertheless, in New York, after they bought Seth's cello, they looked Francie up. At a bar called The Rooster, where Francie worked, they ordered something to eat while they waited for Francie to come on stage and sing. When the girl had finally appeared, the narrator was shocked, because Francie had been pregnant. As the narrator looked at her old friend, she saw the same thin face, but realized that "beneath the straight lines of the red dress I had seen her wearing for years, was a baby growing. It didn't seem a part of her" (341). Then the narrator remembered what Francie had told her when she was packing to go to New York to become an actress: "If I were a boy, I wouldn't just be good. I'd be great. The parts men get to play, my God! And the way I could do them—" (341).

Finally, Francie had begun to sing, singing the folk song "Five Hundred Miles" as if she were singing for the narrator. Although she looked at the narrator, it was as if she weren't looking at her. Seth and the narrator then got up to leave. When they arrived home, their mother had asked about Francie, but didn't press them when they didn't answer.

That night the narrator and Seth were sitting outside. Seth wasn't playing with the other children, so his sister asked why. He said he didn't know why, but when she mentioned that she and Francie used to play in the leaves together like the children were doing Seth went inside and started crying. The story ends with the narrator remembering how she and Francie used to throw leaves at each other and laugh.

identity. ("Baltimore," "Base-Metal," CN, CW, MP, SM) Every person ultimately must answer the question, "Who am I?" In Anne Tyler's fiction, it is natural to assume that many of her younger characters would search for their identity. In *Saint Maybe*, Ian Bedloe, as a teenager and later as a young man, as well as Daphne Bedloe, his niece, both struggle to achieve an awareness of who they are and their place in life. By the time he is 40, Ian has finally solidified his identity through his marriage to Rita diCarlo and the birth of their son Joshua. At the end of the novel, although she seems to be making progress, Daphne, however, still seems to be searching to find herself. This search for identity is not limited to the young. In "The Baltimore Birth Certificate," Miss Maiselle Penney feels an inexplicable need to locate her birth certificate. The story ends with Miss Penney waiting in a lawyer's office for him "to bring her birth certificate" (45), as if that would validate her existence. Thus, identity, for Tyler, is always in flux. No person, no matter what age, seems to have completely achieved a definitive sense of his or her own identity.

If Morning Ever Comes. *If Morning Ever Comes,* Tyler's first novel, introduces many of Tyler's major themes: individual versus family, time, change, escape, isolation, and the limitations of language. As Ben Joe Hawkes discovers when, during a family crisis (his sister Joanne's separation from her husband Gary), he returns home to Sandhill, North Carolina, from New York, where he is attending Columbia Law School, Ben Joe does not really understand his family. Even though he had spent six years working in a bank to support his mother, grandmother, and six sisters following his father's death, they all seem separate from him. In fact, except for the tradition-minded Gram, none of these women seem particularly concerned over Joanne's decision.

What has developed in Ben Joe's absence is an assertion of a strong matriarchal order, which had, unknown to Ben Joe, already supplanted the traditional patriarchy when Ben Joe's father, Dr. Phillip Hawkes, had moved out of the family home. After her husband's departure, Ellen Hawkes, Ben Joe's mother, had refused to compromise her dignity by asking Phillip back. Since then she has managed on her own quite well and has passed this independent spirit on to her daughters.

Joanne Hawkes Bentley, who has left her husband of seven years, goes so far as to go out on a date with another man, despite her husband coming to North Carolina to get her. Ben Joe's other sisters have their own jobs and schedules that run outside of Ben Joe's knowledge and control. Ben Joe's return to this matriarchal stronghold only further confuses his sense of order, control, and identity. Thus his response is to flee back to New York.

At novel's end, however, the patriarchal paradigm is reestablished, at least in Ben Joe's life. Taking his old girlfriend, Shelley Domer, "his own little piece of Sandhill transplanted" (IMEC 265), back to New York with him, Ben Joe feels that he is restoring a sense of order and balance to his life. Yet perhaps even this view is not unchanged, for in his final vision of Shelley and their future son dancing away from his reach, Ben Joe realizes that any traditional sense of order is no longer viable. All things will eventually change with time. Not attempting to stop Shelley and their son in his vision, Ben Joe accepts this inevitable change.

For Further Reading

Croft, Robert W. *Anne Tyler: A Bio-Bibliography*. Westport, CT: Greenwood Press, 1995. 25–27.

Evans, Elizabeth. *Anne Tyler*. New York: Twayne, 1993.

Petry, Alice Hall. *Understanding Anne Tyler*. Columbia: University of South Carolina Press, 1990. 22–52.

Voelker, Joseph C. *Art and the Accidental in Anne Tyler*. Columbia: University of Missouri Press, 1989. 15–27.

Selected Book Reviews

Gloag, Julian. "Home Was a House Full of Women." *Saturday Review* 26 Dec. 1964: 37–38.

Long, John Allan. " 'New' Southern Novel." *Christian Science Monitor* 21 Jan. 1965: 9.

Prescott, Orville. "Return to the Hawkes Family." *New York Times* 11 Nov. 1964: 41. [Reprinted in *Critical Essays on Anne Tyler*. Ed. Alice Hall Petry. New York: G. K. Hall, 1992: 61–62.]

Ridley, Clifford A. "From First Novels to the Loves of William Shakespeare." *National Observer* 16 Nov. 1964: 21.

Saal, Rollene W. "Loveless Household." *New York Times Book Review* 22 Nov. 1964: 52.

Sullivan, Walter. "Worlds Past and Future: A Christian and Several from the South." *Sewanee Review* 73 (Autumn 1965): 719–26.

"I'm Not Going to Ask You Again." *Harper's* Sept. 1965: 88–98. This early Tyler story establishes a familiar theme in Tyler's work: the adjustments that time forces everyone to make. In Noona Long's case, her own personal dreams have been scaled down considerably from personal glory when she was young to producing one good music student now in her middle age. Thus, the loss of Paul Harberg, her one promising pupil, is a crushing blow to Noona's last dream. Her one last defense against time's ravages is the music itself, which somehow manages to sustain her, despite life's disappointments. It seems that no matter what time takes away, her love of music always remains.

Synopsis: One Saturday morning Noona Long wakes up at about 10:30 in her neat bedroom and realizes that her favorite music student, Paul Harberg, has a lesson at 11:00. Once Noona had been very fat, but she had gone on a diet at the insistence of her doctors a few years ago. Now her skin hangs down on her arms. She is obsessively neat, but the neatness serves a purpose: It keeps "her mind in order too" (89).

As Noona rushes about finishing her coffee and getting ready for Paul's lesson, she sets out vanilla wafers on a plate for him, something she does for none of her other pupils. At 11:05 Paul has still not arrived, so Noona sits down and begins to wait for him. She thinks about how she used to play the piano for her parents and how her father had said that she was "going to go somewhere" (89). Yet thirty years later Noona is still here in this house willed to her by her dead parents.

At 11:45, Paul still has not shown up. Noona can't imagine Paul forgetting his lesson, but she won't call him. His mother has recently switched him to taking lessons only every other Saturday because he's getting so highstrung. Mrs. Harberg had told Noona that Paul has started snapping his wrist in his sleep at night, as if he were playing the cello.

To give herself something to do while she waits, Noona decides to dye her bedspread. As she works on the spread, she hears violins in "the music part of her mind" (90). She often feels that this part of her mind has "already selected a piece of music to accompany every moment of her life, past and present" (90).

Sarah Cobbett, Noona's friend, arrives for their Saturday lunch date. Sarah wants to show off her new tweed suit, but Noona is too preoccupied to notice because Paul hasn't shown up for his lesson. Sarah, a history teacher, blames Paul's behavior on his being a boy: "all through life it's the girls who study (boys sit in the back of the class and throw spit-wads) but who is it that ends up famous? The boys" (92). Sarah asks about lunch. Then the doorbell rings, and Sarah goes to answer it.

It is Mr. Harberg, with Paul. Noona, standing at the sink stirring the bedspread tells him she is dyeing and then quickly explains that she is "dyeing material" (92). Mr. Harberg has brought Paul to apologize for missing his lesson because he was playing baseball instead. Noona suggests that she give Paul his lesson right then, but Paul insists that he has to go play ball. He's playing shortstop.

Mr. Harberg offers to pay for the missed lesson, but Noona abruptly refuses. She stands there, awkwardly holding the dripping bedspread. Mr. Harberg helps her hang it up, even though he gets a blue stain on his shirt. Not wanting to miss out on being with Paul, Noona suggests that she and Sarah walk back with Paul and his father. When Sarah protests, Noona tells her that they can eat out at a restaurant.

As they walk down the street, Noona wishes that she could be alone with Paul. Explaining to Mr. Harberg that "*music* is what [she] was *really* born for" (94), Noona shares her hopes for Paul, who runs ahead of them to the playground. At the Harbergs' house they say goodbye.

Walking toward the restaurant with Sarah, Noona realizes that she has forgotten her money for lunch and becomes upset that she hasn't had a chance to talk to Paul. Sarah knows how Noona feels about Paul. She's had students in her class that were special like him. But Noona isn't really talking about Paul. Instead, she is thinking about her own past dreams. At age 10 she had wanted to be "Queen of the Western Hemisphere" (95); then at 20 she had wanted to be "the world's greatest violinist" (95). Now, nearly thirty years later, her one dream is just to "turn out one good pupil" (95).

Upset, Noona decides not to eat lunch. Instead, she heads for the playground to tell Paul that she doesn't expect any more from him than he wants to give and that he shouldn't be afraid of her. But when she reaches the playground she can't distinguish Paul from the other children, so she runs away.

At home, Noona gives a piano lesson to Betty Jo Frankel, a little girl more interested in the way she looks sitting at the piano than in the music she bangs out. As Betty Jo haltingly plays her simple piece, Noona looks at the dyed bedspread and listens to "a Processional she had composed once, tinkling far away in the music part of her mind" (98).

impostors. (BL, LY, MP) In *Ladder of Years*, Delia Grinstead jokes with Adrian Bly-Brice that they should open up a service called Impostors Are Us. Although this business might not succeed in real life, in Tyler's fiction there would be a constant demand for it. When reality is not up to par, Tyler's characters often take on disguises, using costumes to change themselves into someone else. They become, in that sense, impostors, creating another identity for themselves in place of the unsuitable real one. In many instances, however, these impostors find that their disguised identity is either completely preposterous or inappropriate. In *Breathing Lessons*, Maggie Moran's idea to dress Serena Gill's mother up as a clown for Halloween, the day that she is to enter a nursing home, backfires, only embarrassing the poor old woman since the home has held its party the previous day. Tyler's most famous impostor, however, the man of multiple disguises, is Morgan Gower of *Morgan's Passing*. Morgan's identity shifts with the many hats that he keeps in his closet. From priest to physician to hardware handyman, Morgan moves effortlessly from one life into another. In the end, his life changes permanently when he leaves his old life and becomes a permanent member of Emily Meredith's life, as well as her puppet troupe.

Mrs. Inman. (BL) director of Silver Threads Nursing Home, who is pushing Mr. Gabriel's wheelchair when Maggie Moran is caught riding in the laundry cart.

insomnia. (AT, "Holding," IMEC, SC, SM, TCT, "Teenage") Tyler herself suffers from insomnia, so it is no surprise that many of her characters share this same malady. The causes for Tyler's characters' insomnia vary. In *The Tin Can Tree*, both James Green and Miss Lucy Potter have trouble sleeping at night because they worry about others. In *If Morning Ever Comes*, when Ben Joe Hawkes returns to his family home late one night, he is amazed to find almost everyone up. In "Teenage Wasteland," Mrs. Coble lies awake wondering where her runaway son Donny is. In *The Accidental Tourist*, Macon Leary lies awake worrying about everything under the sun from the oxidation of tin cans in his refrigerator to the real cause of his insomnia, the violent death of his only son Ethan. To fight the insomnia, he watches old movies. Looking out his window, however, he finds comfort in seeing another light on, someone else who can't sleep.

intertextuality. In Tyler's fictional world sometimes characters show up in later works. Dr. Felson, the kind old Roland Park physician who can be trusted not to report Elizabeth Abbott's gunshot wound in *The Clock Winder*, turns out to be Delia Grinstead's father in *Ladder of Years*. Ezra Tull's Homesick Restaurant is the setting of a Christmas dinner in *Saint Maybe*. Jeremy Pauling's boardinghouse in *Celestial Navigation* also turns up in *Dinner at the Homesick Restaurant*, as the home of Ruth Spivey. Eli Everjohn, who locates Caleb Peck in *Searching for Caleb*, also helps Ian Bedloe to determine the fate of the children's real father in *Saint Maybe*. Ben Joe Hawkes/Hayes and his family appear in *If Morning Ever Comes*, "Nobody Answers the Door," and "I Never Saw Morning." The Ardavi family shows up in "Uncle Ahmad" and "Your Place is Empty." Mary Beth Polk and her mother are characters in "The Base-Metal Egg" and "Foot-Footing On."

Iola. (DHR) one of Pearl Tull's relatives in her old photographs.

isolation. (AT, "Bridge," CN, DHR, "Flaw," "Geologist," "Knack," "Nobody," "Saints," SDL) Almost all of Anne Tyler's works present people who are in some way isolated from themselves, their own feelings, or the people around them. In "A Flaw in the Crust of the Earth," Peter imagines building a bridge with an ironing board between his apartment and the apartment of the woman next door. But he knows that even this drastic measure would not really break his isolation because the woman never looks in his window. In "Nobody Answers the Door," Joanne Hawkes, who has called to inform her family of her recent marriage, hangs up on her mother. Her brother Ben Joe, who realizes that Joanne's marriage will irrevocably change his relationship with his sister, sits by himself with no desire to come to the phone to speak to Joanne. In "The Geologist's Maid," Bennett Johnson's life is isolated physically due to his illness. Emotionally, however, he is even more isolated, forced to live vicariously through the stories of Maroon, his maid. In *The Accidental Tourist*, the Learys live a very insular and isolated existence, afraid to venture out into the outside world. Only Macon, with the help of Muriel Pritchett, ultimately succeeds in breaking out of this isolation. Even Rose, who for a time through her marriage to Julian Edge breaks away from her family, reverts back to her isolation when Julian moves in to the Leary home and begins to play Vaccination, the Leary family game. The most isolated character in Tyler's fiction is Jeremy Pauling of *Celestial*

Navigation. Jeremy's agoraphobia, and, to a greater extent, his immersion in his art, isolate him from his children, whom he can never understand, and from Mary Tell, the woman who briefly manages to breech Jeremy's psychic barriers.

J

Jacob. ("Neutral") 10-and-a-half-year-old boy in the fifth grade whose parents are divorced.

Jamal. ("Uncle") Ahmad Ardavi's son, who was sheltered as a boy by his mother and who now works in Bank Melli; he never sees his father.

Claire Jamison. (EP) Oliver Jamison's pregnant wife.

Mrs. Jamison. (EP) Oliver Jamison's mother; a widow who opens a motel in Perth, Florida.

Oliver Jamison. (EP) friend of Jake Simms' in training school who makes bombs.

Jane. ("Linguistics") Claire and her foreign husband's twin daughter.

Janice. (MP) young woman in Off the Cuff improvisational troupe.

Mrs. (Julia) Jarrett. (CN) an old widowed woman who boards at the Paulings'; she dials the phone for Jeremy Pauling to tell his sisters about their mother's death.

jealousy. (DHR, MP) Sibling rivalry caused by Beck Tull's desertion and Pearl Tull's favoritism results between two brothers, Cody and Ezra Tull, in *Dinner at the Homesick Restaurant*. Ultimately, Cody's jealousy drives him to steal Ezra's fiancée, Ruth Spivey, away from him. In *Morgan's Passing*, Morgan's jealousy of the Merediths' spare life leads him to replace Leon Meredith as Emily's husband and fellow puppeteer.

Jeannie. (SM) Mr. Brant's niece who comes to work at the cabinet shop.

Uncle Jed. (IMEC) Phillip Hawkes' uncle, who was a farmer and had taken Phillip to the Farmers' Market in Raleigh when Phillip was a boy.

Jeff. (BL) Linda's husband; Serena Gill's son-in-law.

Jenny. ("Some Sign") Sam Simmons' sister, who sends him their father's effects.

Jeremy. (IMEC) Ben Joe Hawkes' roommate in New York; he is not yet 21 and still an undergraduate; he is from Maine.

Jeremy. ("Respect") 16-year-old boy who breaks into Mrs. Willard's house and lives there for over a week even after she returns home.

jewelry. ("Base-Metal," SM) Unlike the pearls that her mother wishes her to purchase, an imaginary egg-shaped locket appeals to young Mary Beth Polk's search for identity in "The Base-Metal Egg." Similarly, in *Saint Maybe*, Lucy Dean's mustard seed necklace is about all that remains of her to remind Agatha and Thomas Bedloe of their mother.

Jiggs. (EP) abandoned baby brought home by Saul Emory and unofficially adopted by the Emorys.

Jimmy Joe. (CW) Margaret Emerson's first husband; a grocery delivery boy.

Joe. ("Tea-Machine) Sandra's cousin who tells John Paul Bartlett about Sandra's good fortune in striking oil.

Joel. ("Common") Miss Lorna Love Johnson's son-in-law; married to her daughter Melissa; he works as an insurance salesman.

Joel. ("Holding") a tall blond boy who is a mechanic at the Exxon station where Lucy Simmons takes her car; he calls her "Mrs. S."

John. ("Linguistics") Claire and her foreign husband's twin son.

Dr. Bennett Johnson. ("Geologist") an invalid geology professor, recovering from a heart attack.

Mr. Billy Johnson. ("Common") Miss Lorna Love Johnson's thin, slightly balding husband; he is a successful businessman.

Miss Lorna (Love) Johnson. ("Common") a fat woman who sits on her front porch eating Sunshine biscuits in her wicker chair because she is angry that her married daughter, Melissa, has gotten pregnant.

Gunther Jones. (CW) Georgia veteran, whom P. J. Grindstaff Emerson knows, who visited home before going to Vietnam, where he was killed.

Quality Jones. (IMEC) a large, mentally handicapped boy, the son of one of the farmers at the Farmers' Market in Raleigh.

Tommy Jones. (TCT) soda jerk at the Larksville drug store who checks Joan Pike's bags for the bus.

Junior Jordan. (SC) neighbor who watches Duncan Peck's goats while he is away.

Mrs. Jordan. (SC) neighbor next to Duncan Peck's goat farm who buys cheese from Justine Peck.

Mrs. Jordan. (SM) the Bedloes' neighbor who is at their house when Danny Bedloe brings Lucy Dean to meet his parents; she succeeds in getting Thomas Bedloe to recall his father's name.

Josephine. (TCT) tobacco hander to Mrs. Hall.

Joshua. ("Feather") Charles and Lucy Hopper's grandson, who accompanies them on their cross-country trip the summer before he goes off to college; he is the son of their only daughter, Charlotte.

Jules. ("Laps") Sue Ellen's son.

Julie. (CW) Polly and Carl's chubby baby daughter; Elizabeth Abbott's niece.

Aunt Junie. (MP) Claire's mother; she had married Aunt Mercer Dulaney's brother.

K

Molly Kane. (DHR) girl in wheelchair whom Josiah Payson wheels to class in high school.

Laura Lee Keller. (MP) Morgan Gower's first love; she had gone to the prom with him.

Mr. Kenny. (MP) chairman of the Fund-Raising Committee for the Presbyterian Church's Easter Fair in 1967.

kidnapping. (EP, SDL) Neither of the kidnappings in Tyler's fiction endangers its intended victim. In *A Slipping-Down Life*, Drumstrings Casey is kidnapped as a publicity stunt, but is forgotten when Evie Decker's father suffers a heart attack. In *Earthly Possessions*, Charlotte Emory's childhood kidnapping is shortlived, and as an adult her plan to escape from her restrictive family is unintentionally aided by the ineptitude of her reluctant kidnapper, Jake Simms.

Miss Kimmel. (BL) Maggie Moran and Serena Gill's first grade teacher.

Sister Bertha King. (SM) member of the Church of the Second Chance; Eli Everjohn's mother-in-law.

Dr. Kitt. (TCT) the Pikes' family doctor.

Mr. George Kitt. (SM) a former alcoholic vagrant; now a member of the Church of the Second Chance.

"A Knack for Languages." *New Yorker* 13 Jan. 1975: 32–37. One of Tyler's stories about foreigners, which grew perhaps out of her experience with her Iranian husband, "A Knack for Languages" explores the limitations of language as a means of communication. No matter how many languages Mark Sebastiani learns, it seems that the growing isolation that his wife Susan feels will never be broken. This isolation started, however, when Susan was a child in a family that spoke only English. Her parents' marriage, as we learn, also lacked communication. Consequently, Susan has grown up incapable of expressing her feelings. Her later feeling of isolation, therefore, seems not such a product of any language barrier, but an inherently human condition, unrelated to or restricted by any one tongue.

Synopsis: Susan, the narrator, begins by noting that her husband Mark is a linguist who teaches Italian at the University, knows several other languages, and is now learning Arabic. They had met when she began auditing his Italian classes. To her surprise, Mark asked her out, although she always wondered what he saw in her. Now that they are married she still audits his class, but her Italian does not improve very much, and she wonders if Mark wishes "he had married someone with a knack for languages" (32).

Mark's parents visit from Italy for a month and a half. Although Mark's mother tries to learn English, his father knows just one sentence: "Already I love you like a daughter" (33). When he is introduced to Susan he says these words, words that go "about as far as language can go" (33), taking Susan aback by their forthrightness. In reply she can manage only a belated "thank you." Yet when Mr. Sebastiani meets Dodie, Susan's ex-roommate, and repeats these same words, she instantly responds that she loves him, too.

Then Mark's sisters, Anna and Giulia, come for a visit. Although they speak English fluently and ask Susan many questions about her life, they speak to Mark in what sounds to Susan like very passionate Italian. Again, Susan cannot rise to this level of emotion and feels like an outsider.

At Christmas, Susan and Mark drive to Virginia to visit her father, who lives alone in a shabby farmhouse. Her mother had killed herself by taking poison when Susan was a freshman in college. Susan had not gotten along well with her mother, who was too moody and always attempted to change Susan and her father. Susan had not even returned home for the funeral; instead she had written her father a condolence letter, choosing her words very carefully. Therefore, Mark and Susan sleep in her old bedroom with its twin bed rather than her mother's old room with the double bed. During their entire visit Susan never enters her mother's old room.

Susan's father, whose health has deteriorated, shows Mark around the farm. Mark enjoys spending the day helping his father-in-law with the chores. Yet Susan and her father, as usual, cannot talk about anything except the farm machinery. Susan's father had often been told by his wife that the rest of the world was different, more feeling: "*Some* people, dear man, plunge joyfully in, and some dampen a toe first, testing the temperature, and you are one of the latter" (35). Her mother had also expressed this attitude to Susan, who is more reserved in temperament like her father.

On Christmas Day, Susan's father gives her a locket that had belonged to her mother. Inside are photographs of her parents when they were young. Susan notices how moved her father is, but she cannot reach out to him. For her part, she gives him a Swiss army knife, another of the gadgets that they both love. Christmas dinner is sad because Susan's father is thinking of her mother. The next day Mark and Susan leave. Although Susan wants to tell her father that she loves him, she can't. All she can do to show that she cares is to leave behind baggies of leftover sliced turkey for her father to warm up for the many lonely meals to come.

Back at home, Susan feels isolated because Mark is practicing his Arabic, a language that she does not understand. She thinks that her husband "is drifting farther and farther, leaving me behind, and there is nothing I can think of to say that will call him back" (37).

Mrs. Knowlton. (BL) owner of Alluring Lingerie Shop, where Serena Gill worked before she married.

Kurosh. ("Uncle") Hassan Ardavi's cousin, whom Ahmad forgets to un- invite to a party.

Dermott Kyle. (SM) 10-year-old boy who attends Camp Second Chance; Thomas Bedloe looks up to him.

L

Ladder of Years. At the beginning of *Ladder of Years*, Delia Grinstead tells Adrian Bly-Brice that she has "a life to get back to" (12) when he tries to convince her to continue their charade of fooling his wife into thinking that they are going together. Yet, very soon Delia does feel compelled to leave her life, which has been a restrictive one. The daughter of a Roland Park doctor, she had married her father's assistant twenty-two years earlier and has lived in the same house all her life. Thus, after a brief, unconsummated affair with Adrian, Delia takes off on her own, leaving her life and her family behind during their annual vacation to Bethany Beach, Delaware.

Like Tyler's other runaways, Delia feels misunderstood by the people in her life, especially her husband Sam and her children. In Delia's case, however, she does not merely run away and then return to her old life. She first establishes a whole new life for herself in Bay Borough, Maryland. What she soon discovers, though, is that this new life contains just as many burdensome responsibilities and problems as her old life. Eventually, she even takes on the task of raising another child, 12-year-old Noah Miller. Before Delia realizes it, sixteen months have passed and, although she had never intended to leave her family permanently, she is stuck in her new life. As she tells her daughter Susie, she just got "separated from [them], and then . . . [couldn't find] a way to get back again" (LY 293).

The opportunity arises, however, in the form of Susie's wedding. When Delia returns to Baltimore for the ceremony, she quickly slips back into her old roles: umpire, negotiator, mediator, cook, scheduler—in other words, wife and mother.

In the end Delia even manages to patch things up with Sam. After learning that he had scratched off an appeal to do whatever she wanted to bring her back home in a letter he had written her shortly after she left him, Delia relents and returns to her old life and to Sam's bed. As she lies there, home again, she realizes that she had not been running away from her family. Instead she had been trying to cope with her father's death, Sam's health problems, and her children growing up and leaving home. Lying there next to Sam, Delia now considers the past sixteen months as a "time trip" (LY 326) that has helped her understand that the family that she thought she had left behind has actually journeyed farther than she herself has. Thinking back to the day she walked off down the beach, leaving Sam and her children behind, she now understands what was really happening: Her children had been looking at the horizon, "poised to begin their [own] journeys," and she, left behind for the first time in their lives, had simply been trying to understand how to tell them goodbye (LY 326).

Selected Book Reviews

Caldwell, Gail. "The Marriage Fled." *Boston Globe* 7 May 1995: 47.

Eder, Richard. "Trying on a New Life." *Los Angeles Times Book Review* 7 May 1995: 3.

Gray, Paul. "The Intentional Tourist." *Time* 15 May 1995: 80.

Harrison, Kathryn. "Adventures of a Wayward Wife." *Washington Post Book World* 16 Apr. 1995: 1.

Lehmann-Haupt, Christopher. "Leaving a Life But Not Quite Escaping." *New York Times* 27 Apr. 1995: C17.

Oates, Joyce Carol. "Time to Say Goodbye." *Times Literary Supplement* 5 May 1995: 22.

Rubenstein, Roberta. "The Woman Who Went Away." *Chicago Tribune* 30 Apr. 1995: sec. 14: 1.

Schine, Cathleen. "New Life for Old." *New York Times Book Review* 7 May 1995: 12.

Shone, Tom. "Runaway." *New Yorker* 8 May 1995: 89–90.

Horace Lamb. (LY) Belle Flint's other boarder and eventual husband; a traveling storm window salesman, he occupies his room only on weekends.

Lamont. (BL) Mr. Otis' nephew, who works at the Buford Texaco.

Edward Landing. ("Bridge") Harriet Landing's brother, who lives in Grover.

Harriet Landing. ("Bridge") a 46-year-old artist who is striking but no longer beautiful.

language. (AT, BL, DHR, IMEC, "Knack," "Linguistics," LY, SC, TCT, "Your Place") As a writer herself, Anne Tyler has a love of words and an ability to use words to convey delicate shades of meaning. In her novels, however, her characters' uses of language are much more limited. In fact, most of her characters experience language barriers that hinder communication more often than they succeed in overcoming those barriers. Although Macon Leary, in *The Accidental Tourist*, labors over the wording of each entry in his travel guidebook, faithfully eradicating all uses of the passive voice, in his personal life he finds it harder to communicate with the people around him. Macon's wife Sarah accuses him of not "even communicat[ing] when [he] communicate[s]" (AT 137). In "A Knack for Languages," Susan Sebastiani has a similar problem breaking through the language barrier. Although her husband Mark speaks several languages, Susan never feels that she understands him at all. These limitations of language make communication very difficult, for without precise tools to convey feelings and emotions Tyler's characters find it hard to express these with any accuracy.

Mr. Lanham. ("Teenage") principal of the private school Donny Coble attends.

"Laps." *Parents* Aug. 1981: 66–67+. "Laps" is a story that stems from Tyler's personal experience as the mother of two daughters. The story transcends the mundanity of a trip to the neighborhood pool, however, through Tyler's skillful use of three of her favorite themes—time, aging, and memory. Through the interweaving of these themes into the events of the story, Tyler produces a poignant blend of past and present. Time and, more to the point, the passage of time seems at once both imperceptible and yet relentless in its effects. It has passed as surely as the laps swum by Mrs. Bond's teenaged daughter, but with much more significant impact.

Synopsis: As always, the narrator (Mrs. Bond) and her friend Sue Ellen arrive at the neighborhood pool with their children just as it opens at 10 A.M., loaded down with the paraphernalia they need for spending the day at the pool: towels, toys, and sandwiches.

Immediately, the children head for the water while their mothers find places for their belongings and lie down on their towels. The two women take turns watching the smallest children—Biddy and Brook—in the baby pool. The boys—Nicholas and Jules—begin diving for pennies. Lindy, Mrs. Bond's oldest daughter, starts gracefully swimming laps.

Sue Ellen describes a dream she had last night in which they were back in high school dissecting frogs. Then Mrs. Bond recalls her dream: A man in a suit rings her doorbell and asks her if she is ready. She replies that she will be ready as soon as she gets changed. The man follows her upstairs and, when she turns around, he is taking off his clothes, carefully hanging them up in her closet.

Lindy finishes her laps and smiles at the lifeguard, who smiles back at her. Mrs. Bond thinks back to the days when she was the only female lifeguard at the old city pool back in the fifties. Snapping out of her reverie, she begins to think about the variety of body types represented at the pool and wonders what Martians would think about this diversity if they landed here. Would they consider all these various people the same species? She notices, too, that Sue Ellen, whose figure has always been better than hers, has begun to look more like a middle-aged woman.

After lunch the adults swim for an hour while the children nap. Sue Ellen points out an old acquaintance of theirs, Dabney Bell Sheridan, who is now fat and drab. After 2 P.M. the children start swimming again. Then at 3 o'clock the older teenagers arrive, and the activity in the pool gets rowdier.

Mrs. Bond and Sue Ellen watch as some of the other women's husbands begin to arrive at the pool for a quick swim after work. Unlike their husbands, Buck and Ned, these men do not have to work late every night. The two women discuss what they are going to fix for supper.

Then it is time to gather their belongings and head home. The children are tired and cranky. Mrs. Bond calls to Lindy, who is ignoring her and swimming a few last laps even though her mother has told her that they are leaving. Mrs. Bond just watches her daughter and thinks, "From here, she seems made of silver. Her stroke is beautiful—slow and effortless. It's clear she has no idea she will ever have to leave the water" (130).

large families. (CN, CW, EP, "Genuine," IMEC, MP, "Nobody," SC, SM) Tyler has a fondness for portraying large families. The Hawkes family in *If Morning Ever Comes* numbers seven children (not to mention a live-in grandmother), the Emersons in *The Clock Winder* include seven siblings, the Bennetts in "The Genuine Fur Eye-Lashes" are at least five with another on the way, the Gowers in *Morgan's Passing* have seven daughters followed by a son, the extended Emory family in *Earthly Possessions* expands through returning brothers and down-on-their-luck church members, and the Pauling family in *Celestial Navigation* increases to six children, not to mention the many boarders who come and go.

Larkin sisters. (BL) two old ladies who are neighbors of the Morans, who used to put a rocking horse on their porch whenever Maggie Moran would stroll by with Leroy.

Kenny Larson. (SM) Thomas Bedloe's best friend; Thomas prays that the boy's earache will get better so that he can come back to Camp Second Chance.

Howard Potter Laskin. (TCT) Miss Faye and Miss Lucy Potter's cousin who used to draw group silhouettes.

"Laura." *Archive* Mar. 1959: 36–37. Set in a collective "community" similar to Celo, North Carolina, where Tyler lived with her parents for several years, "Laura" is Tyler's first published story, published in *Archive*, Duke University's literary magazine. Like many of Tyler's early stories, "Laura" concentrates on the viewpoint of a child coming to grips with the adult world. Here the 11-year-old girl must come to terms with the knowledge of death. At the end of the story, however, what seems most surprising to the girl is the knowledge that, despite the death of someone she knows, life still goes on.

Synopsis: The Saturday before Christmas, Arle Brooks comes in to warm himself and tells the family about the death of Laura, one of the older members of the Community. Inexplicably, the narrator, an 11-year-old girl, begins to laugh. The young girl cannot understand why she responds to the news so inappropriately since Laura's death is not a surprise. The old woman had been "the sort of person who in old age becomes devoutly religious . . . and [who] in the last year had made such dramatic preparations for her departure that it would have been embarrassing had she lasted the winter" (36).

Instead the narrator is surprised at herself for feeling the way she does about Laura's death. She and her brother Ty used to take cookies to Laura and, on their mother's orders, sit with her for an hour while Laura read the Bible to them. Other members of the Community rarely read the Bible, or, if they do, they read it as literature. Laura, however, treated it like "some terribly personal letter" (36). Because of her fundamentalism, the more liberal-minded Community had not known what to do with Laura, but they had tolerated her nonetheless.

Although the narrator tries to remember something profound that Laura had said or done, she cannot recall anything out of the ordinary. To the young girl, Laura just seems "depressingly realistic" (37). Even so, the narrator is amazed that her father walks about tending the fire and getting the mail when someone has just died. She is pleased, however, when her parents announce that she can attend the funeral, her first, and even happier when they do not allow her brother to go because he is too young.

The funeral is held two days later. Laura is buried next to Jeremy MacDonald, the slaveholding owner of the whole valley a century earlier. Because of his ownership of slaves, Laura had called him a "heathen" (37), but Arle had pointed out to her that she and the slavemaster would one day be neighbors. And indeed, in death, they are.

While Arle delivers the eulogy, the narrator fears that she will laugh out loud again. The only child present, she begins to think an odd, "totally irrelevant thought" (37). Then she realizes that her response had been "the only way . . . of expressing this thing that was bursting out of [her]—this sudden new feeling of growing up and having things happen to change [her] life" (37).

Smiling, the narrator takes her mother's hand. Her mother tells her that she needs to have a hot lunch before they decorate their Christmas tree.

Laura. ("Laura") the old woman who dies in the story.

Laura. ("Woman") Dudley's wife.

Laurie. ("Neutral") a girl in Jacob's class, whom he begins to call on the pretext of getting homework assignments.

lawyers. (SC) The proper Pecks' perfect profession, only Caleb and Justin manage to avert careers in this dull life's work.

Alicia Leary. (AT) Macon, Rose, Charles, and Porter's peripatetic mother, who constantly craves change; she has been married four times; in 1950 she sent the children to Baltimore to be raised by their Leary grandparents.

Charles Leary. (AT) Macon Leary's oldest brother, a little portly; he is divorced; he oversees production at the family bottle cap factory.

Danny Leary. (AT) Porter and June Leary's 16-year-old son, who lives in Washington with his mother.

Ethan Leary. (AT) Macon and Sarah Leary's 12-year-old son, who was killed during a holdup at a Burger Bonanza a year before the novel opens.

Grandfather Leary. (AT) Macon, Rose, Charles, and Porter Leary's gruff grandfather; he was known as the Bottle Cap King.

Grandmother Leary. (AT) Macon, Rose, Charles, and Porter Leary's grandmother; she dies before her husband, leaving him in Rose's care.

June Leary. (AT) Porter Leary's ex-wife, who ran away and married a hippie stereo salesman while she was pregnant with their youngest daughter, Liberty; she now lives in Washington.

Liberty Leary. (AT) Porter and June Leary's 8-year-old daughter, born after June left Porter; ironically, she looks more like Porter than their other two children.

Macon Leary. (AT) 42-year-old writer of a series of travel guidebooks for people who hate to travel.

Porter Leary. (AT) Macon Leary's brother; the best looking of the three; he is the financial wizard of the family and works at the family bottle cap factory; he is divorced and has three children.

Rose Leary. (AT) Macon Leary's 38-year-old sister, who lives in the Leary family home and takes care of first her grandparents and then her brothers after their divorces; she marries Julian Edge.

Sarah Leary. (AT) Macon Leary's wife, also 42, who leaves him after twenty years of marriage.

Susan Leary. (AT) Porter and June Leary's 14-year-old daughter, who lives in Washington with her mother; she accompanies her uncle Macon Leary on his trip to Philadelphia.

Ardle Leigh. (EP) girl from Charlotte Emory's childhood whose parents had been very close.

Lem. (SC) Alonzo Divich's mechanic at the carnival, who had robbed a bank in 1969.

Lem. (TCT) Missouri's husband, who did not tell her that he had previously been married.

letters. (AT, BL, CW, DHR, "Dry," IMEC, "Knack," LY, MP, "Outside," "Saints," SC, SM, "Some Sign," "Spending," "Your Place") Tyler often includes portions of or even complete letters to and from various characters in her works. Like most of the communication between characters, however, these letters don't communicate as much as they intend. Like Sam Grinstead's letter to his wife Delia in which he scratches through the most important line in *Ladder of Years*, these letters usually hide more than they reveal. In *If Morning Ever Comes*, Ben Joe Hawkes receives frequent letters from his family in North Carolina, yet these letters fail to tell him what he really wants to know: how his family is getting along in his absence. Instead, the letters are filled with the mundane and trivial aspects of their lives. In Tyler's epistolary tour de force, chapter seven of *The Clock Winder*, Tyler presents a series of letters to and from Elizabeth Abbott, which skirt the salient issues that led to her leaving the Emerson family.

Dr. Lewis or Loomis. (EP) the surgeon who operates on Charlotte Emory's mother, Lacey Ames.

Father Lewis. (CW) Episcopalian priest who conducts Timothy Emerson's funeral service.

Liddie. (DHR) Mag's difficult 14-year-old daughter.

"The Lights on the River." *Archive* Oct. 1959: 5–6. This story opens with the following biographical remark: "Anne Tyler sits quietly but attractively in most of her courses, saying little to demonstrate her intellectual and emotional depth. She is the kind of person who would be lost to all but her closest friends if it were not for her writing" (5).

Tyler's second published story, "The Lights on the River" concentrates on the viewpoint of a young girl, Betty Catherine, who has to incorporate the knowledge of death into her world. Much like the young girl in John Crowe Ransom's poem "Janet Waking," Betty Catherine's innocence is shattered by the unexpected deaths of her father and her brother.

Using Betty Catherine's memory, Tyler charts the progress of the young girl's transformation. Through the motif of the river, flowing relentless on, unaware of the cataclysmic change that it has wrought in Betty Catherine's life, Tyler portrays the flow of life itself. Tyler skillfully understates the scene in which Betty Catherine realizes that her brother is dead. By having her hear the dredging machines stop on the river, the depth of her feelings is underscored. Therefore, the mother's breaking the news to her daughter later on becomes anticlimactic.

Synopsis. When Betty Catherine's mother tells her that her father is dead, the young girl, through whose perspective the story is told, notices that her mother seems distant and realizes that she also suddenly looks older. Her brother Bobby, who was in the boat with their father, is also missing. So all night Betty Catherine listens to "the giant dark machines scraping the river-bed" (5) to try to locate his body, knowing that as long as she hears the machines there is still a chance that her brother is alive.

The next day Betty Catherine goes outside after her mom tells her to. While she waits for news of her brother, she reminisces about throwing all his toys into the lot next door and about his learning to swim. This last thought causes her to hope that he somehow made it safely to shore after the boat capsized. Although she remembers her father, too, she seems to have accepted the fact of his death. But not Bobby's. She imagines herself in his place in the mud at the bottom of the river. As she plays with her dolls, she prays for him.

Betty Catherine's mother comes out and sits with her and talks to her distractedly about her doll. When the young girl asks her mother about whether lemon juice will take off freckles, however, the mother chastises her for asking such an inappropriate question. Then Betty Catherine remembers how her father and Bobby had not returned from their boating trip in time for supper on Sunday and the worried look that had come into her mother's eyes. Even that was better, though, than the way her eyes looked now, "with nothing in them at all" (6).

As Betty Catherine and her mother eat a warmed-over lunch, the young girl drinks lots of milk and feels happy that her prayers are going to make Bobby all right. She also thinks vaguely of her father, but not about "anything definite like the way he looked" (6).

Afterwards Betty Catherine lies down to take a nap. Before she falls asleep, however, she hears the motors out on the river stop, confirming for her Bobby's death. Not surprised, therefore, when her mother comes in to tell her the sad news, she just stares out the window and thinks about the lights on the river.

Lily. (TCT) Missouri's daughter, who, along with Joan Pike, hands tobacco to Missouri.

Linda. (BL) Serena Gill's overweight daughter, who lives in New Jersey with her husband Jeff and their two children.

Linda Lou. (DHR) classmate of Pearl Tull's who has an affair with a male teacher during her senior year.

Doris Lindsay. (SDL) Fay-Jean Lindsay's younger sister who assists in Drum Casey's kidnapping.

Fay-Jean Lindsay. (SDL) classmate of Evie Decker's; she is the daughter of a tenant farmer and is very loose with boys; her favorite singer is Joseph Ballew.

Lindy. ("Spending") Joe and Dory Bell's daughter, who now lives in Chicago; she sends them a check for $1,000.

"Linguistics." *Washington Post Magazine* 12 Nov. 1978: 38–40+. One of several stories that Tyler has written that includes foreign characters, "Linguistics" very closely resembles Tyler's own marriage to an Iranian-born, but now Americanized, child psychiatrist.

Initially, the story focuses on the language problems that Claire and her foreign husband experience, as well as the cultural accommodations they make as they build a "shared history" over the years. Ultimately, and more interestingly, however, the story's focus shifts to the foreigner, whose accommodations and compromises with American culture have been far greater than his wife's to his culture. Eventually, Claire realizes that, after their single, long-delayed visit to her husband's country, they will probably never return there again.

Nevertheless, despite this loss, the love that the couple share over the years develops a bond between them that provides compensation for the cultural loss. Such personal connections transcend language barriers, as evidenced by the phone call from Claire's husband's aunt—also a foreigner.

In the end, these personal connections create communication between two people that overcomes obstacles and that speaks without words.

Synopsis: At a party Claire meets an older, foreign graduate student. They discuss language, and he gives her a ride home. As an undergrad, Claire had studied several languages but had settled on a major in biochemistry. Despite being wary of foreigners and in spite of the language barrier, Claire becomes intrigued by this man. Yet she always feels that "this clumsy, choppy-phrased foreigner was not the real person at all; that there was another man inside, no doubt witty and full of poetry, maybe far brighter than [she] was, whom [she] would never know" (39). After she realizes that she loves him, Claire begins to study his language. Her attempt to learn his native tongue greatly pleases the foreigner; still Claire feels that a barrier remains between them.

Despite her Aunt Phoebe's protest that they lack a "shared history" (39), Claire and the foreigner marry. During the first year of their marriage, they begin to grow more alike. Claire continues to study his language, and he, remarkably, begins to sound more like her when he speaks English. To bridge the language barrier, they go to concerts and listen to music or cook. These activities need no words.

Eventually they have twins, John and Jane. At first, Claire and her husband plan to raise them to be bilingual, but that doesn't really work out. Finally, they decide that the children will learn the language when they go to visit their father's native country. So Claire and her husband start saving up for a trip to his country by putting money in a cookie jar. Like other parents, they watch their children grow up and begin to love them more and more.

A few years later, the husband applies for American citizenship. His lab assistant Stuart goes along as a witness and is mistaken for the foreigner. Claire realizes that her husband has really changed and become quite Americanized. On the way home, however, he surprises Claire by saying, "It's not fair . . . I have to give up everything, all I ever knew" (44).

Eventually, the couple develop a system of talking in the husband's language to communicate secrets. Yet it is a system dependent not only upon language but on shared experience as well, their developing "shared history." When the twins are 10, the family finally takes the trip to the husband's country that they have been saving for. After a few days there, however, Claire's husband feels out of place, complaining, "I don't speak the language anymore" (46). Claire comforts him because she has felt the same language barrier here that he has struggled with in America.

Years pass and the couple continue to develop their "shared history" (46). The twins grow older, and Claire doubts that the family will ever visit her husband's country again, especially after his mother dies. One of the few remaining links to her husband's family is an aunt who lives in New Jersey with her son. She often calls to talk to him at times when he is not at home, forcing Claire to try her best to understand the old woman's language. Sometimes they cannot communicate at all, so the aunt just gives up and says the only English words she knows: "Kellaire . . . I love you very much " (46). Claire responds (she can't remember later in which language): "I love you too" (46).

Greggie Linley. (LY) Vanessa Linley's 18-month-old son.

Vanessa Linley. (LY) young single mother, who becomes one of Delia Grinstead's friends in Bay Borough.

Durwood Linthicum. (MP) Jonas Linthicum's son, who inherits the Holy Word Entertainment Troupe upon his father's death.

Rev. R. Jonas Linthicum. (MP) owner of the Holy Word Entertainment Troupe of Tindell, Maryland.

Mr. Linthicum. (EP) an old man Charlotte Emory passes as she runs by with Jake Simms following the bank robbery.

Mrs. Linthicum. (SC) wife of the pastor of Polk Valley Church.

Lisa Michelle. (DHR) Clement and Dotty's first daughter, who dies of crib death.

lists. (AT, "Foot-Footing," IMEC, LY, MP) See ORDER.

The Little House. —Children's book that Tyler read as a child that taught her the way time works.

For Further Reading

Tyler, Anne. "Why I Still Treasure 'The Little House.' " *New York Times Book Review* 2 Nov. 1980: 33–34.

the Lockes. (BL) the Morans' next-door neighbors.

locusts. (CW, "Woman") The seventeen-year cycle of this insect reinforces the passage of time in "A Woman Like a Fieldstone House," and establishes Elizabeth Abbott Emerson's ability to deal with any situation in *The Clock Winder.*

Noona Long. ("I'm Not Going") obese, nearly 50-year-old music teacher.

Lucas Loomis. (AT) overweight computer software salesman and fan of the Accidental Tourist series who sits next to Macon Leary on his flight from San Francisco.

Lorimer. (BL) drummer in Jesse Moran's band.

Old Mrs. Lowell. ("Dry") Samuel Anders' customer who cancelled her paper subscription; she kept her husband's ashes in a vase on her mantle.

Jane Lowry. (DHR) old friend of Cody Tull's whom he meets at the train station when he and Ruth Spivey are running off to get married.

Miss Lucas. ("Neutral") Jacob's fifth grade teacher.

Lucy. (BL) one of the Morans' cats over the years.

Sister Lula. (SM) member of Second Chance whose son Chuckie dies in Vietnam when he jumps out of a plane without his parachute.

Luna. (DHR) one of Pearl Tull's relatives in her old photographs.

Lurene. (BL) Mr. Otis' sister, with whom he now lives.

Lysander. (LY) air conditioning workman who is working on the Grinsteads' house.

M

Mabel. (BL) waitress at Nell's Grocery and Cafe.

Jeremy MacDonald. ("Laura") the slaveholder who once owned the whole valley one hundred years ago; ironically, Laura is buried next to him in the cemetery.

Mr. Mack. (CN) manager of the bookstore where Miss Vinton works.

Madame Azuki. (SC) fortuneteller Justine Peck visits in Blainestown.

Madame Olita. (SC) East Baltimore fortuneteller who teaches Justine Peck how to read Tarot cards.

Julie Madison. ("Misstep") 16-year-old girl who is raped in her own home.

Mrs. Madison. ("Misstep") Julie Madison's mother, who comes home just minutes after her daughter is raped.

Mag. (DHR) woman who gives Luke Tull a ride from Washington to Baltimore.

Magic Marcia. (SC) fortuneteller Justine Peck visits in Buskville.

mail. (CN, CW, MP, SM) One of the highlights of Anne Tyler's day is the visit of the mailman. She loves to receive mail, especially catalogues. This fascination with mail carries over into her novels in the form of the many letters she includes, as well as characters who view mail as visitations from the outside world. At the end of *Morgan's Passing*, Morgan Gower plans to look at the personal mail of a woman who has mistaken him for a mailman. Not opening mail, on the other hand, indicates a character whose life is limited. In *Saint Maybe*, in one of Ian's dreams, Danny castigates Lucy for not opening even her first-class letters.

male viewpoint. ("Artificial," AT, BL, CN, CW, IMEC, MP, SM) In a 1976 book review entitled "Women Writers: Equal but Separate," Anne Tyler asserted her belief that men and women have more similarities than differences. Therefore, she feels that as a writer she has equal license to write about men as well as women. As if to prove her point, she often presents a male viewpoint in her work. In her first novel, *If Morning Ever Comes*, she concentrates on the viewpoint of young Ben Joe Hawkes. In later novels, Tyler presents the views of Morgan Gower in *Morgan's Passing*, Macon Leary in *The Accidental Tourist*, and Ian Bedloe in *Saint Maybe*. In *Breathing Lessons*, however, she actually divides her novel into three sections, the middle part of which concentrates on the viewpoint of Ira Moran. Tyler's even-handed approach in matters of gender stands out in a literary era dominated by feminist approaches.

managing women. (AT, CN, CW, DHR, "Dry," EP, IMEC, MP, SDL) In her novels, Tyler presents a series of strong women who manage to hold their families together with little or no support from men. In *If Morning Ever Comes*, Ellen Hawkes heads the Hawkes family following the desertion and then death of her husband Phillip. In *A Slipping-Down Life*, Evie Decker establishes a home for herself and her coming child. In *The Clock Winder*, Elizabeth Abbott becomes caretaker to the entire Emerson clan. At the end of *Celestial Navigation*, Mary Tell maintains a home for herself and her children. In *Earthly Possessions*, Charlotte Emory holds her burgeoning household together, as does Bonny Gower in *Morgan's Passing*. In *The Accidental Tourist*, Muriel Pritchett, a single mother, holds multiple jobs and threatens possible intruders with bodily harm in the rough neighborhood in which she lives.

For Further Reading

Brock, Dorothy Faye Sala. "Anne Tyler's Treatment of Managing Women." Diss. North Texas State University, 1985.

Stuart Mann. ("Nobody") old friend of Ben Joe Hawkes' who gives him an address book with Ben Joe's name and address in it.

Bart Manning. (CW) young man who gave Elizabeth Abbott a ride from Philadelphia to Baltimore, whom she sees again at the Schmidts' party.

Maria. (MP) cook at Maria's Home-Style pizzeria, who helps Morgan Gower deliver Emily Meredith's baby.

Marie. (MP) the female clerk who used to work for Morgan Gower at Cullen Hardware.

Marie. ("Some Sign") a woman who works at Sam Simmons' drug store.

Marie-Claire. (LY) Linda Felson's 8-year-old daughter; Thérèse's twin.

Marjorie. ("Neutral") Jacob's mother; a plump, dimpled woman, somewhat out of fashion.

Maroon. ("Geologist") African American maid who looks after Bennett Johnson.

marriage. ("Artificial," AT, BL, "Bride," CN, "Common," CW, DHR, EP, "Feather," "Holding," IMEC, "I Never Saw," "Knack," "Linguistics," LY, MP, SC, SDL, SM, "Some Sign," TCT, "Uncle Ahmad") Marriage is one of Tyler's great themes. She has presented portraits of marriage in almost every stage of that institution. In *A Slipping-Down Life*, she portrays a newlywed couple's financial and emotional struggles. Most of her novels, however, deal with more fully established marriages. In some cases, *Earthly Possessions* and *Ladder of Years*, married couples manage to weather the strains of living together for an extended time. In other novels, however, marriages fall apart (*Morgan's Passing* and *The Accidental Tourist*), unable to withstand the pressures of married life. The novel that most fully explores the whole range of married life is *Breathing Lessons*, whose title provides the perfect metaphor for the rhythms, the give and take, the ups and downs of the married relationship. As Maggie and Ira Moran live a day in their lives, they argue, make up, and exhibit all their strengths and weaknesses. Similarly, as they recall the twenty-eight years of their marriage, they remember the feelings and shared experiences that have pulled them apart and held them together.

marriage proposals. (BL, DHR, IMEC, LY, SDL) Tyler's own response to her husband Taghi's marriage proposal was a matter-of-fact "Oh, well. Why not?" Evie Decker responds to Drumstrings Casey's proposal with the same line in *A Slipping-Down Life*. The noncommittal attitude expressed by this response indicates not a lack of interest in the other person but a fear of commitment that the marriage proposal implies. In *Ladder of Years*, Susie

Grinstead agrees to marry her fiance, Avery Driscoll, after postponing the ceremony with much the same deceptively nonchalant lack of interest.

Ned Marsh. (TCT) the person driving the tractor when Janie Rose Pike was hit.

Dr. Martin. ("Under Tree") the Tilghman family pediatrician.

Maryam. ("Uncle") Ahmad Ardavi's first wife.

Mary Lee (or Mary Lou). (DHR) intern's wife who babysits Becky for Jenny Tull when Jenny is in medical school.

Mr. Maxwell. (LY) older patient of Sam Grinstead's who calls him in the middle of the night to come check on his wife; they were Sam's first house call twenty-two years earlier.

Mrs. Maxwell. (LY) Mr. Maxwell's sickly wife, whom Delia Grinstead calls "the Dowager Queen of Hypochondria" (LY 33).

Barry May. (MP) young man in Off the Cuff improvisational troupe, who owns the group's van.

Caroline Peck Mayhew. (SC) Justine Peck's overweight mother; Daniel Peck's youngest child (born 1910); she kills herself by walking in front of a car.

Sam Mayhew. (SC) Justine Peck's father; Caroline Peck Mayhew's husband; he dies of a heart attack.

Lisa McCauley. (CN) one of Jeremy Pauling's art students.

Gracie McClintock. (SM) young member of the Church of the Second Chance who invites her father, Mac McClintock, to the Christian Fellowship Picnic.

Mac McClintock. (SM) a guest at the Christian Fellowship Picnic who talks to Doug Bedloe.

Claude McEwen. (AT) a young man who dates Claire Dugan; Mrs. Dugan nicknames him "the General" because she thinks he's in the army.

Willis Ralph McGee. (SC) movie theater owner that Dorcas Britt is thinking about marrying.

Daffodil McIlwain. (LY) Henry and Pansy McIlwain's 6-week-old baby daughter.

Henry McIlwain. (LY) Belle Flint's new boyfriend who was supposed to come for Thanksgiving dinner but goes back to his wife Pansy instead.

Pansy McIlwain. (LY) Henry McIlwain's wife.

Jason McKenna. ("Outside") 18-year-old boy who leaves his home in Parsley Valley, North Carolina, to tutor a young boy (Billy Douglas) with learning problems in Pulmet, New Hampshire.

Mary McKenna. ("Outside") Jason McKenna's younger sister.

Mr. McKenna. ("Outside") Jason McKenna's father, who raises goats in a cooperative community in the mountains of North Carolina.

Mrs. McKenna. (Outside") Jason McKenna's mother, who had opposed Jason's leaving Parsley Valley because he doesn't know what it's like outside; she and her husband had moved to the community fourteen years earlier to give their children "a better world" (1131).

Ben Meagan. ("Half-Truths") Susanna Spright Meagan's husband, who falls in love with her at a revival when he is 32; he leaves her after she fails to heal their son Benny.

Benjamin (Benny) Meagan, Jr. ("Half-Truths") Susanna and Ben Meagan's son, who is struck by a car and dies.

Susanna Spright Meagan. ("Half-Truths") first-person narrator of the story, who, at age 60, recalls her life as a healer.

Sue Meeks. (DHR) ninth grade classmate of Cody Tull's.

Melinda. ("Two People") adolescent girl, who, to cure her sleepwalking, is sent by her father to stay with her Aunt Sony.

Melissa. ("Common") Miss Lorna Love Johnson's 30-year-old daughter, who arrived late in life and has always been sickly; she marries Joel and, against her mother's advice, becomes pregnant and has a son, William.

memory. (AT, "Average," "Baltimore," BL, "Bridge," CN, "Common," DHR, EP, IMEC, "I'm Not Going," "Laps," "Lights," LY, MP, "Saints," SC, SDL, SM, "Some Sign," "Under Tree," "Woman") One of

Tyler's most effective literary techniques is the use of memory to expand and enhance her plots. Particularly in certain novels, her characters' memories actually become the plots. This technique allows Tyler to move back and forth along the continuum of time, collapsing time and illustrating how thoroughly the past informs the present lives of her characters. In *Breathing Lessons*, Maggie and Ira Moran's memories provide a full-scale account of their twenty-eight–year marriage, despite the novel's plot taking place all on one day in September. In *Dinner at the Homesick Restaurant*, nearly the entire novel takes place in the memories of Pearl Tull and her children. For only by understanding the different way in which each character remembers the same events can Tyler distinguish between the varied individual responses to their lives. In several of Tyler's short stories, memory also plays an important role. In "Laps," Mrs. Bond's memories of her childhood impress upon her the transience of life when she watches her own teenaged daughter methodically swimming laps in the pool. In "Some Sign That I Ever Made You Happy," Sam Simmons' memory of his parents' marriage while looking through his father's diary and letters from the past teach him a lesson about his need to appreciate his own wife and children, although at the same time he realizes that, because of the way that time passes and due to the pressures of life, he will probably never fully express his feelings, just like his father. Thus Tyler uses memory as a tool to express her characters' reflection and regret.

mental handicaps. ("Average," BL, DHR, IMEC) Tyler's sensitive portrayal of people with mental handicaps is evident in the characters of Arnold Blevins in "Average Waves in Unprotected Waters"; Dorrie Moran in *Breathing Lessons*; Josiah Payson in *Dinner at the Homesick Restaurant*, who proves that he can work productively; and Quality Jones in *If Morning Ever Comes*. More significantly, perhaps, Tyler portrays the brave and caring "normal" people whose love and care provide the environments for these mentally handicapped characters to thrive, most notably Ira Moran in *Breathing Lessons*, Ezra Tull in *Dinner at the Homesick Restaurant*, and Bet Blevins in "Average Waves in Unprotected Waters."

mental illness. ("As the Earth," CN, CW, DHR, "Saints") Mental illness strikes a few of Tyler's characters. Mrs. Brauw in "As the Earth Grows Old" reacts with little concern to her daughter's death by fire. Andrew Emerson's disorder leads him to shoot Elizabeth Abbott in *The Clock Winder*, but later to depend on her completely. Jenny Tull's partner, Dan Charles, struggles to cope with his wife's mental illness in *Dinner at the Homesick Restaurant*. And, most significant in the Tyler canon, Jeremy Pauling fights agoraphobia in *Celestial Navigation*.

Burt Meredith. (MP) Leon Meredith's father, a Richmond banker.

Emily Meredith. (MP) young woman puppeteer whose baby Morgan Gower delivers; later she bears his son, Joshua, and leaves her husband, Leon Meredith, to go live with Morgan.

Gina Meredith. (MP) Emily and Leon Meredith's daughter.

Leon Meredith. (MP) Emily Meredith's husband, who helps with the puppet shows.

Mrs. Meredith. (MP) Leon Meredith's mother.

Reverend Merrill. (LY) minister who performs Nat and Binky Moffat's marriage ceremony.

Miggs. (CW) Johns Hopkins student Elizabeth Abbott plans to ride with to New York.

Brewster Miggs. (SDL) Clotelia's militant boyfriend.

Mike. (CW) Bart Manning and Elizabeth Abbott's mutual friend.

Hannah Miles. (MP) young woman who lives across the hall from Emily and Leon Meredith and sometimes babysits their daughter Gina.

Mr. Milledge. (DHR) neighbor of the Tulls in Baltimore who has crazy spells.

Ellie Miller. (LY) Joel Miller's wife, who leaves him after she discovers a lump in her breast; then she becomes a television weatherperson in Kellerton.

Joel Miller. (LY) principal of Bay Borough's high school, Dorothy G. Underwood High; he hires Delia Grinstead to look after his son Noah after his wife Ellie leaves him.

Melanie Miller. (DHR) a girl in Jenny Tull's Bible class at church.

Noah Miller. (LY) Joel and Ellie Miller's 12-year-old son.

Margie Millet. (SM) Lucy Dean's mother-in-law; Thomas Dulsimore's mother, whom Eli Everjohn tracks down in Portia, Maryland; after visiting her, Ian Bedloe determines that she would not make a fit guardian for the children.

Winston Mills. (SM) Ian Bedloe's roommate at Sumner College who has a chair with the print of a gigantic hand on it.

Rev. Arthur Milsom. (SC) Meg Peck's 26-year-old milquetoast assistant minister husband.

Margaret Rose (Meg) Peck Milsom. (SC) See MEG PECK.

Mother Milsom. (SC) Arthur Milsom's mother; Meg Peck's manipulative mother-in-law; a faith healer who always dresses in white.

ministers. (CW, EP, "Geologist," "Half-Truths," SC, SDL, SM) In an interview with Wendy Lamb published in 1981 in the *Iowa Journal of Literary Studies*, Tyler expressed her disapproval of ministers' tendency to think they have the right to change other people's lives. That negative view is most clearly seen in her early work through a series of closed-minded preachers, such as Arthur Milsom in *Searching for Caleb*, Saul Emory in *Earthly Possessions*, and Rev. John Abbott in *The Clock Winder*. In later novels, Tyler's bias against such characters eases. In particular, Rev. Emmett in *Saint Maybe* is portrayed in a very favorable light. In fact, Tyler has admitted that Rev. Emmett's church offers Ian the second chance that he needs. Perhaps what most appeals to Tyler about Rev. Emmett, however, is his development during the course of the novel from certainty to uncertainty. By the end of the novel, he is questioning his own rigid rules and concentrating on the real purpose of religion: ministering to real-life people. This acceptance of his own limitations makes him one of Tyler's most sympathetic characters.

Miriam. ("Teenage") Donny Coble's girlfriend.

mirrors/reflections. ("As the Earth," AT, "Base-Metal," EP, IMEC, SDL, SM, "Spending") As Tyler's characters search for their individual identities, they sometimes pause to take stock of where they are headed. Often that is tied to a reflection of themselves in a window or a mirror. In "The Base-Metal Egg," Mary Beth Polk notices the reflection of herself, her mother, and her boyfriend in a shop window that makes them look like a couple shopping with their mother-in-law. In *Earthly Possessions*, Charlotte Emory sees herself and Jake Simms reflected on an appliance store window as their picture is shown on several television sets at once. The image causes Charlotte to realize that she is trapped and cannot escape. In *Saint Maybe*, Ian Bedloe watches his own face in a mirror as his brother Danny crashes his car into a stone wall. As he looks at his image, Ian realizes that his life will never be the same again once he moves and time starts flowing again.

miscommunication. (AT, BL, LY, DHR, "Neutral," "Some Sign," "Two People") Tyler's characters are forever attempting to communicate with each other, to establish and maintain connections with those they care about. Because of the limitations of language and the inherent isolation of the human condition, however, Tyler's characters' attempts to communicate often result in failure or misunderstanding. In *The Accidental Tourist*, Sarah Leary accuses her estranged husband, Macon, of not "even communicat[ing] when [he] communicate[s]" (AT 137). Other examples of such miscommunication include Joanne Hawkes Bentley's misunderstanding the name of her future husband's boat, the *Sagacity*, which she mispronounced as "the Saga City"; Sam Simmons' inability to express his true feelings for his wife in "Some Sign That I Ever Made You Happy"; 10-year-old Jacob's inability to convey his feelings of loss and concern in "Neutral Ground"; and Pearl Tull's assertion in *Dinner at the Homesick Restaurant* that "a whole separate language" is needed "for words that are truer than other words" (DHR 9). Finally, in *Ladder of Years*, in his letter to his runaway wife Delia, Sam Grinstead marks through the one sentence that would have brought her back to him immediately. Such acts of miscommunication block communication, but are not impossible to overcome. Other characters, even foreign characters, manage to find alternate means of communication that maneuver around these communication barriers.

Missouri. (TCT) African American woman who works in tobacco; she is a fast stringer and likes to talk.

"A Misstep of the Mind." *Seventeen* Oct. 1972: 118–19+. Critics of Anne Tyler's work who dismiss her as a sunny innocent out of touch with the harsh realities of the "real world" have obviously not read "A Misstep of the Mind." In this story, Tyler deals with one of the most awful crimes— rape—with chilling effect. As is typical of Tyler, however, she concentrates not so much on the violence itself as on the aftermath of the violent act. After all, the days and weeks after the attack are the most significant for Julie because it is then that she realizes that the world is not, nor ever has been, as safe as she once naively imagined.

Synopsis: One sunny Tuesday, 16-year-old Julie Madison comes home from school for lunch and finds the front door ajar. When she enters the house, not thinking anything might be wrong, she is grabbed and raped by a black man wearing a yellow windbreaker.

Julie's mother, who works for the Urban League, comes home three minutes later and calls the police. Julie, however, can remember little of the incident, not even the type of gun the man threatened her with. Julie's parents are comforting, but she senses a change in their attitude toward her.

As for other people, few learn about the crime because Julie's name is kept out of the papers. Still, a few of her neighbors know because they are questioned by the police. One even sends her a sympathy note. Julie begins to feel that the world is not what it seems, as if "safety had crumbled in a second, as if it had never been more than a myth" (119). Yet much of her world is unchanged externally. She returns to school and goes to the movies with her boyfriend Peter, who knows nothing of the incident.

On Saturday Julie goes to the police station to look at mugshots, but she cannot identify a suspect because the rapist had told her to shut her eyes. That night she dreams about all the faces she's seen. During the next few days, undercover detectives follow her and keep watch over her.

Then one day the police call with news that they've made an arrest and want her to view a lineup. As she thinks about the lineup, she wonders if the guy had simply made some "misstep of the mind" (172). She also wonders whether or not she could have prevented the rape. Outside everything seems so normal.

At the police station Julie identifies her attacker in the lineup by remembering a scar on his chin. He has been caught committing another burglary with the windbreaker and the gun. Everyone congratulates Julie for identifying the rapist, but they soon forget about her experience. Julie, however, although she eventually forgets the actual experience, always remembers "the capacity for betrayal in a cheerful world" (172) and the chance that one day she might again open the wrong door.

Binky Moffat. (LY) Nat Moffat's 38-year-old wife.

James Nathaniel Moffat. (LY) Nat and Binky Moffat's 8 lb. 11 oz. baby boy, born on Labor Day.

Nathaniel A. (Nat) Moffat. (LY) Noah Miller's 67-year-old grandfather; Ellie Miller's father; he used to be a photographer.

Thelma Moffat. (LY) Nat Moffat's first wife; now deceased; she had been a busybody in her daughters' lives.

Daisy Moran. (BL) Maggie and Ira Moran's intelligent, serious-minded 17-year-old daughter who is going away to college; she plans to become a quantum physicist and has received a full scholarship to an Ivy League school.

Dorrie Moran. (BL) Ira Moran's older, mentally handicapped sister, who has seizures in which her left leg becomes partially paralyzed.

Fiona Stuckey Moran. (BL) Jesse Moran's 25-year-old former wife, who now lives with her mother and her daughter Leroy in Cartwheel, Pennsylvania, where she works in a beauty parlor.

Ira Moran. (BL) Maggie Moran's 50-year-old husband; he runs his father's frame shop, which supports not only his family but his father and two sisters as well; he has a trick back and loves to quote Ann Landers.

Jesse Moran. (BL) Maggie and Ira Moran's handsome 25-year-old rock musician son, who dropped out of high school; he now lives in an apartment uptown on Calvert Street and works at Chick's Cycle Shop.

Junie Moran. (BL) Ira Moran's agoraphobic older sister, who has fainting spells, but will go out if she is in disguise.

Leroy Moran. (BL) Jesse and Fiona Moran's wiry, blonde 7-year-old daughter, who is allergic to cats, but likes fried chicken and baseball; Maggie and Ira Moran's only grandchild.

Maggie Daley Moran. (BL) 48-year-old woman who has been married to Ira Moran for twenty-eight years; she has been working at the Silver Threads Nursing Home since graduating from high school in 1956; her birthday is February 14, 1938.

Rona Moran. (BL) Ira Moran's mother, who died when Ira was 14; she was more interested in religion than in being a mother.

Sam Moran. (BL) Ira Moran's octogenarian father, who quit working in his frameshop the day Ira graduated from high school due to his "weak heart," which has, nevertheless, held up for thirty years.

Morgan's Passing. The title of Tyler's 1976 *Washington Post* article, "Because I Want More than One Life," explains her motivation for writing. She enjoys entering and living, for a time, the lives of people who live lives quite different from hers. In Morgan Gower, the erstwhile hero of *Morgan's Passing*, Tyler created a character with a similar obsession. Not content to live his one life and play the prescribed roles of husband to his wife Bonny, father to his seven daughters, and hardware store manager, Morgan, the inveterate impostor, plays a variety of roles from doctor to priest to puppeteer, donning one or more of a variety of hats and costumes to fit each part. In a 1980 interview with Bruce Cook, Tyler actually worried "that people would be morally offended by [Morgan]" and assured the interviewer that, despite Morgan's being "sort of amoral," he is really harmless.

Morgan's need to play the role of the impostor reinforces Tyler's concern with identity itself. Morgan, whose father had inexplicably committed suicide when Morgan was a senior in high school, has felt adrift ever since. His marriage to Bonny has not given him the opportunity to develop into his own man either. Bonny, whose wealthy family owns a chain of hardware stores that provide Morgan with a sinecure, handles all the necessary upkeep and repairs on their house, bought for them as a wedding present by Bonny's father. She also takes care of raising their seven daughters. Thus, over the years Morgan has become practically extraneous to the life of his own family.

Not surprisingly, then, Morgan's search for identity leads him outside his family in his quest to find someone who needs him to be the hero of her life. Fairy tale imagery abounds in the novel, and it is appropriate to view Morgan as a fair prince in search of a princess to save. Enter the Merediths, Leon and Emily, whose immediate need for a doctor to deliver Emily's baby provides "Dr. Gower Morgan" the opportunity to come to the rescue. Over the course of the next few months, Morgan becomes increasingly fascinated with the Merediths' spartan lifestyle and begins to observe them from afar. Eventually Leon and Emily notice "Dr. Morgan" shadowing them, but they do not intrude upon his privacy. Gradually they adjust to the costumed, lurking figure of Morgan and accept him as a fixture in their lives.

The Merediths' job as puppeteers is what eventually brings Morgan into their actual lives. After the wedding of his oldest daughter, Morgan feels out of place so he goes to the Merediths' apartment on the pretext of buying one of Emily's puppets. This visit leads Morgan to confess that he is not a real doctor, a revelation that upsets Leon. Emily, though, seems to understand Morgan's need "to get out of his life, sometimes" (MP 120).

Emily's Quaker heritage and her simple style of dress and lifestyle mirror Tyler's own. This simplicity is also what draws Morgan, who appreciates her "pure, plain view of things" (MP 230), closer to Emily. Eventually, Morgan insinuates himself further and further into the Merediths' lives, even to the point of inviting them to join his family on their annual beach vacation and repairing the electrical cords and faucets in their apartment. Emily's response to Morgan's advances is slow at first, but they finally begin an affair that results in Emily's becoming pregnant.

Emily's pregnancy precipitates Morgan's ultimate break from his old identity. He leaves Bonny and replaces Leon as Emily's husband and partner in the puppet show. In fact, Morgan even takes on Leon's last name, due to a mistake by the owner of the entertainment troupe he and Emily start working with. This change in identity becomes official when Bonny places Morgan's obituary in the newspaper. Thus, the old Morgan Gower dies, freeing the new "Mr. Meredith" to explore his new life, which looms forth, "luminous and beautiful, and rich with possibilities" (MP 311).

For Further Reading

Croft, Robert W. *Anne Tyler: A Bio-Bibliography.* Westport, CT: Greenwood Press, 1995. 58–61.

Evans, Elizabeth. *Anne Tyler.* New York: Twayne, 1993.

Petry, Alice Hall. *Understanding Anne Tyler.* Columbia: University of South Carolina Press, 1990. 154–85.

Shafer, Aileen Chris. "Beauty and the Transformed Beast: Fairy Tales and Myths in *Morgan's Passing.*" *Anne Tyler as Novelist.* Ed. Dale Salwak. Iowa City: University of Iowa Press, 1994: 125–37.

Taylor, Gordon O. "Morgan's Passion." *The Fiction of Anne Tyler.* Ed. C. Ralph Stephens. Jackson: University Press of Mississippi, 1990: 64–72.

Selected Book Reviews

Disch, Thomas M. "The Great Imposter." *Washington Post Book World* 16 Mar. 1980: 5.

Grier, Peter. "Bright Novel That Overstretches Credibility." *Christian Science Monitor* 14 Apr. 1980: B9. [Reprinted in *Critical Essays on Anne Tyler.* Ed. Alice Hall Petry. New York: G. K. Hall, 1992: 101–2.]

Hoffman, Eva. "When the Fog Never Lifts." *Saturday Review* 15 Mar. 1980: 38–39. [Reprinted in *Critical Essays on Anne Tyler.* Ed. Alice Hall Petry. New York: G. K. Hall, 1992: 95–97.]

Mojtabai, A.G. "A State of Continual Crisis." *New York Times Book Review* 23 Mar. 1980: 14+. [Reprinted in *Critical Essays on Anne Tyler.* Ed. Alice Hall Petry. New York: G. K. Hall, 1992: 98–100.]

Nesanovich, Stella. "Anne Tyler's *Morgan's Passing.*" *Southern Review* 17 (Summer 1981): 619–21.

Prescott, Peter S. "Mr. Chameleon." *Newsweek* 24 Mar. 1980: 82–83+.

Towers, Robert. *New Republic* 22 Mar. 1980: 28+. [Reprinted in *Critical Essays on Anne Tyler.* Ed. Alice Hall Petry. New York: G. K. Hall, 1992: 103–6.]

Updike, John. "Imagining Things." *New Yorker* 23 June 1980: 94+. [Reprinted in his *Hugging the Shore: Essays and Criticism.* New York: Knopf, 1983: 283–92.]

Morris. (CW) Mary Emerson's husband.

Mrs. Harry Mosely. (SC) a rich divorcée who wears jodhpurs and wants to buy Alonzo Divich's carnival.

Lili Belle Mosely. (IMEC) Phillip Hawkes' mistress, who bore him an illegitimate son named Phillip.

Mrs. Mosely. (IMEC) Lili Belle Mosely's mother; Lili Belle and her son live with her.

Kenny Moss. (LY) one of Noah Miller's friends, who gets a golden retriever; he and Noah plan to start a rock band called Does Your Mother Have Any Children?

mother/daughter relationships. ("As the Earth," "Base-Metal," BL, "Common," DHR, EP, "Foot-Footing," "I Play," "Misstep," "Saints," SC, SM) Mother/daughter relationships in Anne Tyler's works are usually portrayed as strained and adversarial. In "As the Earth Gets Old," Mrs.

Brauw's relationship with her daughter Beatrice is downright antagonistic as they compete mercilessly at various board games. In *Dinner at the Homesick Restaurant*, Jenny Tull's relationship with her mother Pearl leads to Jenny's developing anorexia. In other cases, mothers' demands on daughters hinder the daughters' sense of freedom and their ability to develop their own sense of identity. Mary Beth Polk, in "The Base-Metal Egg" and in "Foot-Footing On," feels pressured by her mother to grow up and marry. Other mothers, however, enjoy better relationships with their daughters. Usually this development occurs when the daughter is older and has a family of her own, as with Bee Bedloe and her daughter Claudia Bedloe Daley in *Saint Maybe*. In other cases, however, the mother/daughter relationship proves ineffectual and weak. In *Earthly Possessions*, Charlotte Emory doubts that she is even her mother's daughter until her mother tells her, on her deathbed, that a picture of a young girl is not the picture of her real daughter, but a picture of herself as a child. In *Searching for Caleb*, Caroline Peck Mayhew is too weak to give her daughter Justine enough of a sense of identity and self-assurance to enable her to live outside the Peck family.

motherhood. ("Average," BL, CN, DHR, "Laps," SC, SDL, "Teenage," "Under Tree," "Who Would Want," "Your Place") Motherhood is a demanding role for Tyler's female characters. It changes their lives irrevocably, bringing in worries and concerns that they had never imagined before. Yet despite these problems, most of Tyler's mothers consider the sacrifices they make to be more than compensated for by the enriching effects that children bring to their lives.

mothers. (AT, BL, CN, CW, DHR, EP, IMEC, LY, MP, SC, SDL, SM, TCT) In her fiction, Tyler presents a wide variety of mothers in nearly every situation imaginable from abandonment to the loss of a child to the birth of children to facing children growing up. Each of Tyler's mothers shares a similar concern for her children's welfare and well-being. Yet the mothers respond to their maternal tasks in very different ways. Some mothers attempt to maintain absolute control like Pamela Emerson in *The Clock Winder*; others suspend their control and allow their children to move on with their lives like Ellen Hawkes in *If Morning Ever Comes*. Some are effective in providing a nurturing environment for their children like Bee Bedloe in *Saint Maybe*, whose holiday hors d'oeuvres become a family tradition; others, like Pearl Tull in *Dinner at the Homesick Restaurant*, struggle to provide the bare necessities for their children and become overburdened by the responsibilities of motherhood. Many of Tyler's mothers, such as Evie Decker in *A Slipping-Down Life* and Muriel Pritchett in *The Accidental Tourist*, are single mothers who face even greater financial and emotional challenges in raising their children.

For Further Reading

Farrell, Grace. "Killing off the Mother: Failed Matricide in *Celestial Navigation*." *Critical Essays on Anne Tyler*. Ed. Alice Hall Petry. New York: G. K. Hall, 1992: 221–32.

Kanoza, Theresa. "Mentors and Maternal Role Models: The Healthy Mean between Extremes in Anne Tyler's Fiction." *The Fiction of Anne Tyler*. Ed. C. Ralph Stephens. Jackson: University Press of Mississippi, 1990: 28–39.

mothers-in-law. (AT, BL, CN, EP, LY, SC, SM) Tyler's mothers-in-law fall into two categories: the stereotypical mother-in-law who interferes in her daughter-in-law's life and the type of mother-in-law who acts as a surrogate mother. Most of Tyler's mothers-in-law fall into the first category. Women like Mother Milsom, Meg Peck's controlling mother-in-law in *Searching for Caleb*, and Eleanor Grinstead, Delia Grinstead's dauntingly superefficient mother-in-law in *Ladder of Years*, make the lives of their daughters-in-law miserable. Other mothers-in-law, however, such as Gloria Tell in *Celestial Navigation* and Maggie Moran in *Breathing Lessons*, develop mutually satisfying relationships with their daughters-in-law.

movies. (BL, DHR, "Feather," MP) Movies provide escape from life, not realistic depictions of life. In "A Feather Behind the Rock," the Indian's appearance is always signaled by his feather in the movies that Charles and Lucy Hopper watch each night. Although they can see the Indian's approach, they deny Lucy's approaching death. Instead they continue their cross-country journey. In *Dinner at the Homesick Restaurant*, Jenny Tull's memory of *A Taste of Honey* as the best movie ever seems flawed when she views it years later with her family. Perhaps Morgan Gower's opinion of movies in *Morgan's Passing* best sums up Tyler's skepticism about movies. Morgan dislikes movies because they tie up all the loose ends too neatly by the end of the movie. Life simply doesn't work that way.

moving. (AT, BL, DHR, SC, SM) Anne Tyler's characters are always on the move. They move from one home to the other, as in *The Accidental Tourist* when Macon Leary's marital status changes. In *Saint Maybe*, Ian Bedloe actually works for Sid 'n Ed's Movers, a job that teaches him a great deal about the lives of the families whose possessions he helps to move. The couple, however, who moves around the most is Justine and Duncan Peck in *Searching for Caleb*, who move almost annually from one Maryland or Virginia town to the next. Ultimately, their life becomes one continuous move when they start living in a trailer in a traveling carnival. Moving, then, becomes a metaphor for the change inherent in all Tyler's characters' lives whether they actually change their addresses or not.

Bridget Muggins. ("Genuine") a young school teacher who has been dating lower-class Eugene Bennett since last year.

Mrs. Muggins. ("Genuine") Bridget Muggins' mother, who disapproves of all the Bennetts.

multiple viewpoints. (BL, CN, DHR, SM) Life is very complex and complicated. Anne Tyler understands this concept, for in many of her novels she utilizes multiple viewpoints that present life from different perspectives—age, gender, occupation, economic status, and so forth. In *Celestial Navigation*, Tyler switches her perspective among artist Jeremy Pauling, the center of the novel, and various family members and boardinghouse residents. These other characters present their perspectives on Jeremy, thus producing a more fully rounded view of this complex, troubled artist figure. In *Dinner at the Homesick Restaurant*, Tyler shifts the perspective from one member of the Tull family to the next in order to present each character's individual views on how the same family history has affected each of them in different ways. In *Breathing Lessons*, Tyler divides the novel into three sections, the first and third giving the perspective of a wife and mother, the middle section presenting the perspective of husband and father. Then in *Saint Maybe*, Tyler alternates chapters between Ian Bedloe's evolving viewpoint over twenty years and other family members, who represent different ages and sexes. This multifaceted view of life cannot help but present a more complete and accurate depiction of life.

"Mum." ("Street") Sammy's mother, who clings to him desperately, having been left first by her husband and then by her oldest son, Philip.

Amy Gower Murphy. (MP) See AMY GOWER.

J. R. Murphy. (DHR) soy sauce salesman.

Jim Murphy. (MP) Amy Gower's husband, a lawyer.

Joe Murphy. ("Dry") Jonas Anders' friend, whose father's boat is used to fulfill Jonas' plan to put Uncle Wurssun's ashes in the river.

Lavinia Murphy. (BL) young, serious-minded friend of Daisy Moran's.

Mrs. Murphy. (BL) Lavinia Murphy's mother, whom Maggie Moran calls "Mrs. Perfect" (BL 281).

Mrs. Murphy. ("Dry") Joe Murphy's mother, who like most mothers doesn't think much of Jonas Anders; she forces her son and his friend to make jigsaw puzzles for the Hospital Fund.

Mrs. Murphy. (MP) Jim Murphy's mother.

Pete Murphy. (LY) a private detective sometimes employed by Zeke Pom-fret; he gives Delia Grinstead a stray cat.

Hepzibah Murray. (BL) patient at the Silver Threads Nursing Home who hates having outsiders in her room.

music. (AT, BL, "Common," DHR, "Dry," EP, IMEC, "I'm Not Go-ing," "I Play," LY, MP, SC, SDL, SM, "Some Sign," "Street," "Under Tree") Tyler's work is filled with music. From the Appalachian Mountain folk songs that Gram sings in *If Morning Ever Comes* to the popular songs playing on the radio on the beach in *Ladder of Years*, Tyler uses music to identify and enhance the timeframe of her novels. In some works, however, her music extends beyond mere time to explore the feelings of her charac-ters. In *Breathing Lessons*, Ira Moran has a habit of humming tunes that reveal his thoughts; thus Maggie becomes angry when, just after an argu-ment, he whistles "Crazy." In *Searching for Caleb*, Tyler's use of the musical motif is even more important. One of the chief themes of the novel, music gives Caleb Peck an outlet from the repressiveness of his Peck world. Ulti-mately, he escapes altogether to pursue a life of music. In music he finds the essential elements of joy and creative expression that his Peck life lacked. (Cf. "Songs in Tyler's Novels" in Appendix 2.)

For Further Reading

Currie, Marianne D. " 'Stringtail Man': Music as Motif in *Searching for Caleb*." *South Carolina Review* 24 (Fall 1991): 135–40.

Mrs. Ruby Myrdal. (SM) a woman who babysits the children for Lucy Dean Bedloe, who rents the apartment above Mr. Myrdal's pharmacy; she later tells Ian Bedloe about Lucy's shoplifting.

N

Nana. (SC) old woman who works for Alonzo Divich; she serves dinner to Justine and Duncan Peck when they visit Alonzo.

Naomi. (SDL) the young woman who had worked at the library before Evie Decker.

Natasha. (BL) Peter's sister on the soap opera Maggie Moran and Fiona Moran used to watch; she tried to cause a breakup between Peter and Claudine.

Ned. ("Laps") Sue Ellen's husband, who works too late to come to the pool.

Nell. ("Under Tree") one of Dolly Tilghman's daughters; she now lives out of state.

Nellie. (TCT) the (Roy) Pikes' chihuahua.

Lola Nesbitt. (SDL) classmate of Evie Decker and Violet Hayes who has a fight with her boyfriend.

"Neutral Ground." *Family Circle* Nov. 1974: 36+. In this story, Tyler tackles a contemporary social problem, divorce; but in typical Tylerian style, she takes an unconventional tack by examining not the marriage that failed but the effects of the divorce on a child. Her sympathy for 10-year-old Jacob is readily apparent as he struggles with problems of identity, security, and belonging both at school and at home—whichever parent's home he happens to occupy at any given time.

Jacob's feeling of isolation, although perhaps deepened by the divorce, is not unique to children of divorce. For Tyler, it is the universal human condition, as Jacob finally realizes at the end of the story. The world is a complicated, entirely relativistic place through whose "neutral ground" individuals must navigate as best they can.

Synopsis: After twelve years of marriage, Jacob's parents have divorced. Even though they don't fight, assuring their only child that he will be on "neutral ground" (36), Jacob still has difficulty adjusting to the changes in his life. He "[understands] more than they [think] he [does]" (36), and worries about his mother, whom he overhears tell a friend that "it's difficult to be half a couple" (182).

Every weekend Jacob visits his father in his new apartment. As Jacob sits watching television on Saturday mornings, Jacob's father sits beside him but does not talk. In the afternoons, they sometimes go to a movie and do the shopping. Jacob notices how little his dad knows about housekeeping and dreams about getting married himself, having a big family, and coming home every day to a happy, whole family.

At school, Jacob likes a girl in his class named Laurie. He begins to call her every night, ostensibly to get homework assignments, but she becomes increasingly annoyed by his persistence. Nevertheless, at Christmas, Jacob buys Laurie a flowered wallet. Although he slips his gift under the tree anonymously, Laurie figures out who it's from and returns it to him, telling him that she doesn't want it. At first he's angry at her, but then he notices that she already has a coin purse.

At his father's that night, Jacob cries as he watches television. His father thinks he's upset because of the divorce and tries to comfort him. Jacob, however, thinks to himself that he's not crying about the divorce but "for the fairness of it, the absolute balance, the possibility that no one in the world is right and no one is wrong, and no one can be held to blame" (187).

Jack Newell. (LY) one of Noah Miller's friends.

newspaper articles. (AT, EP, LY, MP, SDL) Tyler incorporates newspaper articles into her plots in *A Slipping-Down Life*, where Drumstrings Casey uses Evie Decker for publicity; in *Morgan's Passing*, where Bonny Gower announces her husband Morgan's "death" through a fake obituary; and in *Ladder of Years*, where Delia Grinstead's disappearance is first revealed in a newspaper article that serves as an epigram for the entire novel. Additionally, Tyler found inspiration for several of her characters in newspaper articles:

Evie Decker in *A Slipping-Down Life*, Morgan Gower of *Morgan's Passing*, and, from *Earthly Possessions*, both Saul Emory and Jake Simms.

Mr. Nichols. (BL) church choir director when Maggie and Ira Moran were in the choir.

"Nobody Answers the Door." *Antioch Review* 24 (Fall 1964): 379–86. This prequel to *If Morning Ever Comes* presents the Hawkes family on the day that the oldest daughter in the family, Joanne, calls to announce her marriage. This news, however, is preceded by scenes in which the family's lack of communication and Ben Joe's isolation (even in such a large family) are already evident. So when Joanne calls and then hangs up after arguing with her mother, it is neither unexpected nor unprecedented. Rather it is merely a symptom of this family's (and perhaps every family's) failure to communicate with those people whom they love the most, live in the closest proximity to, and yet somehow still fail to understand even partially. Here is one of Tyler's favorite conflicts, the individual versus the family, played out for one of the first times in her fiction.

Mrs. Hawkes' attempt to call Joanne back and Joanne's refusal to answer the phone further emphasize this lack of connection. The most interesting response to Joanne's news, however, comes from Ben Joe. Unlike his sisters, who quickly run out to inform the whole town of Joanne's nuptials, Ben Joe feels a sense of loss and further isolation. Yet, ironically, his decision not to speak to Joanne, if and when she finally answers the phone, will only reinforce his isolation.

Synopsis: One Saturday morning just before the start of spring, Ben Joe Hawkes is in the kitchen watching his sister Jenny make coffee when the phone rings. Jenny doesn't answer it because she thinks it's for her sister Susan, who is very popular. Ben Joe tells Jenny that he didn't sleep very well the previous night and had gotten up three times. Jenny tells him that their youngest sister, Tessie, had crawled into bed with her because she had had a nightmare. Then Jenny mentions how she used to crawl into bed with her older sister and how they each used to crawl into bed with their older sisters. Finally, she wonders who Ben Joe, the oldest, crawled into bed with when he had a bad dream.

Not answering her, Ben Joe tells Jenny that a friend of his, Stuart Mann, had given him an address book with Ben Joe's full name (Benjamin Josiah Hawkes) and address in it. Stuart had found the book at a hotdog stand and given it to Ben Joe because there were no other names in it that were familiar.

Jenny asks to see the book, but Ben Joe has it locked up at the bank where he works to support his mother and six sisters since their father's death. Jenny suggests that he call up some of the other names in the book, but Ben Joe says they're too far away. Besides there aren't that many names in the book. What is important to him is that his name is one of the few. He wonders whose book it could have been. He thinks that it might be a hitchhiker in pajamas that he once gave five dollars.

Then he asks Jenny if she remembers his old girlfriend, Shelley Domer. Jenny is more interested in finding her comb. As she searches through the clutter in her room, which used to be Joanne's room, Ben Joe thinks about his sister who is now living in New York. Jenny finds her comb and starts teasing her hair, but she doesn't remember Shelley. Instead, she mistakes Shelley for Gloria, another of Ben Joe's girlfriends, who stuck out in Jenny's mind because she had worn knee-socks to a formal dance.

When Ben Joe describes Shelley, Jenny remembers her as "the one who liked to go on walks" (384). Then he finds a deck of cards Joanne used to use to tell fortunes. He thinks about how Joanne had quit her job and left him alone to support the family.

At this moment Tessie interrupts with the news that Joanne has gotten married. The phone call that Jenny had not answered earlier had been Joanne calling to announce her marriage. Their mother had taken the call. Susan and Tessie had wanted to talk to their sister, but Mrs. Hawkes had gotten into a big fight with Joanne, who finally had hung up on her.

Tessie says that now their mother is trying to call Joanne back, but that Joanne is not answering the phone. So Mrs. Hawkes keeps telling the operator to keep ringing because "*nobody* in this family answers" (385). Tessie asks Ben Joe and Jenny if they want to talk to Joanne. Although Jenny does, Ben Joe says that he wants to get some more coffee. In the kitchen, he stares out the window, where he sees two names drawn in the corner of the window: "Lowell" and "Patty." Wondering who these people were, he finally goes back up to his room by the back stairs, before his sisters can "come rushing past him on their way to tell the town that Joanne was married" (386). He misses Joanne and feels that, in some inexplicable way, he has lost her.

Dr. Norman. (LY) the Bay Borough doctor who tends Delia Grinstead's wounded forehead.

North Carolina setting. (CW, DHR, "Genuine," IMEC, "I Never Saw," "Nobody," SDL, TCT) All of Tyler's early novels and most of her early short stories are set in North Carolina, where she grew up. Even while she was living in Canada shortly after her marriage, she continued to write about North Carolina. It was not until after she had lived in Baltimore for five years that she first set a novel there, *The Clock Winder*. And even then she allows her protagonist Elizabeth Abbott to escape briefly back to North Carolina in the middle of the book. Later books, such as *Dinner at the Homesick Restaurant*, contain North Carolina references. In that book, Pearl Tull hails from North Carolina.

Newton Norton. (SC) customer who buys many of Duncan Peck's antique tools for the farm he's renovating.

numbers. (BL, MP, SC) For Tyler, numbers have symbolic meaning. Particularly in *Searching for Caleb*, Justine Peck's occupation as a fortuneteller causes her to believe in the significance of various numbers. At the end of the novel, Justine is certain that the next year, 1974, will bring good luck because the numbers of the year add up to twenty-one, whose numbers, in turn, add up to three, her lucky number.

O

Oakes. (DHR) headwaiter at Scarlatti's Restaurant.

obesity. ("As the "Earth," "Common" EP, SC, SDL, "Spending," Tea-Machine," "With Flags") Obesity is a sign of a life on hold or a character who has withdrawn from life. Such is the case with Miss Lorna Johnson in "The Common Courtesies," who sits on a porch all day; Evie Decker, who waits for life to bring something interesting to her in *A Slipping-Down Life*; Lacey Debney Ames in *Earthly Possessions*, whose fatness is her defining characteristic; and in *Searching for Caleb*, Justine Peck's mother, Caroline Peck Mayhew, whose inability to cope with life is manifested by her tendency to sit and eat chocolates. Weighted down as much by mental fears and insecurities as by their extra pounds, most of these characters remain incapable of engaging life.

objects. (BL, CN, EP, "Flaw," "Laps," MP, SM, "Tea-Machine") Material possessions often take on added significance for Tyler's characters. In *Breathing Lessons*, Maggie Moran equates an imaginary soap dish with her hopes of getting her son and daughter-in-law back together. Then at the end of the novel, Maggie recalls objects that she has lost and hopes to get back someday, but doesn't really believe that she will. In *Celestial Navigation*, objects in the outside world make impressions on Jeremy Pauling's artistic mind and he incorporates them into his sculptures. In *Saint Maybe*, Lucy Dean's mustard seed necklace is all that her children have left to remember her by. In other ways, however, material objects serve only to burden Tyler's characters. In *Earthly Possessions*, Charlotte Emory attempts to rid herself of two households' worth of furniture. Consequently, Charlotte views her life as a casting off of these encumbrances. In *Morgan's Passing*, Emily Meredith leads a sparse life with few material possessions. To these characters, material objects only burden them with further responsibilities. At the end of "The Artificial Family," Mary Scott leaves her husband, taking only her daughter and their gingham gowns. So, too, at the end of *Breathing Lessons*, Fiona Stuckey leaves with only her purse, her daughter Leroy, and Leroy's baseball glove.

observation. ("Average," BL, IMEC, "Knack") The act of observing is a sign of withdrawal from life in Tyler's fiction. Unable to join the flow of life, some of Tyler's characters sit back and observe life rather than participating in it. This act of observing may bring them added insight, however, and motivate them in the end to reach out to the people around them.

Katie O'Connell. (LY) young woman who had worked as Zeke Pomfret's secretary briefly after Miss Percy's death; she had rented a room at Belle Flint's, but then ran off with Larry Watts.

the O'Donnells. (CW) the couple Elizabeth Abbott is supposed to interview with for a job when she gets hired by Mrs. Emerson instead.

Miss Ogden. (SDL) one of Evie Decker and Violet Hayes' teachers, who gets married and becomes Mrs. Bishop.

Paul Ogle. (SDL) photographer for the Pulqua *Times*.

old age. ("Baltimore," BL, "Feather," "Geologist," IMEC, "Laura," LY, MP, SC, SM, "Some Sign," TCT, "Under Tree," "With Flags") See AGING.

old men. (BL, CN, SC, "With Flags") Tyler once wrote that she thought she could spend her entire career writing about old men. Her sensitivity toward them stems from her close relationship with both her grandfathers. In *Searching for Caleb*, the jacket cover of the man playing the cello in the barn loft came from an old picture of Tyler's grandfather, as does the character of Daniel Peck.

Billy Sam Oliver. ("Bride") Venetia Oliver's now deceased father; she lives in his old place.

Teddy Oliver. ("Bride") Venetia Oliver's imaginary husband, who supposedly works on motorcycles.

Venetia Oliver. ("Bride") a somewhat run-down looking woman in her late twenties who lives in a shack near the boatyard; she creates an imaginary husband for herself.

Olympia. ("Under Tree") Dolly Tilghman's tall girlhood friend who would meet her at the bosom tree.

Rev. Orbison. (BL) minister at Max Gill's funeral, who disapproves of Serena Gill's plan, but gives in when she tells him that a memorial service is for the living.

order. (AT, BL, CN, MP, SM, "Who Would Want") In Wallace Stevens' poem "The Idea of Order at Key West," Stevens expresses a "blessed rage for order." So, too, do Tyler's characters attempt to find order in their lives. Some of Tyler's characters, however, take this desire too far. The Learys in *The Accidental Tourist* stagnate in their orderly lives, making lists, alphabetizing their pantry, and adhering strictly to family traditions. In "Who Would Want a Little Boy," Mrs. Schmidt's list of "dos and don'ts" makes it nearly impossible for any of the series of foster families with which he lives to keep him. This desire for order ultimately comes to naught. In a world of change, absolute order, stability, predictability, or stasis is not possible. Therefore, the most successful of Tyler's characters learn to accept this state of disorder as the norm and, as Ian Bedloe realizes at the end of *Saint Maybe*, the disorder of life imposes a kind of cyclical order of its own.

ordinary. (BL, "Bride," SM, "Street") In *Saint Maybe*, Bee Bedloe laments: "We've had such extraordinary troubles . . . and somehow they've turned us ordinary" (SM 181). The problem with being ordinary for Bee is that it makes her family just like everyone else's. But in Tyler's fiction that is the point. Ordinariness is not bad. Tyler succeeds in elevating the ordinary to the status of the extraordinary. Even the ordinary events of life, no matter how universal or seemingly mundane, gain importance merely by being the stuff that life is made of. The real heroes in Tyler's books and stories are not those who rescue people out of burning buildings, but those who, like Ira Moran in *Breathing Lessons*, go to work every day for thirty years and provide for their families. So, even though Tyler's characters are common, ordinary people, the events of these characters' lives prove that their dreams and hopes and sorrows are just as significant as anybody's. Tyler's use of the ordinary thus reinforces her belief in the common humanity of all people.

For Further Reading

Ross-Bryant, Lynn. "Anne Tyler's *Searching for Caleb*: The Sacrality of the Everyday." *Soundings: An Interdisciplinary Journal* 73 (Spring 1990): 191–207.

Uncle Oswald. (BL) Max Gill's uncle, who had filmed Max and Serena Gill's wedding.

Daniel Otis. (BL) elderly African American man in a red Chevy, whom Maggie Moran yells at and then goes back to help.

Duluth Otis. (BL) Daniel Otis' wife, who gets mad at him because she has a dream in which he steps on her needlepoint chair, shawl, and petticoat.

"Outside." *Southern Review* NS 7 (Autumn 1971): 1130–44. In this 1971 story, Tyler harkens back to her roots in a Quaker community and vicariously allows her protagonist, young Jason McKenna, to escape from the confines of Parsley Valley (and his family). What Jason discovers in Pulmet, New Hampshire, however, is what most of Tyler's characters usually learn: wherever you go, there you are. The Douglas family is as troubled and full of demands as Jason's own family, so at the end of the story his escape turns into a homecoming, in the typical Tylerian escape/return paradigm. Perhaps, though, Jason's experience in the outside world will have given him a new perspective on his home. In many cases, outsiders do bring needed change to Tyler's characters' lives.

Synopsis: Jason McKenna, 18, leaves his home—Parsley Valley, North Carolina, an isolated Quaker community in the mountains, to see what the outside world is like. He takes a job in Pulmet, New Hampshire, tutoring Billy Douglas, a 10-year-old boy with learning problems. Jason likes the town, especially the way the people think of him as a mountain boy, for at home when his family had gone into town, the true mountain boys had thrown rocks at them.

On the night that Jason arrives in town, he meets his employers, Mr. Brandon Douglas, the wealthy owner of a clothing factory, and his wife Melanie, a rather fat, shy woman. The Douglases are sitting in the den watching television and drinking, as, Jason soon learns, they seem to do every night.

Jason slowly becomes accustomed to the routine of life in the small town. He spends his mornings running minor errands, his early afternoons writing letters home, and the hours between 3 and 6 tutoring Billy. Although Billy has trouble reading, he plods through the work goodnaturedly, and Jason grows to like him.

When supper time comes each night, the maid Emily, who is a horrible cook, calls them. As they eat the badly cooked food, they say little, except for Mr. Douglas, who talks incessantly about his work, his past, or anything that comes to mind. After dinner, Billy retreats to his room, but Jason accompanies Mr. and Mrs. Douglas to the TV room. There the couple drink and talk, even Mrs. Douglas, while Jason listens. Sometimes they ask him awkward questions. Although he would like to leave, he cannot because he is mesmerized by the television set, only the second one that he has seen. So he endures their talk, coming to realize that perhaps "he had been hired . . . more as listener than as tutor" (1138).

Not until two months later does Jason finally realize that the family situation is dysfunctional. His friend Tom Bowen, who works at the repair shop, is amazed that Jason has not figured out that Mr. Douglas is an alcoholic. He also tells Jason about Mrs. Douglas' bouts with depression that sometimes require her hospitalization.

With this knowledge, Jason begins to notice other problems such as the state of disrepair and general untidiness of the house. He wonders how he could have lived in the house for two months without noticing these signs. Tutoring Billy becomes the focal point of his days, yet the boy doesn't seem to make much progress. Discouraged, Jason tells Mr. Douglas that Billy needs expert help. Mr. Douglas, however, discounts the notion, pointing out that the boy's grades have gone up since Jason has started tutoring him. He simply tells Jason to keep doing what he's been doing, even after Jason explains that the reason for the rise in Billy's grades is that Jason has been reading his homework assignments aloud to him.

Almost daily Jason writes and receives letters from home, but he tells no one except his girlfriend, Sugar Potter, about the Douglases' problems. Still the words in his family's letters keep echoing in his mind.

One morning Jason walks into town and briefly can't remember the way home. Finally, he remembers "by habit" (1142) and finds the house. Once there he suddenly decides to talk to Mrs. Douglas about Billy's need for expert help. Jason also tells her that he's leaving for New York that morning on the bus. Although she offers more money, as well as no teaching responsibilities, Jason is determined to leave.

On the bus to New York he reads a letter from his grandmother, "a wealthy Republican, who disapproved of everything" (1144). She accuses him of having moved to New England to chase his dreams like his father. Putting away the letter, Jason looks out the window at the rain and tries to think about New York; nevertheless, he finds his thoughts wandering to Parsley Valley.

outsiders. (AT, BL, CN, DHR, EP, IMEC, LY, SC, SDL, SM, "Uncle") Outsiders often influence Tyler's characters in positive ways. Muriel Pritchett, in *The Accidental Tourist*, enables Macon Leary to break away from his restrictive family and his grief over his son's death. Rita diCarlo performs a similar function for Ian Bedloe in *Saint Maybe*, drawing him back into the life cycle and the flow of time. Despite Tyler's characters' fear of such outside influence, sometimes verging on obsession as with Jeremy Pauling in *Celestial Navigation*, the effect of such outsiders is usually positive.

Uncle Owen. (MP) Morgan Gower's Welsh great-great uncle who had drowned in New York harbor.

P

Barbara Pace. (DHR) plump redhead in Cody Tull's ninth grade class who acts as a "central switchboard" (DHR 57) for budding school romances.

Anita Palermo. (BL) Serena Gill's unwed mother, who had had an affair with a married man (Mr. Barrett) and became pregnant.

Pammie. (CW) Mary Emerson and Morris' daughter, who is prone to nightmares; Mrs. Emerson's granddaughter.

parades. (BL, "Bridge," EP, "Street") From the parade of people walking by in the dreams of young Sammy in "A Street of Bugles" to the actual parade passing in front of Charlotte Emory at the end of *Earthly Possessions*, Tyler uses parades as a metaphor for the stream of life, which her characters ultimately decide to rejoin.

parenting. (AT, BL, CW, DHR, EP, SM, "Teenage") As a parent herself, Anne Tyler understands the tremendous demands of time, energy, and emotions that parenthood places on a mother or father. In her work, parents continually worry about their children and work to provide them with the basic necessities of life and to equip them to be able to handle the demands of adulthood. This task is not an easy one, as Ian Bedloe in *Saint Maybe* asserts to his new wife, Rita diCarlo, who wants them to have a child. The effort put forth in caring for children is, ultimately, worth the sacrifice, as Ian discovers through raising his brother's three children.

Pari. ("Uncle") Ahmad Ardavi's second wife.

Emma Parkins. (DHR) fortuneteller Jenny Tull consults prior to her first marriage; she advises Jenny to marry lest she be "destroyed by love" (DHR 96).

Ned Parkinson. (SC) owner of the house Justine and Duncan Peck rent in Caro Mill.

Mrs. Parry. ("Saints") neighborhood woman whom all the other women used to envy because she had a fur coat and a ballpoint pen.

Lu Beth Parsons. (BL) girl Durwood Clegg had started dating after Maggie (Daley) Moran turned him down.

Michael Parton. (BL) Sissy Parton's pink-haired husband, who serves as a bartender at the reception after Max Gill's funeral.

Sissy Parton. (BL) old friend of Maggie Moran and Serena Gill's, who plays "My Prayer" on the piano at Max Gill's funeral, just as she had done at Serena and Max's wedding.

past. (BL, CN, DHR, EP, "Saints," SC, SM) William Faulkner once asserted that the past is not only not dead, it is not even past. Such a view, without Faulkner's overt determinism, could also apply to Anne Tyler's fiction. Through her characters' memories and her cyclical view of time, the past does have a tendency to keep cropping up in her characters' lives. Unlike Faulkner, however, Tyler presents a more hopeful view that, at least some of the time, her characters can learn from the past and change their futures. The three Tull children in *Dinner at the Homesick Restaurant* and Ian Bedloe in *Saint Maybe* all seem to be on the road to recovery from past traumas. Maybe it is true that, as Madame Olita tells Justine Peck in *Searching for Caleb*, while one cannot change what has happened in the past, one can control the "hold" the past has on an individual (SC 129).

Pat. (LY) one of Nat Moffat's four daughters; she refuses to attend his wedding to Binky.

Paula. (MP) young woman in Off the Cuff improvisational acting troupe.

Paula. ("Under Tree") one of Dolly Tilghman's daughters; she now lives out of state.

Abigail (Abbie) Pauling. (CN) Jeremy Pauling and Mary Tell's oldest daughter.

Amanda Pauling. (CN) Jeremy Pauling's oldest sister; an old maid school teacher who lives in Richmond with her sister Laura Bates.

Edward Pauling. (CN) Jeremy Pauling and Mary Tell's son, their fourth child.

Hannah Pauling. (CN) Jeremy Pauling and Mary Tell's daughter, their third child.

Jeremy Pauling. (CN) agoraphobic artist who "pretends" to marry Mary Tell, with whom he has five children.

Mr. Pauling. (CN) Jeremy Pauling's father, who abandoned his family when Jeremy was 4.

Phillipa (Pippi) Pauling. (CN) Jeremy Pauling and Mary Tell's daughter, their second child.

Rachel Pauling. (CN) Jeremy Pauling and Mary Tell's youngest daughter, their fifth child.

Wilma Pauling. (CN, DHR) Jeremy Pauling's overprotective mother, who leaves him her house when she dies. She also appears in *Dinner at the Homesick Restaurant* as Ruth Spivey's landlady.

Josiah Payson. (DHR) Ezra Tull's large, mentally slow friend, who later works at the Homesick Restaurant with him.

Mrs. Payson. (DHR) Josiah Payson's loving mother, who dies a few years after he gets out of high school.

Pearl Joe. ("Dry") friend of Wurssun Anders', who sends his ashes to Wurssun's wife, Lucille.

Alice Peck. (SC) Justine and Duncan Peck's first cousin; the daughter of Mark and Bea Peck; Sally Peck's twin; she never marries and becomes a librarian.

Bea Peck. (SC) Mark Peck's wife; Duncan and Justine Peck's aunt.

Caleb Justin Peck. (SC) Daniel Peck's musical, 88-year-old half-brother, born February 14, 1885, who runs away in 1912 and is not heard from again until Eli Everjohn locates him in 1972.

Claude Peck. (SC) Duncan Peck's hefty brother; Justine Peck's first cousin.

Daniel Peck. (SC) Justine and Duncan Peck's very reserved, nearly deaf, distinguished 92-year-old grandfather; a former judge, he now lives with Justine and Duncan Peck; he was born on June 6, 1880.

Daniel Peck, Jr. (SC) Daniel and Margaret Rose Peck's third child (born 1907); he becomes a lawyer but remains a bachelor.

Duncan Peck. (SC) Justine Peck's tall, blond, blue-eyed 40-year-old husband and first cousin; Meg Peck's father.

Esther Peck. (SC) Justine and Duncan Peck's first cousin; the daughter of Mark and Bea Peck; she never marries and becomes the supervisor of a nursery school.

Justin Montague Peck. (SC) Justine and Duncan Peck's great-grandfather who founded the family's importing fortune in the late nineteenth century; Daniel and Caleb Peck's father.

Justin (Two) Peck II. (SC) Daniel and Margaret Rose Peck's oldest child (born 1905); nicknamed "Two," he marries Lucy Hodges and becomes a lawyer like his father; he is Duncan Peck's father and Justine Peck's uncle.

Justine Mayhew Peck. (SC) thin, blonde, blue-eyed 40-year-old fortune-teller, who marries her first cousin Duncan Peck; she is Meg Peck's mother.

Laura Baum Peck. (SC) Caleb Peck's mother; Justin Montague Peck's second wife, whom he marries in 1881; she dies in 1958 at the age of 97.

Laura May Peck. (SC) Daniel and Margaret Rose Peck's fifth child (born 1909); she remains a spinster.

Lucy Hodges Peck. (SC) Justin Two's wife; Duncan Peck's mother.

Marcus Peck. (SC) Daniel and Margaret Rose Peck's fourth child (born 1908); he marries Bea and becomes a lawyer like his father.

Margaret Rose Bell Peck. (SC) Daniel Peck's wife, who leaves him in 1911 to work as a money launderer in the Treasury Department in Washington, D.C.; she dies the next year in a boardinghouse fire.

Meg Peck. (SC) Justine and Duncan Peck's neat, intelligent 17-year-old daughter; born March 3, 1955; she marries the Rev. Arthur Milsom.

Richard Peck. (SC) Justine and Duncan Peck's first cousin; the son of Mark and Bea Peck; after his brief marriage is annulled, he moves into a downtown apartment.

Sally Peck. (SC) Justine and Duncan Peck's first cousin; the daughter of Mark and Bea Peck; Alice Peck's twin; she divorces after a one-month marriage and becomes a piano teacher.

Sarah Peck. (SC) Daniel and Margaret Rose Peck's second child (born 1906); she remains unmarried.

Sarah Cantleigh Peck. (SC) Justin Montague Peck's first wife, who dies in 1880 after giving birth to Daniel Peck.

Jared Peers. (DHR) man whom Cody Tull hires to look after his farmhouse and, initially, the livestock.

Miss Ariana Pennington. (SM) Daphne Bedloe's attractive fifth grade teacher, whom the children consider a possible wife for their uncle, Ian Bedloe.

Elizabeth (Betsy) Penney. ("Baltimore") Miss Maiselle Penney's 25-year-old niece and Warren Penney's daughter; she works as a secretary and lives in New York.

Miss Maiselle (Maisie) Penney. ("Baltimore") a 62-year-old retired sales-clerk who suffers from asthma; she lives in an apartment in a lower-class neighborhood of New York; she was born outside of Baltimore, Maryland, on April 12, 1900, but doesn't have a birth certificate; she wants one desperately to validate her identity.

Warren Penney. ("Baltimore") Miss Maiselle Penney's younger brother, who now lives in North Carolina; he had been born on a tenant farm and didn't have a birth certificate either, but, unlike his sister, he doesn't care.

"People Who Don't Know the Answers." *New Yorker* 26 Aug. 1991: 26–36. This story is an unabridged version of chapter five of *Saint Maybe*. It centers on Doug Bedloe's life after his retirement.

Miss Percy. (LY) Zeke Pomfret's longtime secretary, who had died recently.

Rosa Perez. (DHR) the nurse who helps Jenny Tull through her labor with her daughter Becky.

Peter. (BL) character on a soap opera Maggie and Fiona Moran used to watch together; he was in love with Claudine.

Peter. (DHR) one of Cody Tull's best friends in ninth grade, who is in the same homeroom.

Peter. ("Flaw") young college dropout from Alberta living in Montreal whose apartment is burglarized.

Peter. (LY) one of Binky Moffat's sons, who acts as an usher at her wedding.

Peter. ("Misstep") Julie Madison's boyfriend, who never learns about her rape.

Darryl Peters. (DHR) sales representative for Peaceful Hills Memorial Gardens.

Millie Peterson. ("Tea-Machine") John Paul Bartlett's girlfriend.

Mrs. Peterson. (MP) customer at Fresco's shoe repair, to whom Morgan Gower tells a fantastic story about drug smugglers using the heels of Italian shoes.

pets. (AT, BL, LY, MP, SC, SM) As a pet owner herself, Anne Tyler incorporates her love of animals, both dogs and cats, into her novels. Especially in her later works, pets play important roles in illuminating their masters' lives. In *Breathing Lessons*, the Moran family includes a succession of cats. In particular, Maggie recalls Thistledown, the kitten Ira gave her that unfortunately died when Maggie forgot to check the dryer before turning it on. In *Saint Maybe*, Tyler reinforces the theme of aging through the death of the Bedloe family dog, Beastie, whose death coincides with Doug Bedloe's retirement. In *Ladder of Years*, Delia Grinstead begins to take on responsibilities for others and to feel connected to life again through her cat George. Tyler's most fully developed use of pets, however, occurs in *The*

Accidental Tourist, where Edward, Macon Leary's dysfunctional corgi, parallels Macon's own psychic recovery from his son Ethan's death.

Philip. ("Street") Sammy's older brother, who had inherited their father's wanderlust and left his mother alone with Sammy.

Aunt Phoebe. ("Linguistics") Claire's aunt, who raised her after the death of Claire's parents; she opposes Claire's marriage to a foreigner because they lack a "shared history" (39).

photographs. ("Artificial," AT, BL, CN, DHR, EP, IMEC, LY, MP, SC, SDL, SM, TCT, "Under Tree," "Who Would Want") Photographs provide a means of arresting time. In a static photograph, the motion of time is temporarily halted, allowing a character to examine his or her own past and to relive old memories, as Pearl Tull does in *Dinner at the Homesick Restaurant* when her son Ezra goes over an old photograph album with her. In other works, photographs provide major clues to the past. In *Searching for Caleb*, the picture of Caleb playing a cello in a barn loft is the Peck family's last picture of him. In *Saint Maybe*, the photograph of Lucy standing with Agatha and Thomas as a baby before a trailer with a rainbow in the background provides the naive, young Thomas with hope of finding his mother. Similarly, the photograph of Lucy that Daphne hangs up on the family picture wall years later installs Lucy as part of the family. In *Earthly Possessions*, an old photograph of Charlotte Emory's mother finally convinces Charlotte that she really is her mother's child. In *The Tin Can Tree*, a limitation of photographs is brought out. Great-Aunt Hattie Hammond does not want her nephew Danny to have a copy of the picture that James Green takes of her, because she doesn't want Danny's view of her to be limited to the two-dimensional, one-moment view that a photograph provides.

photography. (EP, "Flaw," "I Never Saw," "Some Sign," TCT) Two of Tyler's characters work as photographers: James Green in *The Tin Can Tree* and Charlotte Emory in *Earthly Possessions*. James Green's photographs serve the purpose of revealing the personalities of the people that he photographs, such as the picture of his fiancée, Joan Pike, in a dust storm or the picture of Simon Pike with a cigar. Charlotte Emory's clients actually dress up in a variety of costumes, as if to hide their true selves. What Charlotte discovers, however, is that these "disguises" actually reveal much more about her clients' true personalities and identities than they know. Thus, photography serves as a means of exploring and observing other people's lives very closely.

Bess Pickett. (SC) waitress who befriends Caleb Peck.

Luray Spivey Pickett. (SC) Roy Pickett's wife, who places Caleb Peck in the old folks' home in Box Hill, Louisiana.

Roy Pickett. (SC) Bess Pickett's son, who inherits her cafe.

Abby Pike. (TCT) Joan Pike's mother, who sends gladioli to her niece Janie Rose Pike's funeral.

Janie Rose Pike. (TCT) Roy and Lou Pike's 6-year-old daughter, who has been killed in a tractor accident.

Joan Pike. (TCT) 26-year-old woman who lives with Lou and Roy Pike (her aunt and uncle).

Lou Pike. (TCT) Joan Pike's aunt; Roy Pike's wife; Janie Rose and Simon Pike's mother; she works as a seamstress.

Mr. Pike. (TCT) Joan Pike's father, who is becoming hard of hearing.

R. J. (Roy) Pike. (TCT) Joan Pike's uncle; Lou Pike's husband; Janie Rose and Simon Pike's father; he is a construction worker who has been laid off for the month of July.

Simon Lockwood Pike. (TCT) Roy and Lou Pike's 10-year-old son, who runs away from home.

Miss Pleasance. (CW) persona Elizabeth Abbott takes on in her fake telephone survey for the gas company.

Mr. Plum. (BL) nearly deaf man who was at the hospital while Maggie Moran was waiting for her granddaughter Leroy's birth.

Mrs. Plum. (BL) Mr. Plum's wife, who was also at the hospital.

Plymouth. (EP) Mindy Callender's cat.

Andy Point. (TCT) friend of Simon Pike's whose parents get into an argument and aren't speaking.

Mary Point. (TCT) woman who is not speaking to her husband, Sid Point, after an argument over a road sign.

Sid Point. (TCT) Mary Point's husband, whose anger keeps him from making up with his wife.

Mary Beth Polk. ("Base-Metal," "Foot-Footing") In "Base-Metal," she is 17 and about to graduate from high school; In "Foot-Footing," she is 20, engaged to be married, and having second thoughts.

Mr. Polk. ("Foot-Footing") Mary Beth Polk's father.

Mrs. Polk. ("Base-Metal," "Foot-Footing") Mary Beth Polk's mother; in "Base-Metal," she accompanies Mary Beth to find a pearl necklace for graduation; in "Foot-Footing," she is busy with wedding preparations.

Polly. (CW) Elizabeth Abbott's younger sister, who is married to Carl.

Polly Pomfret. (LY) Zeke Pomfret's prim and proper wife.

Zeke Pomfret. (LY) the attorney Delia Grinstead works for in Bay Borough.

Mr. Pond. ("With Flags") Mr. Carpenter's roommate at the retirement home.

Pooky. (LY) senile old woman at Senior City who rides the elevator up and down all day.

Porter. ("Street") one of the children who follow Sammy down to the wharf to launch the sailboat.

Dr. Porter. (EP) the Emorys' family doctor.

Miss Faye Potter. (TCT) a fat woman in her sixties who lives with her sister Lucy Potter in the middle section of the three-part house shared by the Pikes and the Green brothers.

Miss Lucy Potter. (TCT) Faye Potter's sister, also in her sixties and fat; she suffers from insomnia and paces all night.

Mr. Potter. (MP) owner of a used instrument shop; he thinks Morgan Gower is a street priest.

Mrs. Potter. (DHR) waitress who serves the Tull family at their last dinner.

Sugar Potter. ("Outside") Jason McKenna's girlfriend in North Carolina, who writes him while he is away in New Hampshire.

Kitty Potts. (MP) classmate of Gina Meredith's, whom she claims to dislike.

pregnancy. (BL, CN, DHR, EP, "I Play," MP, SC, SDL, SM) In *Celestial Navigation*, Mary Tell claims that her "natural state" is pregnancy (CN 69). Like Mary Tell, most of Tyler's characters enjoy their pregnancies, anticipating the birth of their children, although there are some natural apprehensions and worries. In *A Slipping-Down Life*, Evie Decker's pregnancy is the catalyst for her to break off from her irresponsible husband and establish a stable life for herself and her coming baby. In *Breathing Lessons*, Fiona Stuckey's pregnancy brings her together with Jesse Moran and allows Jessie's mother, Maggie, to develop a bond with her daughter-in-law. In *Saint Maybe*, Rita diCarlo Bedloe's pregnancy, though unplanned, is a welcome development because it completes her sense of family and, in Ian's case, brings him back into the flow of time.

Dr. Prescott. (SM) the minister of Dober Street Presbyterian Church, Bee and Doug Bedloe's church; he marries Lucy Dean and Danny Bedloe, and then later preaches at their funerals.

Alice Printz. (SC) neighbor of Justine and Duncan Peck's in Semple, Virginia.

Sister Priscilla. (SM) Reverend Emmett's mother, who attends his church in her Episcopalian finery.

Alexander Pritchett. (AT) Muriel Pritchett's allergy-prone 7-year-old son.

Muriel Pritchett. (AT) the frizzy-haired divorcée who works at the Meow-Bow Animal Hospital; she trains Edward and falls in love with Macon Leary.

Norman Pritchett. (AT) Muriel Pritchett's ex-husband, whom she had married while they were still in high school; he divorces her after their son Alexander is born.

privacy. ("Bridge," CN, DHR, "I'm Not Going," "I Play," "Respect") Like Tyler herself, Tyler's characters feel a need for privacy and usually respect other's privacy in return. The dilemma that they face is knowing when to breech that tacit agreement to maintain the privacy of another person. In the short story "Respect," Jeremy develops a feeling of privacy for Mrs. Willard, whose house he is living in unknown to her, and feels betrayed when she finds him out. In *Dinner at the Homesick Restaurant*, Pearl Tull guards her own privacy and instills in her children a need to maintain their own closeness about family secrets, such as Beck's desertion. In "The Bridge," Harriet Landing respects the privacy of the young girl she sees, but her reticence to speak to the girl causes the girl to remain a stranger to her; therefore Harriet is unable to put a face on the girl when she paints her picture. That lack of personal connection is the downside of privacy, for it ultimately isolates people from each other.

private detectives. (SC, SM) Private detective Eli Everjohn appears in two of Tyler's novels. In *Searching for Caleb*, he locates long-lost Caleb Peck. In *Saint Maybe*, he discovers that Thomas Dulsimore, the children's father, is dead.

Alice Gail Pruitt. (CW) redhead whom Dommie Whitehill is engaged to briefly before he goes back to Elizabeth Abbott.

Mrs. Pruitt. (CN) church friend of Wilma Pauling's.

Mrs. Puckett. ("Average") Bet Blevins' older neighbor, who babysat for Bet's mentally handicapped son, Arnold, until he grew too big for her to manage.

Pumpkin. (BL) one of a succession of the Morans' family cats; Pumpkin ate the children's gerbil after Maggie Moran set it free.

puppets. (MP) Morgan Gower's interest in puppets draws him to Emily and Leon Meredith. In the end he replaces Leon as Emily's husband and becomes a member of the troupe. His many identities in life transfer to playing characters on stage. Like Tyler, who writes because she wants to lead more than one life, Morgan's puppets allow him to experience multiple identities.

Mr. Purdy. (DHR) vegetable buyer for the Homesick Restaurant.

Mrs. Purdy. (DHR) Mr. Purdy's wheelchair-bound wife.

puzzles. (SC) Duncan Peck's attempt to put together complex jigsaw puzzles parallels his attempt to make sense out of his wandering life.

Q

Quakers. (BL, MP, "Outside," SC) Tyler's Quaker heritage is a subtle influence on all her work. In *Morgan's Passing*, Emily Meredith's plain dress and simple lifestyle stem in some part from her Quaker beliefs. In addition, Tyler's Quaker pacifism is evident in the lack of military connections in Tyler's work. Ian Bedloe misses out on Vietnam due to a heart murmur in *Saint Maybe*. Ezra Tull gets sent home from the army for sleepwalking in *Dinner at the Homesick Restaurant*.

For Further Reading

Voelker, Joseph C. "The Semi-Miracle of Time." *World and I* Feb. 1992: 347–57.

quilts. (IMEC) Ben Joe Hawkes hides under the warmth of Shelley Domer's quilt, which protects him, temporarily, from the uncertainty of the future.

R

B. J. (Rick) Rackley. (LY) young, muscled black man who owns Rick Rack's cafe; he used to be a professional football player until he hurt his knee; he is married to Teensy.

Teensy Rackley. (LY) Rick Rackley's red-haired wife; she works as a waitress at his cafe.

radios. (BL, SDL, SM, TCT) Besides setting the mood or timeframe of a scene through the songs played on the radio, radios play important roles in three Tyler novels. In *The Tin Can Tree*, Janie Rose Pike gets a long-awaited call from a radio station contest only after her death. In *A Slipping-Down Life*, Evie Decker first hears Drum Casey when he is being interviewed on the radio. In *Breathing Lessons*, the novel's theme is brought out as Maggie Moran listens to a radio call-in show, whose topic of the day is marriage. On this same show, Maggie mistakes one of the callers for her ex–daughter-in-law, Fiona Stuckey, a coincidence that sets in motion much of the novel's subsequent plot.

rain. (AT, "Outside," "Saints") Like fog, rain sets the bleak mood for several scenes in Tyler's fiction, mirroring the despair that her characters are feeling at that moment.

Abel ("White-Eye") Ramford. (SC) blind, black guitar player whom Caleb Peck played blues with on the streets of New Orleans.

Monty Rand. (BL) the boy who had really been killed in the army training accident instead of Ira Moran.

Tucker Randolph. ("Foot-Footing") Mary Beth Polk's fiance, a lawyer who is six years older than she.

rape. ("Misstep") The violence of this most violent act is muted in Tyler's short story "A Misstep of the Mind." Instead Tyler chooses to concentrate on the after-effects of the rape on its victim, Julie Madison.

Raymond. (DHR) sauce maker at Scarlatti's Restaurant.

religion. (BL, CN, CW, DHR, EP, "Half-Truths," IMEC, "Laura," SC, SDL, SM) As one might expect of a person who was raised a Quaker and is married to a Muslim, Tyler's religious views are quite tolerant. In her early works, however, she does satirize religious intolerance, in cases such as the traveling evangelist Brother Evan Hope in *A Slipping-Down Life*; Elizabeth Abbott's preacher father, Rev. John Abbott, in *The Clock Winder*; and Saul Emory, another fundamentalist preacher in *Earthly Possessions*. In her later works, though, her satiric fervor wanes so that in *Saint Maybe* her depiction of Rev. Emmett is quite favorable. Furthermore, she views Ian Bedloe's religious beliefs as a positive force in his life.

T. J. Renfro. (LY) high school student who, despite being suspended, still comes to Delia Grinstead for tutoring in math.

repairs. (AT, BL, CW, DHR, "Holding," LY, MP, "Outside," SC, SM) In an attempt to maintain order in their lives, many of Tyler's characters become adept at repairing their homes in an effort to shore them up from the ravages of time. The Learys in *The Accidental Tourist*, Doug Bedloe in *Saint Maybe*, Morgan Gower in *Morgan's Passing*, and Pearl Tull in *Dinner at the Homesick Restaurant* all work on repairing their homes. In their personal lives, however, they are undergoing crises that cannot be so easily fixed. The transference of their energies to these manual tasks diverts them from working on the more important emotional crises that they are experiencing. Or, perhaps, the time spent on these repairs allows them time to work through their emotional and psychological problems. In "Holding Things Together," the ability to make repairs is equated with responsibility. Therefore Lucy Simmons feels that her husband is completely dependent on her because of his utter lack of mechanical ability.

"Rerun." *New Yorker* 4 July 1988: 20–32. This story is a slightly abridged version of chapter two of *Breathing Lessons*. It recounts Serena Gill's unconventional funeral for her husband Max.

"Respect." *Mademoiselle* June 1972: 146–47+. "Respect" tackles two common Tylerian themes: privacy and routines. When Jeremy breaks into Mrs. Willard's house on a sudden whim, he is subconsciously yearning to escape from his mundane life (running errands for his mother). Yet once inside this other world, he quickly sets up a routine that is, if anything, more restricted than the life he led outside the house. The routine, however, satisfies him by giving him a feeling of power over his life, something that perhaps at 16 he is beginning to feel that he is losing—or perhaps never had to begin with.

When Mrs. Willard returns, Jeremy's world and hers do not collide at first. Each respects the other's privacy: a key concern for Tyler both in her fiction and in her private life. Yet privacy is problematic. When should one invade another's privacy? For never breaking through another's outer shell ultimately condemns both that person and one's self to complete isolation. So while Tyler's characters yearn for privacy because it gives them control over their lives, they simultaneously and contradictorily desire to break out of the isolation that privacy—taken to the extreme—necessarily promotes. Therefore, Jeremy eventually begins to wonder how Mrs. Willard cannot feel his presence in the house, even as they circle each other in their own separate "orbits." And his capture at the end of the story provides that inevitable confrontation between, and resolution of, his conflicting desires.

Synopsis: On an errand to get some fresh corn for supper for his mother, 16-year-old Jeremy walks by a house that is closed up for the summer and decides to break into it. After climbing in a window on the sun porch, he looks around the house. Upstairs he lies down on a bed, imagining his mother waiting at home and wondering what's taking him so long to get the corn. He falls asleep, and it is dark when he wakes up. Although Jeremy imagines his worried parents calling the police, he just turns over and goes back to sleep.

The next morning Jeremy awakens to find that his watch has stopped. And with no sense of time, he can no longer imagine what his parents might be doing. For breakfast he eats something from a can because the refrigerator is empty. Then he starts exploring the house from top to bottom, opening every drawer and cabinet. He begins to consider this house as "a sort of halfway house where he could get his bearings before he started moving" (165). He plans to hitchhike west soon.

For five more days he stays at the house, developing an orderly routine to his days. In the morning he cleans up, in the afternoon he reads one of the many novels on Mrs. Willard's book shelves (he learns the owner of the house's name from a Christmas card), and in the evenings he listens to a talk show on the radio.

On the sixth day, Mrs. Willard returns, but she doesn't notice anything different. At first Jeremy feels that his privacy has been invaded, but then he decides that he likes the old lady. So Jeremy stays on. Learning her schedule, he manages to remain undetected. Yet he wonders how Mrs. Willard can possibly not know that he is there. Perhaps she does and they are "like two ancient married people [who] filled the same geographical space but spun in their own private orbits," each making "little adjustments" for the other (166). Best of all, each is "*respectful*" (166) of the other's privacy. Soon he is imagining himself living this way indefinitely.

Three days later, however, Mrs. Willard is showing the gas man down the stairs into the basement when she catches a glimpse of Jeremy and screams. Although Jeremy attempts to run past them up the stairs, the gas man catches and holds him while Mrs. Willard calls the police, "dashing all their faith in each other" (166). Caught in the gas man's iron grip, Jeremy realizes "that he was never going to go anywhere at all" (166).

responsibility. ("Artificial," AT, CN, DHR, EP, "Holding," "Laps," LY, MP, SC, SM, "Street") Many of Tyler's characters feel restricted by their family situations or by life in general. They respond to these restrictions in different ways. Some pack up their bags and leave, such as Mary Scott in "The Artificial Family." Others stay put, allowing the restrictiveness to build up around them until they can stand it no longer, such as Mary Tell in *Celestial Navigation* or Charlotte Emory in *Earthly Possessions*. In *Morgan's Passing*, Morgan Gower feels restricted by his life because it allows him to live only one life. His response is to become an impostor who takes on multiple identities. In *Saint Maybe*, Ian Bedloe feels restricted by the responsibility of parenting his brother's three children and wonders when these responsibilities will ever ease. Ultimately, many of these characters, after their doubts or escape, find that they can return to their families and that they can endure their lives once they achieve a new perspective and understanding of their place in life. See also DEPENDENCY.

restaurants. (AT, DHR, EP, LY, SM) Restaurants provide opportunities for characters to get together to work out differences, as when Macon and Sarah Leary meet in *The Accidental Tourist*; bring families together, as in Ezra Tull's repeated dinner attempts in *Dinner at the Homesick Restaurant*; or substitute for family connections, as Rick Rack's cafe does for Delia Grinstead in *Ladder of Years* or Ezra's Tull's Homesick Restaurant does for the Bedloe family in *Saint Maybe* on the Christmas following Bee's death.

restrictiveness. ("Artificial," BL, CN, EP, "Foot-Footing," IMEC, MP, SC, SM, "Street") Anne Tyler's characters often feel restricted by their families and/or by situations that life has thrust upon them. As early as her short story "A Street of Bugles," Tyler has explored this tension between freedom and restriction. In this story Sammy feels trapped in the town of Balton, Maine, and yearns to escape. Although he heads out to sea, he ultimately returns. Similarly, Charlotte Emory in *Earthly Possessions* feels restricted by her households of furniture and burgeoning family members, prompting her escape and eventual return. So, too, Ira Moran in *Breathing Lessons* feels restricted by the demands of providing for not only his immediate family, but his father and sisters as well, demands that have caused him to give up his plan to attend medical school. In *Saint Maybe*, Ian Bedloe spends twenty years caring for his brother's three children rather than living a life of his own. At times he comes close to despairing of ever having a life of his own. Yet despite these characters' desires to escape the restrictiveness of their lives, and their brief escapes in some instances, they ultimately return to their families, having learned that the compensations for their lost freedom—love and family connections—outweigh their losses.

retirement homes. (BL, IMEC, LY, "With Flags") Tyler's use of retirement homes as the setting for some scenes in her novels allows her respect for the elderly to shine through. In particular, she loves to write about old men, including Mr. Gabriel, Maggie Moran's favorite patient in *Breathing Lessons*; Jamie Dower, who has come home to die in an old folks' home in his hometown in *If Morning Ever Comes*; Nat Moffat, whose life continues as he remarries and starts a new family, despite living in Senior City in *Ladder of Years*; and Mr. Carpenter, who decides to move into a nursing home in "With All Flags Flying" to avoid becoming a burden to his family.

revivals. (CW, "Half-Truths," SDL) Religious revivals are treated with some skepticism by Tyler, for their dubious motivations and results. Only in her short story "Half-Truths and Semi-Miracles," in which the self-effacing Susanna Meagan heals some but not all who come to her for help, is this attitude eased.

Richard. (CW) Mrs. Emerson's African American handyman of twenty-five years, whom she fires for peeing on her roses.

rivers. ("Dry," "Lights") Rivers act as symbols of life flowing by. They also represent opportunities to join the flow of life, as the boys do by dumping Uncle Wurssun's ashes in the river in "Dry Water."

Mr. Robb. (EP) the Ameses' first boarder; a factory watchman who stays only three weeks.

Brindle Gower Teague Roberts. (MP) Morgan Gower's sister, who had been married to Horace Teague for seven years, but left him and came to live at Morgan's; she reads tarot cards; later she marries and then divorces Robert Roberts.

Clemson Roberts. ("Saints") old friend of Mary Robinson and Laura Gates'.

Robert Roberts. (MP) Brindle Gower's boyfriend throughout school; she marries and then divorces him years later.

Jim Robinson (or Robertson). (AT) director of the summer camp in Virginia that Ethan Leary was attending when he was killed.

Mary Robinson. ("Saints") young woman who works in a New York publishing firm; she comes home for vacation and visits her old friend Laura, who has suffered a nervous breakdown.

romance. (AT, BL, DHR, "I Never Saw," LY, MP) Although Tyler's novels do recount some examples of romance (Ira Moran's gasp when he first sees Maggie on their wedding night in *Breathing Lessons* or Robert Roberts' return to reclaim his childhood sweetheart, Brindle Gower, in *Morgan's Passing*), for the most part Tyler's depictions of romance are rather lackluster. Romance is mostly illusion anyhow. What keeps Maggie and Ira Moran together for twenty-eight years is a bond that surpasses romance. Even Tyler's couples' marriage proposals and responses are matter-of-fact without much fanfare.

Rosalie. (LY) Velma's quiet 6-year-old daughter.

Mr. Rosen. (DHR) customer Ezra Tull dreams about.

routines. (AT, LY, "Respect") See ORDER.

rowhouses. (AT, CN, DHR) Baltimore's famous downtown rowhouses appear as settings in *Celestial Navigation* (the Paulings' boardinghouse), in *Dinner at the Homesick Restaurant* (the Tulls' home), and in *The Accidental Tourist* (Muriel Pritchett's rundown home).

Murray Rumford. (SM) the typewriter salesman whom Lucy Dean Bedloe tries to get interested in her after her husband Danny Bedloe's death; he reconciles with his wife, however.

"The Runaway Wife." *Ladies' Home Journal* Apr. 1995: 130+. This story is an edited version of chapter five of *Ladder of Years*. Editors added explanatory information about some characters and summaries of earlier events, especially those dealing with Delia's encounters with Adrian Bly-Brice and his mother-in-law's visit to the Grinsteads' house.

runaways. (DHR, "Dry," EP, IMEC, LY, "Runaway," SC, TCT, "Teenage") See ESCAPE/RETURN.

S

Dominick Saddler. (AT) neighborhood boy who fixes up Muriel Pritchett's car in exchange for using it on certain nights of the week and Sundays; he later dies in a car wreck.

Saint Maybe. Until the publication of *Saint Maybe* in 1991, Anne Tyler had generally steered clear of overtly religious themes. Yet, as its title suggests, *Saint Maybe* does address the theme of religion as it chronicles the redemptive process of its main character, Ian Bedloe. In the novel, Ian changes from an uncertain young man to a mature adult with a strong Christian faith. The process of becoming "Saint Maybe" requires Ian, by means of faith and a greater openness to the world around him, to shed his old self and take on a new belief in God, in himself, and in other people.

While not avoiding religious subjects altogether in previous works, Tyler has typically treated ministers in her previous novels with skepticism. In a 1981 interview with Wendy Lamb published in the *Iowa Journal of Literary Studies*, Tyler noted, "It's not that I have anything against ministers, but that I'm particularly concerned with how much right anyone has to change someone, and ministers are people who feel they have that right" (Lamb 61). Tyler faults people other than ministers, too, for pretending to know more than they really do. She views anyone who claims to know all the answers with much the same caution. Appropriately, one of *Saint Maybe*'s chapters is titled "People Who Don't Know the Answers." All of Tyler's characters are people seeking to find themselves, to stake out an identity for themselves, and to find a connection to the people around them and a deeper understanding both of themselves and others. In *Saint Maybe*, this focus on the individual falls on Ian Bedloe as he experiences similar needs, most especially his need for forgiveness for his role in the death of his brother, Danny. In order to achieve forgiveness, Ian must pass through three stages: recognition, repentance, and redemption.

The first stage in the process of Ian's redemption begins with a psychological recognition of his wrongdoing. The 17-year-old boy whom Tyler presents at the beginning of her novel is too immature and self-absorbed to admit his wrongdoing. In fact, his immaturity ultimately precipitates his brother's death when he blurts out his suspicions about Danny's wife's infidelity, thus triggering Danny's reaction—suicide. Up to this point, Ian has believed that he knows all the answers and acts accordingly. Consequently, it comes as a shock to Ian to hear his devastated brother crashing his car into a stone wall. Ian's recognition, coming most significantly as he gazes into a mirror, causes him to understand "that nothing in his life would ever be the same" (SM 46). This introspective realization of himself as he really is for the first time marks the beginning of Ian's recognition stage.

The nagging guilt Ian suffers as he struggles to admit his role in Danny's death forces him to make his first psychological adjustment, slowly integrating into his consciousness (through fragmented, manageable bits of information) the full consequences of his actions first toward Danny and then, later, toward Lucy. In confronting the horror of a reality that he has helped to create through his negligence and overbearing certitude, Ian reacts to this new reality with a growing need for spiritual release.

And thus, coincidentally—or providentially—Ian's psychological search turns religious at about the same time he stumbles upon the Church of the Second Chance. Sensing his need for some sort of spiritual recognition of his wrongdoing, Ian first needs forgiveness, an easing of his guilt. Then his search widens to encompass a search for meaning and purpose in his life. Ian's redemption requires that he use spiritual insight to make changes in himself and in the way he responds to the world. Some of the changes concern religion and morality. Others are more individual, requiring that he let down some of the self-imposed psychological barriers constructed to protect himself from being hurt. The first stage in the process comes quickly; the second, repentance, has to be worked out slowly over the next twenty years as he works out his ultimate redemption.

The person most influential in prompting Ian's religious redemption is Reverend Emmett, the church's minister, whom Tyler presents sympathetically, unlike other preachers in earlier Tyler novels. Ian immediately senses Reverend Emmett's inner peace and desires to gain a similar redemption. Yet, this minister is not one who offers all the answers, and he does not make it easy for Ian. After Ian confesses his role in Danny's death, Reverend Emmett shocks Ian by telling him that he is not forgiven until Ian "offer[s] reparation—concrete, practical reparation, according to the rules of our church" (SM 122). Reverend Emmett acts as a catalyst to Ian, spurring him on to make the hard sacrifices that lead to his redemption, first quitting college and then caring for his brother's children. The choice must be Ian's. His ultimate redemption requires both spiritual assistance from God as well a psychological adjustment on Ian's part. In his advice to Ian, Reverend Emmett is actually urging Ian to make connections with those outside himself, first the children and then the other members of the church. Though Ian's choice is in some ways forced upon him, Anne Tyler has explained, the choice he makes is "literally, his Second Chance at a moment when he had given up hope."

Psychologically, Ian's religious decision is reflected in his dreams, the first of which are accusatory: Danny's assertion that he knew of Lucy's infidelity and Lucy's complaint that Ian considers her "not a bit first-class" (SM 106). After repenting, however, Ian experiences his final dream about Danny. In contrast to the earlier dreams, this last one is very comforting. In the dream, as Ian is lifting a heavy carton, Danny appears and offers to help him carry it. Then Danny lifts his end, Ian lifts his, and they smile at each other. Yet, despite the psychological implications of this last dream, its clearly religious import and what it reveals about the change in Ian's consciousness should not be overlooked. This dream about Danny is the final one because Ian has exorcised the demon of his guilt. Ian now sees himself and his condition in religious terms, imagining himself resting "all his weight on God, trustfully, serenely, the way his [college] roommate used to rest in his chair that resembled the palm of a hand" (129). With God's help, Ian feels sure that he can handle the responsibilities that face him as he moves on to the next stage of his redemption: the long, difficult phase of repentance.

The trials and temptations Ian endures during this next stage reveal a deeper problem standing in the way of his ultimate redemption. Ian enjoys his job at a cabinetmaking shop because it involves working with "inanimate objects . . . that he couldn't mess up. Or if he did mess up, it was possible to repair the damage" (SM 126). Ian's attitude toward the furniture he builds reveals his hesitation to become involved in the lives of others.

In addition, Ian struggles with issues of fidelity and responsibility. His girlfriend breaks up with him because she can't understand the new Ian, "Mr. Holiness" (SM 149). But, despite rejecting other propositions, psychologically, Ian cannot completely suppress his sexuality. He fantasizes about a "Church Maiden" (SM 201) and is tested by Eli Everjohn, a private detective, who, after learning that Ian is raising someone else's children, tempts Ian (much as Satan tempted Christ in the wilderness) with escape by offering to locate their missing father. But, spiritually, if Ian's faith is real, he must withstand this temptation. And, psychologically, he must also resist the temptation to retreat into himself by shedding connections with the outside world, which the children represent.

But Ian's greatest burden is not the children. It is his need for complete forgiveness, especially to forgive Danny and Lucy for saddling him with the children. So, again at Reverend Emmett's urging, once Ian accepts the need for this further forgiveness, this time on *his* part, not someone else's, he feels like "an arrow—not an arrow shot by God but an arrow heading toward God, and if it took every bit of this only life he had, he believed that he would get there in the end" (SM 225). Ian's faith here matures to the point that he can wholeheartedly, unreservedly give his "only life," much as Christ, to a greater degree, gave His. At this point, giving himself completely, Ian can realize full repentance and move on to the last stage of his spiritual journey toward redemption. The Christian implications here, again, are unmistakable. Though Ian's faith is not unwavering, he always views himself in relation to God as he moves from one stage to the next in the process of his redemption.

Yet the final stage of Ian's redemption cannot be complete until he risks immersing himself in the lives of others. Up to this point in the novel, Ian has managed to maintain a distance between his true self and the chaos of the outside world with its dangers and responsibilities. Though he has involved himself in the lives of the children and in the lives of his fellow church members, Ian has not really stepped over the line, which requires his risking his personal commitment, with its concomitant dangers both of rejection by and of harm to the other party. As long as Ian retains this cautious, self-protective posture, he remains, ultimately, uncommitted.

"Saint Maybe," as his niece Daphne accurately dubs Ian, has learned caution as to when and where to intrude in the lives of others. He becomes increasingly ascetic, monk-like, maintaining both his psychic distance and ultimate deniability of responsibility. If he is to reach the final stage of his redemption, however, Ian must move beyond Saint Maybehood to an understanding of his place in the world and in the lives of the people around him.

Again the catalyst for Ian's development, Reverend Emmett confronts Ian with the possibility of training for the ministry. In a scene reminiscent of the Last Supper, with potato chips and onion dip instead of bread and wine, Reverend Emmett explains his vision for the church's future with Ian as its new pastor, but Ian doubts his ability to give people the answers they are searching for. He is still unwilling to take complete responsibility for other people's lives. Because Ian cannot at this point make such a commitment, he declines Reverend Emmett's offer. The impossibility of getting *the* answer, though, does not preclude Ian's remaining true to his faith. He still falls back on his faith, praying "not forming actual words but picturing instead this green planet safe in the hands of God, with the children and his parents and . . . himself small thrusting dots among all the other dots" (SM 266).

Locked in his static trust, Ian must take one more step before his redemption is complete. Ian, who has withdrawn from involvement with the lives of others, must reenter the larger world outside himself and his family. And, as is so often the case in Tyler's novels, it is an outsider who forces the issue. In *Saint Maybe*, the person who moves Ian on to the final stage of his redemption is Rita diCarlo, an Italian "Clutter Counselor" who arrives to set the Bedloes' house in order after Ian's mother's death and finally convinces him to risk reaching out to another person and building a life of his own with her.

Rita's almost immediate pregnancy reinforces the forward direction of Ian's decision, with its emphasis on the future, not the past. Ian's willingness to launch out into new areas is evident in the cradle he begins building for the baby. In the past he had always preferred to work on furniture "with straight lines" (SM 315), but now Ian finds a particular satisfaction in the curving lines of the cradle. The change in Ian's attitude toward furniture-making mirrors the change in his personal attitude. He is now willing to accept the uncertainties and the risks of life as they curve out of sight into the future, into the unknown. He no longer feels the need to see everything in long, straight, predetermined linear fashion. With faith, and a newfound trust in himself and the people he loves, he can accept life's risks because he understands that to avoid them is to miss life itself.

Ian's redemption, his reconnection to the world, is completed as he holds his son Joshua, named after the man who led the Israelites into the promised land. Ian notes Joshua's frailty—that is, the human condition—and yet he also realizes that Joshua is not alone in the struggles that life will bring. The baby has his parents and his family and other people who will touch his life in mysterious and exciting ways.

Thus, by accepting his place in this uncertain everyday world, Ian achieves his final redemption, although it may be a somewhat tenuous redemption—appropriate for a saint named "Maybe." In his final epiphany, the Ian who had retreated from involvement with other people's lives because of shame and guilt over his past at last accepts his role in the lives of others, through faith in God, in himself, and also in the people around him. Once he makes this decision to accept life, his redemption is as complete as it can ever be. Though trials may come and though he will certainly continue to grow and change, this redemption will enable Ian to participate fully in the lives of the people around him. And, with such an attitude, he will find, maybe, a full measure of happiness.

For Further Reading

Caesar, Judith. "The Foreigners in Anne Tyler's *Saint Maybe*." *Critique: Studies in Contemporary Fiction* 37.1 (1995): 71–79.

Croft, Robert W. *Anne Tyler: A Bio-Bibliography*. Westport, CT: Greenwood Press, 1995. 87–91.

Evans, Elizabeth. *Anne Tyler*. New York: Twayne, 1993.

Koppel, Gene. "Jane Austen and Anne Tyler, Sister Novelists under the Skin: Com-

parison of *Persuasion* and *Saint Maybe.*" *Persuasions: Journal of the Jane Aus-*
ten Society of North America 15 (1993): 164–69.
Voelker, Joseph C. "The Semi-Miracles of Time." *World and I* Feb. 1992: 347–57.

Selected Book Reviews

Bawer, Bruce. "Anne Tyler: Gravity and Grace." *Washington Post Book World* 18
Aug. 1991: 1–2.
Cherry, Kelly. "The Meaning of Guilt." *Southern Review* 28 (Winter 1992): 168–
73.
Eder, Richard. "Quiescence as Art Form." *Los Angeles Times Book Review* 8 Sept.
1991: 3+.
Gardner, Marilyn. "Ordinariness as Art." *Christian Science Monitor* 25 Sept. 1991:
13.
Kakutani, Michiko. "Love, Guilt and Change in a Family." *New York Times* 30 Aug.
1991: C21.
Morey, Ann-Janine. "The Making of Saint Maybe." *Christian Century* 20–27 Nov.
1991: 1090–92.
Parini, Jay. "The Accidental Convert." *New York Times Book Review* 25 Aug. 1991:
1+.

"The Saints in Caesar's Household." *Archive* Apr. 1961: 7–10. One of
the five early stories Tyler published in *Archive*, Duke University's literary
magazine, "The Saints in Caesar's Household" introduces several Tylerian
themes that would continue to appear in her more mature work.

Mary's reticence to visit her old friend Laura is as much an expression of
the isolation Mary feels in her own life as it is respect for Laura's privacy.
When Mary finally does visit Laura, their conversation centers around the
issue of connectedness. Obviously deeply depressed, Laura feels completely
unconnected to the world around her—family, friends, and townspeople.
Yet, as Laura points out, Mary, whether she realizes it or not, is just as
unconnected in her failure to reach out to the people around her.

Laura's accusation affects Mary deeply, as profoundly in its way as Mary
Grace's challenge to Mrs. Turpin in Flannery O'Connor's short story "Revelation." Leaving her friend in the rain, Mary soberly returns home to con-
template Laura's bleak vision, aware of her own isolation as never before.

Synopsis: Mary's mother does not write her in New York to tell her about
the breakdown of her old friend Laura Gates. When Mary finally comes
home for a visit in the fall, she learns about Laura's problem from Clemson
Roberts, an old friend, on the bus ride home. Although Mary tells her
mother about what Clemson had said, to her mother's surprise, Mary
doesn't ask many questions about Laura.

The next day Mary's aunt reminds her of the time when Mary and Laura
stole smudgepots from the road construction crew. She thinks that it is
Mary's duty to go see Laura. Nevertheless, Mary waits four days before
going to see Laura. It is raining, so she asks her mother to use the car. At

Laura's house, Laura lets Mary in and offers her some breakfast, but Mary refuses because she's already eaten. Laura looks much thinner and is dressed in shabbier clothes than the bright colors Mary remembers her wearing when they were younger.

A little defensive at first, Laura tells Mary that if she's come to watch her that there's not "much to watch any more" (8). Laura also lets Mary know that she knows Mary's been home for five days and is just now getting around to visiting her. Laura tells Mary about hearing a strange noise in the middle of the night that no one else in her family heard. When Mary suggests that it was probably just the house settling, Laura replies testily, "Of course it was. . . . Do you think I hear *voices*?" (8).

Expressing her connectedness to her mother, Mary says that her mother has "touched people who've touched other people all the way back to Babylon, all those generations touching hands" (8). When Mary suggests that Laura has the same connections, however, Laura says she doesn't feel that way. She's not like her mother who can remember everything, including how Mrs. Parry was envied by all the neighborhood women because she had a fur coat and a ballpoint pen when they used to be so expensive. Then Laura laughs and Mary joins her.

Despite the rain, Laura suggests that they go sit in the town's amphitheater. Laura asks Mary if her aunt had asked her about the time they stole the smudgepots. Next she asks Mary if she wants to be like her mother, who visits the sick, especially the aged and insane. Mary says no, but then Laura asks her if she was afraid to come visit her. In the increasingly heavy rainfall, Laura stands up and starts turning around and around. Then she tells Mary how she had gone to a confessional and offered to let the priest confess to her and how she had put her sister Jennifer's clothes in the garbage can so Jennifer would have to talk to her. Laura feels that Jennifer can't or won't stop long enough to talk to her.

As Laura continues to talk about how people are too busy to stop and talk to each other, she walks up onto the stage of the amphitheater, while Mary remains seated in the top row. Laura quotes a Bible verse: "The saints salute you . . . and especially they that are of Caesar's household" (9). She says that she will always remember the feeling you get "when you catch people and say, 'wait,' " but they pull away and keep going. She concludes, "Nowadays there is too much love in the world; it goes floating around and nobody wants it" (10).

Noticing that the rain has made Mary cold, Laura suggests that she go home. Then suddenly she shouts at Mary: "Who did *you* ever reach out for as they went by?" In response, Mary puts on her coat and leaves. Although she looks back once, Laura is not looking after her.

The next line of the story reads: "People say . . . that it was a heartless thing to leave a disturbed person out there alone in the rain, with the stones all around her and the gray sky pressing in" (10). That day, however, despite both Mary's mother and aunt castigating her for leaving Laura in the rain, Mary insists that she doesn't worry about Laura. As she looks out the window at the rain, Mary understands Laura's vision of people alone in the world.

Sally. ("Half-Truths") one of Susanna Spright Meagan's sisters, who worked in their father's pharmacy, but soon married.

Sally Ann. (CN) one of Jeremy Pauling's art students; a fat girl who once offered to pose nude for him.

Joe Salter. ("Flaw") Peter's friend, also from western Canada, who allows Peter to sleep on his couch after Peter's apartment is burglarized.

Sammy. ("Street") young ship engine mechanic who yearns to escape the town of Balton, Maine, and his restrictive existence.

Sandra. ("Tea-Machine") a fat, lazy girl in John Paul Bartlett's graduating class who struck oil and now lives in Paris.

Mrs. Saunders. (DHR) Cody Tull's ninth grade English teacher.

Billy Scarlatti. (DHR) Mrs. Scarlatti's son, who is killed in the Korean War.

Mrs. Scarlatti. (DHR) the dignified owner of Scarlatti's Italian Restaurant, who leaves her restaurant to Ezra Tull when she dies of cancer.

Christopher Edward Schmidt. (CW) Ian and Lisa Schmidt's six-month-old son.

Ian Schmidt. (CW) classmate of Timothy Emerson's who throws a party.

Jason Schmidt. ("Who Would Want") 5-year-old boy who has been sent from one foster home to the next; he comes to stay with the Burns family.

Lisa Schmidt. (CW) Ian Schmidt's wife.

Lorena Schmidt. (DHR) one of Cody Tull's cheap girlfriends in the summer before the ninth grade.

Martin Schmidt. ("Bride") Sarah Mellor Schmidt's husband, a teacher.

Sarah Mellor Schmidt. ("Bride") young woman recently married to Martin Schmidt; she meets Venetia Oliver at the boatyard.

Sophie Schmidt. ("Who Would Want") Jason Schmidt's mother; she is a foreigner and works as a nurse.

Gary Schneider. (EP) television news reporter who interviews Saul Emory after his wife Charlotte's kidnapping.

Abner Scopes. (BL) Mr. Gabriel's roommate at the Silver Threads Nursing Home.

Mary Glover Scott. ("Artificial") young woman with a 5-year-old daughter (Samantha Glover) who works in an art gallery; she marries and then leaves Toby Scott.

Mr. Scott. ("Artificial") Toby Scott's father, who tacitly agrees with his wife's assessment of Toby's new family.

Mrs. Scott. ("Artificial") Toby Scott's mother, who comes for a visit at Christmas and doesn't like the artificiality of her son's new family.

Toby Scott. ("Artificial") graduate student in chemistry who marries Mary Glover Scott.

Dana Scully. (AT) former boyfriend of Muriel Pritchett's before she married Norman Pritchett.

Searching for Caleb. *Searching for Caleb* covers a longer timeframe than any of Tyler's other novels—nearly a hundred years. It is also notable for its tribute to Tyler's grandfather, who provided the model for Daniel Peck. The novel explores the dual aspects of family, in this case the Peck family of Roland Park in Baltimore, which was founded by Justin Peck in the late nineteenth century and has flourished and then floundered by the time the novel opens in 1972. At that time Daniel Peck, Justin's now 92-year-old son, and Daniel's fortunetelling granddaughter, Justine Peck, are in search of Daniel's long-lost brother Caleb, who has not been heard from since 1912.

Daniel represents the staid, conservative side of the Peck family nature while Caleb symbolizes the untamed, creative counterbalance, which the Pecks who stay behind in the family's Roland Park enclave never allow to develop. Daniel has spent his life responsibly working as a lawyer and judge, but wound up alone raising his five children after his wife, Margaret Rose, deserted him and thereafter died in 1912, shortly before his brother Caleb left home for good. Now at the end of his life, Daniel finds himself searching for his brother desperately in a race to find this lost part of himself before he dies. As it turns out, Caleb is located before Daniel's death, but because

Daniel insists on contacting him by letter, according to Peck etiquette, Daniel does not get to see Caleb before he dies. That is left for Justine to do, who brings Caleb back home for a visit only to discover that he doesn't want to stay, although he reveals himself to be a true Peck in the way he leaves: the obligatory Peck bread-and-butter thank you note. In the end, then, neither Daniel nor Caleb has succeeded in reconciling the two warring sides of the Peck nature in their own lives.

Justine, however, seems to have managed to meld the two elements of her heritage effectively into her life. On the one hand, she marries her own first cousin, Duncan Peck, thus assuring that she will remain a Peck forever. Yet she also follows the unsettled Duncan around from town to town, living a nomadic life that brings her into contact with strangers that she must turn into friends on a yearly basis. Worse yet, she chooses a seedy occupation, fortunetelling, that her conservative Peck relatives meet with suspicion and downright distaste. For Justine, this blending of the two sides of her nature results in a happy life. At the end of the novel, she and Duncan have discovered the perfect lifestyle for themselves, living in a trailer and working for a traveling carnival.

For Further Reading

Croft, Robert W. *Anne Tyler: A Bio-Bibliography.* Westport, CT: Greenwood Press, 1995. 49–52.

Currie, Marianne D. " 'Stringtail Man': Music as Motif in *Searching for Caleb." South Carolina Review* 24 (Fall 1991): 135–40.

Evans, Elizabeth. *Anne Tyler.* New York: Twayne, 1993.

Petry, Alice Hall. *Understanding Anne Tyler.* Columbia: University of South Carolina Press, 1990. 128–53.

Ross-Bryant, Lynn. "Anne Tyler's *Searching for Caleb*: The Sacrality of the Everyday." *Soundings: An Interdisciplinary Journal* 7 (Spring 1990): 191–207.

Voelker, Joseph C. *Art and the Accidental in Anne Tyler.* Columbia: University of Missouri Press, 1989. 89–105.

Selected Book Reviews

Howes, Victor. "Freedom: Theme of Pecks' Battle Hymns." *Christian Science Monitor* 14 Jan. 1976: 23.

Just, Ward. "A 'Wonderful' Writer and Her 'Magical' Novel." *Washington Post* 10 Mar. 1976: B9.

Peters, Catherine. "Opting Out." *Times Literary Supplement* 27 Aug. 1976: 1060. [Reprinted in *Critical Essays on Anne Tyler*. Ed. Alice Hall Petry. New York: G. K. Hall, 1992: 80–81.]

Pollitt, Katha. "Two Novels." *New York Times Book Review* 18 Jan. 1976: 22. [Reprinted in *Critical Essays on Anne Tyler*. Ed. Alice Hall Petry. New York: G. K. Hall, 1992: 82–83.]

Updike, John. "Family Ways." *New Yorker* 29 Mar. 1976: 110–12. [Reprinted in *Critical Essays on Anne Tyler*. Ed. Alice Hall Petry. New York: G. K. Hall, 1992: 75–79; and in his *Hugging the Shore: Essays and Criticism*. New York: Knopf, 1983: 273–78.]

Patty Sears. (DHR) one of Dan Smollett's old girlfriends; she lives in Washington, D.C.

Mark Sebastiani. ("Knack") Susan Denneson Sebastiani's Italian husband; a linguist who teaches Italian at the University, he also knows French, Spanish, Russian, and Greek and is learning Arabic.

Mr. Sebastiani. ("Knack") Mark Sebastiani's father, who comes for a visit from Italy.

Mrs. Sebastiani. ("Knack") Mark Sebastiani's mother, who comes for a visit from Italy.

Susan Denneson Sebastiani. ("Knack") Mark Sebastiani's American wife; she is a graduate student in geology.

self-reliance. (CW, DHR) Even the name of Tyler's Emerson family in *The Clock Winder* conjures up visions of self-reliance. Ironically, however, Tyler's Emersons are anything but self-reliant, depending on Elizabeth Abbott for almost every aspect of their lives. See also DEPENDENCY.

For Further Reading

Marovitz, Sanford. "Anne Tyler's Emersonian Balance." *Critical Essays on Anne Tyler*. Ed. Alice Hall Petry. New York: G. K. Hall, 1992: 207–20.

Serena, Mistress of the Occult. (SC) fortuneteller Justine Peck visits in Blainestown.

Seth. ("I Play") the narrator's 12-year-old blue-eyed brother, who accompanies his sister to New York to buy a cello.

Uncle Seward. (DHR) Pearl Tull's uncle who offers to send her to Meredith College in Raleigh.

sex. (AT, BL, DHR, EP) There is no heavy breathing in Anne Tyler's novels. She is not a writer interested, as Faulkner noted in his Nobel Prize speech, in writing "not of the heart but of the glands." Her only interest is the heart. Even so, the physical aspects of love are noticeably absent, especially when her works are compared to other contemporary writers. In her early works, Tyler's reticence to broach this delicate subject is near absolute. In later works, however, she has ventured into the sexual corners of the marriages she describes, if delicately, to hint at a passion that constitutes an integral part of married life. In *Earthly Possessions*, Charlotte Emory plots to get her preacher husband Saul into bed on Sunday afternoons. In *The*

Accidental Tourist, Macon and Sarah Leary break in their new sofa bed. And in *Breathing Lessons*, Maggie and Ira Moran's passion erupts at a most unexpected time—the wake of an old friend. In each of these encounters, however, Tyler is careful to maintain her characters' privacy, respecting the act of sex itself as the personal act that it is.

For Further Reading

Gornick, Vivian. "Anne Tyler's Arrested Development." [Rev. of *Dinner at the Homesick Restaurant*.] *Village Voice* 30 Mar. 1982: 40–41.

sexism. (CN, "I'm Not Going," "I Play") In Tyler's work she is usually very evenhanded in dealing with matters between the sexes, attempting to show that both genders suffer, for the most part, from the same universal human problems. In a few instances, however, she has presented the viewpoint of women who feel repressed because of their sex. In "I Play Kings," Francie Shuford, pregnant and presumably abandoned by the child's father, asserts that she could have played more roles if she had been a boy. In "I'm Not Going to Ask You Again," Sarah Cobbett, a school teacher, notes the many advantages that life gives to boys.

Dabney Bell Sheridan. ("Laps") old classmate whom Sue Ellen spots at the pool; she is visiting from Atlanta.

shoes. (CN, EP, TCT, "Under Tree") See ESSENTIALS.

shoplifting. (SM) Lucy Dean Bedloe's shoplifting to support her family serves as a commentary on the plight of single mothers struggling to raise their children without the proper means of support. As an integral aspect of the novel's plot, however, Lucy's shoplifting proves to Ian how wrong he was to suspect Lucy's fidelity. This revelation heightens his feelings of guilt.

Francie Shuford. ("I Play") 20-year-old girl who moves to New York to pursue an acting career, but gets pregnant.

Mrs. Shuford. ("I Play") Francie's mother, who gives the narrator Francie's address in New York so that she can check on her.

sibling rivalry. (DHR, LY) The tension between siblings in the same family is an inevitable condition of the closeness of family life. In *Dinner at the Homesick Restaurant*, however, this natural rivalry goes beyond the normal. Jealous of his mother's favoritism toward his brother Ezra since childhood, Cody Tull sets out to steal Ezra's fiancée, Ruth Spivey, away from him and succeeds.

For Further Reading

Madden, Deanna. "Ties That Bind: Identity and Sibling Relationships in Anne Tyler's Novels." *The Significance of Sibling Relationships in Literature.* Ed. JoAnna Stephens Mink and Janet Doubler Ward. Bowling Green, KY: Bowling Green State University Popular Press, 1992. 58–69.

Paula Sidey. (AT) Sarah Leary's mother.

Alfred Simmons. ("Holding") Lucy Simmons' 40-year-old husband, a school principal who is not good with tools.

Brenda Simmons. ("Some Sign") Sam Simmons' busy wife.

Darwin Simmons. ("Base-Metal") Mary Beth Polk's previous boyfriend, whom she had dated because his name was the same as Darwin Two's.

Donnie Simmons. ("Some Sign") Sam and Brenda Simmons' son.

Eddie Simmons. ("Some Sign") Sam and Brenda Simmons' son.

Lucy Simmons. ("Holding") 25-year-old woman who now works in a library; she is married to Alfred Simmons, who she has discovered is not a responsible person; the mechanics at the Exxon station call her "Mrs. Simmons."

Miss Simmons. (SDL) librarian at Pulqua's public library.

Molly Simmons. ("Some Sign") Sam Simmons' mother, who had died in 1959, years before her husband.

Mr. Simmons. (BL) Morans' neighbor across the street, who looks like an insurance or real estate salesman.

Mr. Simmons. ("Some Sign") Sam Simmons' recently deceased father; a chicken farmer.

Mrs. Simmons. (BL) Mr. Simmons' wife, who is childless and happy.

Mrs. Simmons. (DHR) neighbor of Pearl Tull's in Baltimore.

Nicky Simmons. ("Some Sign") Sam and Brenda Simmons' son.

Samuel (Sam) Allen Simmons. ("Some Sign") owner of Simmons Drugstore.

Benny Simms. (CW) neighborhood college boy who becomes interested in Elizabeth Abbott.

Jake Simms. (EP) demolition derby driver turned bank robber who kidnaps Charlotte Emory.

Stuart Simms. (SM) Agatha Bedloe-Simms' incredibly handsome doctor husband.

Lollie Simpson. ("With Flags") former school teacher of Mr. Carpenter's.

Terry Simpson. (BL) Serena (Palermo) Gill's date to the Harvest Home Ball on October 22, 1955, the night she met Max Gill.

Mrs. Jeffrey Simpson-Jones. ("Geologist") former employer of Maroon's for seventeen years.

single mothers. (AT, "Average," BL, CN, DHR, SDL, SM) Tyler's sympathy for the tremendous burdens of single parents is evident in her portrayals of Muriel Pritchett in *The Accidental Tourist*, Bet Blevins in "Average Waves in Unprotected Waters," Mary Tell in *Celestial Navigation*, and Lucy Dean in *Saint Maybe*. These women face financial and social stresses without much support, yet most manage, somehow, to survive.

Dr. Arthur Sisk. (EP) physician contemplating suicide who moves in with the Emorys.

Skipper. (LY) Rosemary Bly-Brice's boyfriend; an accountant who had done the Bly-Brices' taxes.

sleep. (AT, BL, TCT) See DREAMS and INSOMNIA.

sleepwalking. (DHR, "Two People") In *Dinner at the Homesick Restaurant*, Ezra Tull's sleepwalking prevents him from remaining in the army. In "Two People and a Clock on the Wall," 12-year-old Melinda's sleepwalking is an inexplicable sign of unrest.

A Slipping-Down Life. Written when the younger of Tyler's two daughters had just started nursery school, *A Slipping-Down Life* is Tyler's shortest novel. It recounts the story of the growth of young Evie Decker from adolescence to young womanhood and budding motherhood. Overweight and unprepossessing, Evie first seeks to establish her identity by cutting the name of a local rock singer on her forehead. Tyler had read about a similar story of a girl in Texas who cut Elvis' name on her forehead.

Evie Decker's uncertain, insecure teenage life is sensitively portrayed. Ever since her mother's death (at Evie's birth), Evie has been raised by her ineffectual father and by a surrogate mother, the family's maid, Clotelia. Thus, more so than even other teens, overweight, unnoticed Evie has had to struggle to find herself. When she sees Drumstrings Casey performing on stage at a local nightclub, she sees her chance to change her lackluster life. In an attempt to achieve the identity and validation she is missing, Evie goes into the restroom and carves Drum's last name on her forehead. Typical of her ineptness, however, since she looks in a mirror to see what she is doing, she winds up carving his name backwards.

Nevertheless, Evie's scheme meets with initial success. Evie starts to appear at Drum's performances for publicity. Over the next few months Evie becomes an integral part of Drum's act. Eventually, even Drum comes to view Evie as a necessary element and, following a brief breakup, asks her to marry him to make their partnership permanent. Evie's response to Drum's marriage proposal is the same answer that Tyler gave to her husband Taghi's proposal, "Oh, well. Why not?" (SDL 131).

After they have been married only a few months, however, Evie quickly learns that Drum is not a dependable provider. Instead, he becomes increasingly dependent on her, urging her to quit school and opposing her working at the local library. Although she is beginning to tire of his immaturity, Evie tries to accommodate Drum, dropping out of school, but not quitting her job. When she becomes pregnant and then discovers Drum's infidelity, however, Evie, now more mature, realizes that she must put her child ahead of her irresponsible husband. With her job at the library to support herself, Evie moves back into her father's house, which she has inherited following her father's unexpected death of a heart attack. There she plans to build a life for herself and her child, making "a circle of herself, folding more and more inward" (SDL 185).

Although Evie asks Drum to accompany her back to her home, he refuses and accusingly questions her ability to care for the child on her own, as well as her motivations in cutting his name on her forehead in the first place "just for purposes of *identification*" (SDL 212). Hurt but undeterred, Evie leaves. Now sure of her own identity, she feels confident enough to build a life for herself and her child without Drum, although ironically the scar from his name will always be on her forehead.

For Further Reading

Croft, Robert W. *Anne Tyler: A Bio-Bibliography*. Westport, CT: Greenwood Press, 1995. 33–34.

Evans, Elizabeth. *Anne Tyler*. New York: Twayne, 1993.

Petry, Alice Hall. *Understanding Anne Tyler*. Columbia: University of South Carolina Press, 1990. 53–72.

Voelker, Joseph C. *Art and the Accidental in Anne Tyler*. Columbia: University of Missouri Press, 1989. 40–47.

Selected Book Reviews

Edelstein, Arthur. "Art and Artificiality in Some Recent Fiction." *Southern Review* NS 9 (July 1973): 736–44. [Reprinted in *Critical Essays on Anne Tyler*. Ed. Alice Hall Petry. New York: G. K. Hall, 1992: 65–66.]

Lee, Hermione. "Frantic Obsessions." (London) *Observer* 29 May 1983: 30.

"New and Noteworthy." *New York Times Book Review* 3 Apr. 1977: 53–54.

Sloan. (DHR) Cody Tull's business partner, who invents time-saving gadgets.

Harriet Smith. (DHR) ninth grade classmate of Cody Tull's.

Mr. Smodgett. (CW) Matthew Emerson's boss; owner of a small country newspaper; he drinks too much.

Dan Smollett. (DHR) high school English teacher who is traveling around the country visiting his old girlfriends; he gives Luke Tull a ride from Richmond, Virginia, to Washington, D.C.

Sammy Smollett. (DHR) Dan Smollett's son.

Dr. Snell. (AT) Alexander Pritchett's allergy doctor.

Dr. Soames. (LY) minister who is supposed to perform Susie Grinstead and Driscoll Avery's marriage ceremony.

soap operas. (AT, BL, SDL) The fictional lives of soap opera characters provide escape for Tyler's characters, but the shows also provide time for characters to bond. For instance, Maggie Moran and Fiona Stuckey's mother/daughter-in-law relationship grows closer as they watch a soap opera together each day, as does the relationship of Clotelia and Drum Casey in *A Slipping-Down Life*.

Mr. Somerset. (CN) an old man who is a longtime boarder with the Paulings.

"Some Sign That I Ever Made You Happy." *McCall's* Oct. 1975: 90+. One of Tyler's most affecting stories, "Some Sign That I Ever Made You Happy" captures the poignancy of the passage of time and examines the conflicting emotions of married couples as they strive to maintain the most intimate of all relationships in the face of the relentlessly mundane minutiae of everyday life. Sam's marriage to Brenda is a happy one, but even this happy marriage illustrates the lack of understanding and inevitable miscommunication inherent in the human condition. To paraphrase Tolstoy, "All marriages are unhappy in their own way."

This sobering fact comes home to Sam in the form of his father's notebooks. Given the rare opportunity to catch a glimpse of his parent's marriage through his father's letters, Sam realizes that his father struggled with the same problem of communicating his feelings toward his spouse just as he does. Having learned his lesson from his father, a wiser Sam returns home, inspired to break through the communication barrier and openly express his love for Brenda. Yet Sam's attempt at communication is thwarted by Brenda's attention to household chores. So, oddly relieved, Sam gives up the effort. Having failed to express what he had hoped to tell his wife, Sam settles back into his old pattern of isolation, yet he can't shake the nagging feeling of somehow having lost a valuable opportunity.

Synopsis: Breakfast at the Simmons home is always hectic. Sam Simmons wonders how his wife Brenda can be so cheerful in the midst of the commotion of getting their three boys—Eddie, Donnie, and Nicky—fed and ready for school. She even sings snippets of songs and advertising jingles. She also has an annoying habit of relating her odd dreams to Sam. This morning she tells him one in which she has a houseful of guests to feed but no food in the house, so she considers feeding them nasturtiums for dessert. Sam listens patiently to Brenda's dream, but, as soon as she finishes, he rushes the boys to get ready so he can drop them off at school on his way to work.

Sam owns Simmons Drugstore. Arriving at work, he smells a stale, musty odor and then notices several cartons in the storeroom. Marie, one of the store's employees, informs him that they are marked personal. After examining the boxes and noticing that they are addressed to him in his sister Jenny's handwriting, Sam realizes that they contain his dead father's personal effects. He tells Marie that he will sort through them later. All morning, though, their musty odor reminds him of his father's house.

At lunch time Sam opens a few boxes and finds many books, as well as all his father's personal belongings. Sam starts to remember his father, a chicken farmer with only an eighth grade education who had nonetheless been a voracious reader. Mr. Simmons was a man who was "desperate to know everything" (127), so he had books on every subject imaginable. His favorite book was *Tess of the d'Urbervilles*, which he kept by his bed. Having opened only a few of the boxes, Sam leaves his lunch half eaten and goes back to work.

When business slows down at about 5:30, Sam calls Brenda to let her know that he will be home late because he has to finish going through his father's boxes. For a minute, Sam considers giving away all the boxes because they seem to contain nothing but more old books. Nevertheless, he decides that he should at least sift through all of them in case he should find something of value. Then he finds a box full of old diaries. Although most of the diary entries are merely weather reports, he locates one for the day he was born, June 8, 1935, and another for the day his mother died, October 5, 1959.

In another box, Sam discovers a notebook containing a series of letters his father began writing a month after his wife Molly's death. In the letters Mr. Simmons apologizes over and over to her for his neglect and his failure to let her know how much he really loved her. He continued to write these letters for years, stopping only six weeks before his death. Then Jim Bayles, the evening pharmacist, interrupts Sam to tell him that it is time to close up.

At home Brenda has supper waiting for Sam. He sits down to eat, and she goes off to put the boys to bed. Sam begins reading the diaries again and is deeply touched to learn how much his father missed his mother after her death. One letter in particular describes how Mr. Simmons had looked at old photographs of his wife, searching for "some sign that I ever made you happy" (133).

When Brenda returns, Sam wants to talk to her and tell her that he loves her, but she is busy cleaning out the refrigerator. Before he realizes it, Sam is starting a fight by criticizing the way she fails to organize the refrigerator. But Brenda understands that he has had a hard day and tells him to go read the paper. The moment passes, his opportunity to communicate his true feelings to her. Life, with all its cares and responsibilities, has intervened once again. So Sam goes to the quiet living room to read the paper, surprisingly relieved and yet sad, too. For a few minutes he stands there, "hoping against hope that the sorrow was the kind that would lessen as time went on" (133).

Lena Sparrow. (DHR) one of Dan Smollett's old girlfriends; she lives in Washington, D.C.

sparseness. (MP) Emily Meredith's simple dress and spartan living quarters appeal to Morgan Gower's sense of wishing to cast off his responsibilities. See also ESSENTIALS.

"Spending." *Shenandoah* 24 (Winter 1973): 58–68. "Spending" expresses both Tyler's antimaterialism and her dislike of extraneous material objects that serve no purpose, merely burdening people. Very few, if any, of the Bells' purchases can be justified by actual need. Consequently, after their buying frenzy they wonder if somehow their daughter is not trying to buy them off with material goods as a means of balancing her emotional accounts.

Synopsis. Lindy sends her parents (Joe and Dory Bell) a check for $1,000 to spend "selfishly" (58). At first Mr. and Mrs. Bell debate whether or not they should accept the money, but they decide that it might hurt their daughter's feelings if they return it. Having finally determined that they will keep the money, they decide that they should immediately put such a large sum in the bank. Therefore, they take the bus to the bank and deposit the money.

On the way home they notice a man's coat in a store window. Dory urges Joe to buy it. He agrees so long as she buys herself a new coat, too—a red one. That night Dory models the coat in front of the mirror, but she does not like her image: "a dumpy little woman about to pop out of a coat size 20 1/2" (60–61). Wondering why she ever bought the coat, she begins writing a thank you note to Lindy. Her writing is bold, "the writing of a woman in control of things" (61).

That night she dreams about the past, when she was helping out at the hardware store because Lindy was in teacher's college. When she awakens she goes to the bathroom and looks in the mirror. Her fatness displeases her, and she decides to go on a diet. The next morning she eats no breakfast, yet she is not hungry, feeling "stuffed" (62).

When the Bells go to the grocery store, however, Dory's resolve weakens. First they buy a bag full of pastries and then cakes and breads. At a wine shop they buy champagne and caviar. At last they go to a fancy department store, where they begin to buy everything in sight—from a black lace bra to a German cuckoo clock. When the buying frenzy is over, Joe totals up what they've spent—$1,007.29. Yet Dory continues to think of more things she'd like to have. They don't even have money left to pay the taxi home, and the driver is angry because he has to accept a check.

That night, sitting in their ridiculous clothes and sipping champagne, they realize how silly they've been. Dory wonders why Lindy sent them the check and asks, "Why did she do it? Does she consider us paid back now? Does she think we're quits?" (68). In response, Joe comforts her.

Spindle. (SDL) Clotelia's old boyfriend who had drunk too much and mooched off her.

Ruth Spivey. (DHR) "the country cook" (DHR 140); Ezra Tull's red-haired fiancée, who runs off with his brother, Cody Tull; she is Luke Tull's mother.

Mel Spruce. (BL) host of radio call-in show "AM Baltimore" on WNTK.

Greta St. Ambrose. (DHR) Joe St. Ambrose's wife, who deserts him, leaving him with six children.

Jacob St. Ambrose. (DHR) Joe and Greta St. Ambrose's son.

Jane St. Ambrose. (DHR) Joe and Greta St. Ambrose's daughter.

Jenny St. Ambrose. (DHR) See JENNY TULL.

Joe St. Ambrose. (DHR) Jenny Tull's third husband, whose first wife deserts him, leaving him with their six children to raise.

Peter St. Ambrose. (DHR) Joe and Greta St. Ambrose's son.

Phoebe St. Ambrose. (DHR) Joe and Greta St. Ambrose's daughter.

Quinn St. Ambrose. (DHR) Joe and Greta St. Ambrose's youngest son.

Slevin St. Ambrose. (DHR) Joe and Greta St. Ambrose's oldest son, who has learning problems.

Sister Myra Stamey. (SM) member of the Church of the Second Chance whose house is used for Camp Second Chance, the church's summer children's camp.

Harvey Stample. ("Feather") a college roommate of Charles Hopper's in the summer of 1913.

Lottie Stein. (BL) patient at the Silver Threads Nursing Home, where Maggie Moran works, who walks about with a walker.

Mr. Stevens. (TCT) owner of the Esso station where James Green stops for gas on his trip to Caraway.

Mrs. (Ida) Stimson. (CW) Mr. Cunningham's daughter.

Jerome Stimson. (CW) Mrs. Stimson's husband.

"A Street of Bugles." *The Saturday Evening Post* 30 Nov. 1963: 64–66. [Reprinted in *The Saturday Evening Post* July-Aug. 1989: 54–57+]. In an opening headnote, Tyler explains the source for this story, a summer she spent in the coastal town of Camden, Maine, which "seemed unusual [because] . . . no one, not even the young people, appeared to want to leave it. Most of them seemed bound to that one place forever" (64). That situation was what she "wanted to write [about] as soon as [she] left the town" (64).

"A Street of Bugles" is one of Tyler's classic escape/return stories. In it she explores the tension between an individual's overwhelming desire to escape the restrictiveness of life and the ultimately stronger urge he or she feels compelled to obey, the pull of family that causes the individual to return to that same life after a brief escape. Although family life may be dull and confining at times, it still offers security, stability, and—most of all—love to the individual. Therefore, like Sammy, almost all of Tyler's characters ultimately return home, older and wiser, and with a new perspective on life.

Synopsis: Each night before he falls asleep, Sammy imagines the townspeople who have known him all his life walking before him in a parade. Taking out a pistol, he imagines shooting them like ducks in a shooting gallery, a catharsis that leaves him feeling "tired and peaceful and his mind . . . cleared for sleeping" (64).

In the morning, Sammy's mother awakens him. As he dresses, he listens to the familiar sounds from the harbor. At breakfast his mother almost smothers him with attention, pressing him to eat something. She clings to Sammy almost desperately, because her husband and then her older son, Philip, have both left her. But Sammy refuses everything she offers to fix him except coffee.

Followed by a group of admiring children, Sammy heads down to the dock where he and his boss, Barney, are to ride a new boat, the *Odessa*, out when it's launched. One of the children, Porter, asks if he can accompany them, but Sammy tells him no. He says that the launching won't take more than fifteen minutes anyhow, so he won't be missing much. Nevertheless, the boy is very envious of Sammy's status.

At the boatyard about fifty people have gathered for the launching. Sammy makes his way though the crowd to the boat. Barney, Sammy's boss, introduces him to the boat's owner, Mr. Flint. Barney brags about how Sammy is so smart and could have gone to college if he hadn't had to take care of his mother. Mr. Flint seems more interested in Captain Harding's instructions to his wife, who is to christen the boat with a bottle of champagne.

Sammy and Barney go aboard the boat. As they wait, Sammy admires the boat's workmanship and wants to hug it. Amazingly, Mrs. Flint manages to break the champagne bottle on the boat's bow. As the boat moves down the rails, Sammy feels "like some god, standing where no one else could stand, above all the ordinariness of iron and boat grease" (66). Someone on the shore starts blowing a bugle, which seems to be "speeding the boat away and yet, at the same time, sadly, calling it back" (66).

For some inexplicable reason, instead of turning the boat back to the harbor, Sammy has a sudden urge to head out to sea. For a few minutes he rides out toward the open Atlantic, despite Barney's protests. When Barney stops objecting, Sammy finally turns the boat back to the dock. He mentions how the town's many bugles always seem to keep calling him home even though he is "crying to go" (66). Nevertheless the bugles blow and he always comes back to the restrictiveness of "such a damned *loving* town" (66).

Barney says that he will make up an excuse about a noise in the engine to explain Sammy's behavior. At the dock, people comment on the ride he has had. They admire the boat and talk about other boats from the past. Sammy doesn't listen to them. Instead, "in his own private echoing silence, he polished the pistol of his dreams" (66), while the seagulls "called beyond the shore" (66).

Stuart. ("Linguistics") Claire's husband's lab assistant who accompanies him when he applies for U.S. citizenship.

Crystal Stuckey. (BL) Fiona Moran's sister, who gets off work to take Fiona to the abortion clinic.

Mrs. Stuckey. (BL) Fiona Moran's mother, who smokes heavily and dislikes Jesse Moran.

subways. (SC) See TRAVEL.

Vernon Sudler. (LY) the handyman Delia Grinstead meets at the beach house in Bethany Beach; he gives Delia a ride to Bay Borough in his brother Vincent's RV.

Vincent Sudler. (LY) Vernon Sudler's older brother, who owns the RV.

Sue Ellen. (CW) Elizabeth Abbott's childhood friend who experienced multiple religious conversions.

Sue Ellen. ("Laps") friend who accompanies the narrator to the neighborhood pool.

suicide. (CW, "Dry," "Knack," MP, SC, SM) A surprising number of Tyler's characters commit suicide. But, unconcerned about the act of violence itself, Tyler concentrates her attention on the aftereffects of the death on the survivors: In *Morgan's Passing*, Morgan Gower's search for identity following his father's suicide; in "A Knack for Languages," Susan Sebastiani's feeling of disconnection ever since her mother's suicide; in *Searching for Caleb*, Justine Peck's grief and guilt over her mother's tragic death; and in *Saint Maybe*, Ian Bedloe's struggle to overcome his guilt for contributing to his brother's and sister-in-law's deaths. See also DEATH.

Brady Summers. (CW) Margaret Emerson's second husband; a law student.

Margaret Carter Emerson Summers. (CW) See MARGARET CARTER EMERSON.

Susan. (CW) Margaret Emerson's daughter.

swimming. ("Laps," LY, MP) Tyler's love of the beach appears in several novels in which characters take vacations to the beach, most notably *Ladder of Years* in which Delia Grinstead's family vacation to the beach, during which she avoids the water, ends up with Delia's running away. While she is on her own the next summer, however, Delia makes a trip to the beach by herself and makes a point of swimming in the ocean each day. More confident, she is no longer afraid of the water. In "Laps," the act of swimming becomes a metaphor for the passage of time, in its relentless and re-current motion.

Edith Taber. (DHR) dark-haired ninth grade girl Cody Tull likes.

Deborah Palmer Tabor. (SC) Paul Tabor's widow, who remembers nothing about Caleb Peck.

Paul Jeffrey Tabor. (SC) Caleb Peck's childhood friend, who dies on December 18, 1972, in New York City; Daniel Peck goes to see his widow.

Horace Teague. (MP) Brindle Gower's husband for seven years; he dies of a stroke six months after she leaves him.

"The Tea-Machine." *Southern Review* NS 3 (Winter 1967): 171–79. The southern setting of "The Tea-Machine" is its most obvious point of interest, for the influence of Tyler's North Carolina upbringing is readily apparent. From a literary standpoint, however, the story is also an intriguing character study of a young man coming of age, wrestling with identity, paternal control, and the possibility of future romantic attachments (and their concomitant responsibilities). Uncertain of exactly which direction to proceed in his life (or perhaps afraid to grow up), John Paul Bartlett prefers to daydream and spin around on his stool, maintaining his present status as long as he can.

Synopsis: John Paul Bartlett works as an assistant at his father's auction warehouse. It is a boring job, so he daydreams a good bit. As he sits on his stool, he particularly likes to think about Sandra, a fat girl who graduated from high school with him three years earlier. She had claimed that she would strike oil. And she did—while digging in the garden behind her grandmother's house. When John Paul starts spinning his stool, his father, busy auctioneering, orders him to stop. John Paul slowly stops spinning, but notes that "his father couldn't keep him from thinking, though" (172).

John Paul no longer has quite so much to do during the early stages of the auction because Katy, his brother Bill's wife, has taken over the job of handing the china to his father. John Paul and Bill used to do that, but would break too much and anger their father, Homer, who, in the midst of rattling off bids, would call them names that only they could understand. Now they just move all the merchandise into the warehouse before the auction and then handle the heavy objects at the end of the auction. That leaves plenty of time at the beginning of the auction for daydreaming.

Tonight they are auctioning off an entire household. John Paul's father is getting red in the face from all the activity. He is overweight and has recently had a stroke, but refuses to teach John Paul how to auction, despite John Paul's strong voice.

Sitting there with nothing to do, John Paul asks Fong, the Chinese man who has worked for the Bartletts for years, what he's thinking about. Fong says he's thinking about what he ate and needs a cup of tea. John Paul teases him about making tea and points out the teapots that are to be auctioned off.

John Paul's girlfriend, Millie Peterson, comes in with a Coke for him, sits beside him, and inquires about his thoughts. He replies that he is pondering oil wells and starts imagining finding oil the way Sandra did; only he'll find his digging potatoes on land given to him by his father. Sandra points out that this is North Carolina, not Texas. She is, however, interested in how much money he has. Every month she checks his bankbook to see how much he's saved. When he has enough to build a house, they're supposed to get married.

Dissatisfied with working for his father, John Paul complains that the job doesn't even have a name. Millie points out that the job does pay well, though. Meanwhile Homer carries on with the auction. Millie asks John Paul, "Aren't you ever satisfied?" (178). Looking at her, sizing her up the way his dad measures bidders, John Paul replies that he wants to leave "free, not laying a cent down on any of them" (178). Millie says she believes he would because he never cares about anyone. The auction continues. John Paul looks out the window, imagining the houses down the road becoming possessions to be auctioned off.

Millie points out that Sandra's cousin Joe probably made up the story about the oil well. John Paul laughs, spinning around on his stool.

Ted. ("Woman") Virginia's husband, who works as an insurance salesman.

"Teenage Wasteland." *Seventeen* Nov. 1983: 144–45+. "Teenage Waste-land" tackles the thorny problem of raising teenagers. With great sensitivity to the parents, Tyler describes Matt and Daisy Coble's efforts to help their son Donny through this difficult stage of his life. Hindered by a lack of communication with their son, Matt and Daisy ultimately have to face failure when Donny runs away. Another of Tyler's runaways, Donny leaves his parents, especially his mother, broken and racked with guilt, wondering how they could have broken through the barriers he put up and helped him. Donny's exact motivation for leaving is left unclear, and the reader, like Daisy, never figures out exactly what his problem is. In the final analysis, that is appropriate because Tyler's focus remains on the effect of Donny's running away on his parents.

Synopsis. As he has grown up, teenager Donny Coble has changed not only in appearance but also in behavior. In October, Mr. Lanham, principal of the private school Donny attends, calls and requests a conference with his parents to discuss Donny's problems. Donny's mother, Daisy, goes alone to the conference because her husband Matt is busy. At the conference she feels shamed as if she were a "delinquent parent" (144). During the next month, Daisy, herself a former teacher, spends extra time with Donny and checks his homework daily. This additional attention to her son, however, leaves little time for her daughter Amanda.

Despite Daisy's best efforts, by December Donny's behavior has only worsened. Both she and Matt are summoned for another conference and are shocked to learn that Donny's disruptive behavior now includes skipping school and drinking beer. Daisy thinks that, to the principal, she and Matt must look like "failures . . . the kind of people who are always hurrying to catch up, missing the point of things that everyone else grasps at once" (145). They finally agree to send Donny to a psychologist, who recommends that he start working with a young tutor, Calvin Beadle, who has had some success working with troubled teens.

That night, unable to sleep, Daisy wonders what she did or didn't do when Donny was growing up to nurture his "self-worth" and wishes for some kind of time machine that would allow her a second chance to raise her son more "perfectly" (145).

Donny starts going to Calvin's for tutoring on Monday, Wednesday, and Friday nights from 7 to 8, and his attitude improves somewhat. Calvin, who is younger looking than Daisy expects, acts almost like a teenager himself and insists that Donny call him Cal. At the tutor's insistence, Daisy and Matt also begin to allow Donny more freedom. According to Cal, this additional freedom will boost Donny's self-esteem by proving that they trust him.

But then Donny's history teacher, Miss Evans, informs Daisy that Donny is failing her class and suggests that Daisy should resume supervision of his homework. Cal, however, tells Daisy that she should not be so "controlling." Ultimately, Daisy relents, allowing Donny to continue going to Cal's, although he seems to just hang out with the other teens there rather than study. Donny soon acquires a girlfriend named Miriam, whom Daisy does not really approve of, especially when the girl starts accompanying Donny to his tutoring sessions at Cal's.

Then in April, the principal calls to say that Donny has been expelled from school because beer and cigarettes have been found in his locker. Instead of coming home, Donny goes to Cal's house. When Donny fails to show up at home, Daisy, worried and almost frantic, calls Cal, who tells her that Donny is at his house and suggests that she come over to hear Donny's side of the story. Cal unquestioningly defends Donny and even blames the school. Daisy, though, finally sees through Cal and realizes that he is not helping Donny, only excusing or perhaps even perpetuating her son's rebellious behavior.

Deciding to get tough, Daisy and Matt end Donny's tutoring sessions and place him in public school. In the new school, he earns average grades, but to Daisy there seems "something exhausted and defeated about him" (169). In June, Donny runs away. Despite the police's best efforts to locate him, three months go by without any word from Donny. The loss of their son ages Daisy and Matt noticeably. Every night Daisy lies awake wondering who is to blame for her son's running away. But she has no answers.

teenagers. ("Base-Metal," BL, DHR, "Laps," LY, "Respect," SC, SDL, SM, "Teenage") With two daughters of her own, Anne Tyler is well aware of the difficulty of raising teenagers from a parent's point of view. In *Breathing Lessons* and *Dinner at the Homesick Restaurant*, she clearly illustrates the anguish of parents trying to cope with teenagers' raging hormones and volatile emotions. Yet Tyler is also able to look at this stage of life from a teenager's perspective. In *A Slipping-Down Life*, she explores Evie Decker's and Drum Casey's searches for identity. In most of her works, teenagers somehow manage, like Daphne Bedloe in *Saint Maybe*, to negotiate the minefield of the teenage years successfully and to develop into promising adults. Such a positive outcome is not always assured, however. In "Teenage Wasteland," young Donny Coble runs away from home, leaving his mother to lie awake at night wondering where he is.

telephones. (AT, BL, CW, LY, "Nobody," SDL, TCT) The telephone is an instrument of communication, but more often than not, for Anne Tyler, the telephone serves as a device to block communication. In *The Tin Can Tree*, when the radio station calls about the contest that the now-dead Janie Rose Pike had been trying to win, the call pushes Mrs. Pike back into her withdrawn state. In "Nobody Answers the Door," Joanne Hawkes hangs up after her call to announce her recent marriage results in a fight with her mother. Then she refuses to answer the phone when her mother tries, repeatedly, to call her back. In *The Accidental Tourist*, the Leary family makes it a practice not to ever answer the phone because they live in an insular world and do not want the outside world to intrude. Their reasoning is that all their acquaintances know that they never answer the phone and, therefore, would never attempt to call them in the first place. No one else would bother to call. Thus, their cocoon, as well as the lack of communication that it perpetuates, remains intact.

television. (BL, CN, EP, LY) Television, that form of entertainment around which so many Americans center their lives, in Anne Tyler's works does not play a major role, with a few notable exceptions. In *Celestial Navigation*, Jeremy Pauling and various boarders in his boardinghouse, most notably Olivia, sit around watching the boob tube blankly. Is this an escape from their lives or an attempt to find, in the fictional lives of television characters, a more interesting life? In *Breathing Lessons*, Maggie and Fiona bond as they watch a soap opera together. In *Ladder of Years*, the act of watching television provides Joel and Noah Miller one of their few opportunities to see their absent wife/mother, Ellie Miller, who now serves as a weatherperson on a local television station.

Darcy Tell. (CN) Mary and Guy Tell's daughter.

Gloria Tell. (CN) Guy Tell's peroxide blonde mother, who was so helpful to Mary Tell during and after her pregnancy with Darcy; Guy and Mary lived with Gloria for a while after they were married.

Guy Alan Tell. (CN) Mary Tell's first husband; Darcy's father.

Mary Darcy Tell. (CN) Jeremy Pauling's "pretend" wife, with whom he has five children.

Jimmy Terry. (TCT) Mr. Terry's son, who takes the full tobacco sticks to the barn.

Mr. Terry. (TCT) tobacco farmer who employs Joan Pike, Roy Pike, and James Green.

Thérèse. (LY) Linda Felson's 8-year-old daughter; Marie-Claire's twin.

Thistledown. (BL) kitten Ira Moran gave to Maggie as his first present when they were dating; it died when Maggie forgot to check her mother's clothes dryer before she put a load in.

Carol Thompson. (TCT) Dan Thompson's wife, who delivers the Larksville newspaper.

Dan Thompson. (TCT) editor of the Larksville newspaper.

Reverend Thurman. (DHR) minister who officiates at Pearl Tull's funeral.

Melissa Tibbett. (MP) Mrs. Tibbett's daughter, who is turning 6.

Mrs. Tibbett. (MP) woman who hires Emily and Leon Meredith for their first puppet show for her daughter Melissa's birthday.

Bernice Tilghman. (AT) Muriel Pritchett's overweight best friend who works at the Gas and Electric Company.

Betsy Tilghman. ("Under Tree") Lou and Peg Tilghman's second daughter, who is somewhat overweight.

Dolly Tilghman. ("Under Tree") Lou Tilghman's recently widowed 67-year-old mother; she lives in a downtown Baltimore rowhouse.

Doug Tilghman. (SC) policeman in Caro Mill.

Elizabeth (Sugar) Tilghman. (BL) old friend of Maggie Moran and Serena Gill's, the class beauty, who sang "Born to Be with You" at the wedding, but refuses to sing it at the funeral; she sings "Que Sera Sera" instead.

Jim Tilghman. ("Under Tree") Dolly Tilghman's husband, who died four months earlier.

Laurie Tilghman. ("Under Tree") Lou and Peg Tilghman's third daughter.

Lou Tilghman. ("Under Tree") Dolly Tilghman's oldest son; a teacher.

Peg Tilghman. ("Under Tree") Lou Tilghman's wife.

Robert Tilghman. (BL) Sugar Tilghman's husband, who could not attend Max Gill's funeral.

Winnie Tilghman. ("Under Tree") Lou and Peg Tilghman's oldest daughter; she is at the difficult age of 11.

Tillie. (BL) old woman patient at the Silver Threads Nursing Home, who wanders around the home.

time. (AT, BL, CN, "Common," CW, DHR, EP, "Feather," IMEC, "I'm Not Going," "I Never Saw," "I Play," "Laps," LY, MP, SC, SDL, SM, TCT, "Under Tree," "Woman") The flow of time and the changes it brings about constitute, for Tyler, the most intriguing plot twists of all. To Tyler, time is circular. Yet time is also a spiral because her characters, through memory, can call up events from the past so that they seem a part of the present. Thus, Tyler's view is Faulknerian in the sense that the past is never completely over, although without Faulkner's determinism. For instance, in her novel spanning the longest stretch of time, *Searching for Caleb*, Tyler moves her plot back and forth over almost one hundred years. By contrast, in *Breathing Lessons*, Tyler telescopes twenty-eight years of Maggie and Ira Moran's marriage, indeed almost the entire forty-eight years of Maggie's life, into the Aristotelian timeframe of a single day. Thus, time for Tyler becomes, as with Thoreau, a river that she navigates through memory.

Even so, Tyler does not forget that time produces changes in her characters' lives. These changes are usually subtle, imperceptible in the immediate present, but when observed from a longer temporal perspective, as she does so effectively in "A Woman Like a Fieldstone House," these changes are clearly monumental, for they make up the cycle of life itself.

For Further Reading

Elkins, Mary J. *"Dinner at the Homesick Restaurant*: The Faulkner Connection." *Atlantis: A Women's Studies Journal* 10 (Spring 1985): 93–105.
Linton, Karin. *The Temporal Horizon: A Study of Time in Anne Tyler's Major Novels.* Uppsala, Sweden: Acta Universitatis Upsaliensis, 1989.
Voelker, Joseph C. "The Semi-Miracle of Time." *World and I* Feb. 1992: 347–57.

time travel. (LY, "Teenage") Time, of course, is a major theme in Anne Tyler's work. Many of her characters wish for the ability to travel through time, whether to journey into the past to correct old mistakes or into the future to discover what will happen to them. In *Ladder of Years*, Adrian Bly-Brice even publishes a newsletter on time travel entitled *Hurry Up, Please*.

The Tin Can Tree. Anne Tyler's second novel, published in 1965 while she was still living in Canada, is nevertheless set in North Carolina. Its characters are typically Southern, with an extended sense of community symbolized by the unusual three-part house occupied by the Pikes, the Greens, and the Potters. Despite their closeness physically, however, each of these characters remains essentially alone. Young Simon Pike, whose sense of abandonment while his mother struggles to cope with the loss of his sister Janie Rose, asks if there is an x-ray camera that can take a picture of his house and "have the people show up from inside" (TCT 28). Unfortunately, no such camera exists and each person's real life remains hidden.

This lack of understanding is highlighted by the recurrent photographic images throughout the novel. James Green is a photographer, but his two-dimensional photographs, as Great-Aunt Hattie points out, do not capture the true essence of his subjects. No one really knows anyone else. James and Joan Pike, who have been going together for several years, remain single. Simon eventually runs away, after warning several people of his plans. Joan, too, runs away and returns with no one except Simon and James' brother Ansel knowing that she has even left.

The central action in the novel revolves around the death of 6-year-old Janie Rose Pike in a tractor accident. Lou Pike, her mother, sinks into a depression so deep that neither her husband Roy nor her niece Joan can pull her out of it. Finally, however, Simon's running away draws her out of her near catatonic state. When she realizes that she might lose Simon, she insists on driving with James to look for the boy. Her son is the one connection strong enough to pull her back into the mainstream of life. Simon also needs his mother's attention to reassure him that he is wanted after his sister's death.

The novel's main theme is expressed by Missouri, the black woman who works in tobacco with Joan: "Bravest thing about people . . . is how they go on loving mortal beings after finding out there's such a thing as dying" (TCT 106). This life-affirming philosophy offers the only consolation that Lou or Joan can hope for. So, in the end, Lou returns to her maternal role and reconnects herself to her son. For her part, Joan returns to the people she loves, although she comes to realize that, like each of them, she will never really connect with them. Each one will remain separate individuals. In the novel's final scene this separateness is emphasized when Joan replaces James as photographer for a group photograph commemorating Simon's return. As she looks through the camera's lens, Joan sees the people who mean so much to her look to her "like figures in a snowflurry paperweight who would still be in their set positions when the snow settled down again" (TCT 273). Thus, even as the photograph brings these people together, life keeps them separate.

For Further Reading

Croft, Robert W. *Anne Tyler: A Bio-Bibliography*. Westport, CT: Greenwood Press, 1995. 28–29.

Evans, Elizabeth. *Anne Tyler*. New York: Twayne, 1993.

Petry, Alice Hall. *Understanding Anne Tyler*. Columbia: University of South Carolina Press, 1990. 22–52.

Voelker, Joseph C. *Art and the Accidental in Anne Tyler*. Columbia: University of Missouri Press, 1989. 27–40.

Selected Book Reviews

Bell, Millicent. "Tobacco Road Updated." *New York Times Book Review* 21 Nov. 1965: 77.

Frankel, Haskel. "Closing a Family Wound." *Saturday Review* 20 Nov. 1965: 50. [Reprinted in *Critical Essays on Anne Tyler*. Ed. Alice Hall Petry. New York: G. K. Hall, 1992: 63–64.]

Gardner, Marilyn. "Figurines in a Paperweight." *Christian Science Monitor* 10 Feb. 1966: 7.

Ridley, Clifford A. "Spark and Tyler Are Proof Anew of Knopf Knowledge of Top Fiction." *National Observer* 29 Nov. 1965: 25.

Todd. (MP) Morgan and Bonny Gower's grandson.

Tom. (DHR) co-owner of the body shop where Josiah Payson works.

tools. (AT, CW, DHR, "Holding," LY, MP, SC, SM) In *Death of a Salesman*, Willy Loman states that "a man who doesn't know how to handle tools is not a man." Anne Tyler would seem to agree, for one of the qualities that she prizes above all others is the ability to fix things. Even the eccentric Learys in *The Accidental Tourist* all can handle tools. In fact, Rose fixes her elderly neighbors' plumbing. Similarly, in *The Clock Winder*, Elizabeth Abbott becomes Mrs. Emerson's handyman. In *Dinner at the Homesick Restaurant*, Pearl assiduously maintains the Baltimore rowhouse where her family resides after her husband Beck deserts her. In "Holding Things Together," Lucy Simmons modifies her opinion of her husband's competence, when after a few years of marriage, she realizes that he has no mechanical ability. In *Searching for Caleb*, Duncan Peck's natural mechanical abilities gain him job after job, and ultimately land him the perfect job, mechanic for Alonzo Divich's carnival. In *Saint Maybe*, Doug Bedloe's retirement years are salvaged when his mechanical skill finds an appreciative outlet at the foreigners' house.

trailers. (EP, LY, MP, SC) Most people consider trailers small, cramped domiciles occupied only by those who can't afford sturdier housing. No so Tyler's characters, who see trailers as less demanding than regular houses. In *Ladder of Years*, Delia Grinstead is delighted by the miniature appliances and efficiency of Vernon Sudler's RV. Another element that appeals to her is the trailer's portability, for she makes her escape from her family in Vernon's RV. At the end of *Morgan's Passing*, Morgan and Emily Meredith are living in a trailer. So, too, at the end of *Searching for Caleb*, Justine and Duncan Peck have found the perfect home for their traveling lifestyle, a small carnival trailer.

trains. (AT, "Average," "Baltimore," DHR, "Flaw," IMEC, SC) While Tyler was living in New York, she fell in love with riding the subway. Many of Tyler's characters ride trains of various types. Whenever possible, in *Searching for Caleb*, Justine and Daniel Peck ride trains on their trips to check out clues as to the whereabouts of Daniel's lost brother, Caleb. The train, with its set schedule, gives Tyler's characters a sense of order and permanence that they seek in their lives. In "The Baltimore Birth Certificate," Miss Maiselle Penney is impressed when her niece Betsy holds back the door of the train as if she were holding back time itself.

travel. (AT, BL, DHR, EP, "Feather," LY, "Outside," SC, TCT) Whether by bus, plane, train, subway, or automobile, Anne Tyler's characters are often on the move. Travel represents for them the opportunity to step out of the restrictiveness of their own lives. In "The Feather Behind the Rock," an elderly couple, nearing the end of their lives, travel across the United States with their grandson. Much of the action in *Searching for Caleb* occurs on Justine and Daniel Peck's trips. In addition, Justine and Duncan Peck live a mobile lifestyle, moving to a succession of Maryland and Virginia towns, never staying in one place much more than a year. In *Dinner at the Homesick Restaurant*, Cody Tull becomes, like his father before him, a traveling salesman. Unlike his father, however, he moves his family around the country with him. In *The Accidental Tourist*, Macon Leary's vocation involves constant travel, although ironically he writes a travel book for people who hate to travel.

Tyler's characters have contradictory impulses where travel is concerned. They yearn to escape their mundane existences in their restrictive families, yet when they escape through travel, or by other means, they almost always return, having realized either that escape is impossible or that they don't really want to leave in the first place. In *Earthly Possessions*, Tyler's escape novel, Charlotte Emory is kidnapped and forced to travel. Yet, at the time of her kidnapping, she was planning to run away anyhow. At the end of the novel, however, it is she who makes the decision to return home. Later when her husband Saul suggests that they might do a little traveling themselves, Charlotte declines his offer and states: "We have been traveling . . . all our lives" (EP 200).

traveling light. ("Artificial," EP, MP) See ESSENTIALS.

trees. (TCT) Janie Rose Pike's tin can tree, a Southern tradition whose variation is the bottle tree, serves as a constant reminder of her even after her death.

Clarine Ramford Tucker. (SC) Abel Ramford's widow, whom Eli Everjohn interviews in his search for Caleb Peck.

Beck Tull. (DHR) Pearl Tull's husband, who is six years younger than she; he works for the Tanner Corporation as a traveling salesman; in 1944 he deserts her, leaving her to raise their three children alone.

Cody Tull. (DHR) Beck and Pearl Tull's oldest son, who works as an efficiency expert and travels around like his father.

Ezra Tull. (DHR, SM) Beck and Pearl Tull's son; he is Pearl's favorite; he opens the Homesick Restaurant. He appears later in *Saint Maybe*, when the Bedloes eat Christmas dinner at the restaurant in 1988.

Jenny Marie Tull. (DHR) Beck and Pearl Tull's daughter, who becomes a pediatrician; she marries three different men: Harley Baines, Sam Wiley, and Joe St. Ambrose.

Luke Tull. (DHR) Cody and Ruth Tull's son; he is fair-haired like his uncle, Ezra Tull.

Pearl E. Cody Tull. (DHR) 85-year-old woman, now blind, who is on her deathbed at the start of the novel; she is the mother of Cody, Ezra, and Jenny Tull; she married Beck Tull in 1924 when she was 30.

Ruth Spivey Tull. (DHR) See RUTH SPIVEY.

"Two People and a Clock on the Wall." *New Yorker* 19 Nov. 1966: 207–17. Despite its seemingly self-limiting Southern setting, complete with front porch, this story focuses on the universal problems of adolescence. Melinda's sleepwalking is a metaphor for the searching that all adolescents go through. Therefore, the other characters' vain attempts to understand, much less cure, Melinda's malady illustrate yet another Tylerian instance of the failure and limitations of communication.

Synopsis: Melinda, a 12-year-old sleepwalker, has been sent by her father to visit her Aunt Sony Elliott, who lives in the country. Eliza Bowers, Sony's neighbor, comes over to question Melinda about her sleepwalking. In the past three days, she's suggested everything from first love to witnessing a crime as possible reasons for the girl's sleepwalking.

Sony is nervous about having a sleepwalking niece staying with her and had told her brother Ben as much when he sent the child, on doctor's orders, for a bit of fresh country air and rest. Sony is particularly unnerved when the girl sleepwalks about at night so "purposeful . . . with firm, even strides" (208).

Tonight Mrs. Bowers suggests that Melinda's sleepwalking might be caused by a fear of the dark. Melinda, who is very talkative, tells the woman how her brothers and sisters used to scare her when she got up to go to the bathroom at night. But when Mrs. Bowers ascertains that this traumatic event happened back when Melinda was 4, she discounts it as a cause for the girl's sleepwalking.

While Mrs. Bowers talks to Melinda, Sony sits there rocking and locking through the Sears catalogue. Finally, Mrs. Bowers concludes that the cause of Melinda's sleepwalking can be only one thing: The young girl has something she wants to say to people. Sony laughs at that notion because Melinda talks all the time. Melinda agrees with her aunt, but Mrs. Bowers insists that the girl talk: "Every mind has *something* in it, something to tell other people" (214).

Thus prompted, Melinda begins to talk about sleepwalking, which, according to her, "is caused by having two people using the same mind" (214). In this situation, the second person is searching for something he or she can't find. After finishing this odd speech, Melinda goes inside. Astonished, Mrs. Bowers remarks that she thinks Melinda is "maladjusted" (217). Sony, however, seems not to have heard the girl at all; she just keeps turning the pages of the Sears catalogue.

Ty. ("Laura") 10-year-old boy who is too young to attend Laura's funeral.

U

"**Uncle Ahmad.**" *Quest/77* Nov.-Dec. 1977: 76–82. One of Tyler's tales about foreigners, "Uncle Ahmad" reveals what happens when two cultures clash. More importantly, however, it portrays the universal clashing of lives as they weigh on others. Privacy and dependency, it seems, cannot be long maintained outside of the immediate family, at least in the American culture.

Synopsis: Uncle Ahmad calls the Ardavi household to tell them that he has arrived in the United States from Iran. Elizabeth, an American woman who is married to Ahmad's nephew, Hassan, happens to answer the phone. Before Elizabeth can get Hassan to talk to his uncle, however, Ahmad tells her that he is on his way to Baltimore and that Hassan should meet his train at 10 P.M. While Hassan dresses, he recalls how his flamboyant uncle had been the black sheep of the family, disapproved of by the women of the family—including his two ex-wives—and adored by the men for his outrageously funny exploits.

When Uncle Ahmad arrives, Elizabeth thinks he looks like Mr. Clean. He fills the room with his presence. Although Ahmad is disappointed that the children, Jenny and Hilary, are already in bed, he settles for seeing them in the morning. Almost immediately, he makes himself right at home, drinking and smoking and taking off his shoes.

At first everyone is happy to have Ahmad staying at the house. He entertains the children, but when he gets tired he becomes short tempered. Ahmad also begins to complain about his life, everything from his own father's selfish ways to his ex-wives' pickiness to his son Jamal's lack of concern. To Hassan he laments: "I've worn out my life before I've come to the end of it" (79). Soon he begins to impose on the family. The biggest burden falls on Elizabeth, who has to bring Ahmad's drinks and take him shopping, his favorite activity.

Soon, however, Ahmad has bought everything he needs and becomes bored with shopping. So he starts making calls to all his relatives in America. Without Elizabeth's knowledge, one day he invites all their relatives for a huge party. When Ahmad tells Hassan about it, Hassan insists that he call them back and uninvite them. Unfortunately, Ahmad forgets to call two of the relatives back, so Kurosh (with his pregnant wife and two babies) and Hamid show up anyhow. Elizabeth is left to wait on all of them, but she tells herself that, compared to her American friends' ordinary in-laws, hers are quite colorful.

Finally, Elizabeth has had enough, though. One Friday night she is feeding the girls the last of the ice cream, just enough for them to have a small scoop each. Ahmad comes in, however, and picks up Hilary's scoop. Elizabeth defiantly orders him to put it back. Chastened, he obeys, but soon decides that it is time for him to leave.

Although relieved in some ways, Elizabeth can't help feeling a little sad after Ahmad leaves. Until that moment she has not realized how "people who are larger than life become that way by consuming chunks of other people's lives, so they are missed forever afterward like an arm, or a leg, or a piece of a heart" (82).

"Under the Bosom Tree." *Archive* 89 (Spring 1977): 72–77. A touching story, "Under the Bosom Tree" reveals Tyler's sympathy for old people. More than that, however, it explains her view of time as a series of stages that everyone goes through. Perhaps what endears older people to Tyler most is their ability to see that pattern since, like Dolly Tilghman, they have already lived through most of the stages of life.

Synopsis. Dolly Tilghman and her son Lou are shopping for a dress and shoes for her 67th birthday party that night. Dolly buys a dress two sizes too small, but says it will fit when she puts her girdle on at home. Lou has taken the afternoon off from school to take his mother shopping, so he feels a little burdened by this familial responsibility. Yet after she selects the dress, he insists that they look for shoes.

While waiting for the clerk to bring the pair of navy pumps that she likes, Dolly tells Lou the story of how she and her girlfriend Olympia used to go to stores and try on shoes for fun. She also reveals how they would meet at the "bosom tree" halfway between their houses and "plan for when our real lives would begin" (73). Strangely enough, in her case, her dream of "a husband, children, and a house full of Early American furniture" (73) had all come true, although her husband has been dead for four months.

At home Dolly shows her son pictures from her many picture albums. She had gotten married at 18, but waited twelve years for her first child.

Eventually she had five: Lou, twin boys, and two daughters who now live in other states, Nell and Paula. Dolly notes the changes in styles as evidenced in the photos. Looking at an album from the 1950s, she blames the change in the pace of life on rock-and-roll. To her, during the 1950s, the time when her children were teenagers, "life speeded up so" (75).

At Dolly's birthday party that night, Lou's daughters—Winnie, Betsy, and Laurie—are uncomfortable in their dresses, his wife Peg lovely in her wool suit, and his mother stuffed into her new dress (which is still too tight even with the girdle on). Dolly mentions that this is her first birthday without her husband Jim. She remembers how he had started keeping an hour-by-hour diary in the months before his death, as if he knew that the end was near.

As she cuts the birthday cake, with its thirteen candles—six plus seven for sixty-seven, Dolly reveals how much she misses Jim and how she wishes he could see how well she is managing on her own. Peg hugs her, but Lou just stares off into the distance, not knowing what to say. The girls begin to fight over the cake; Peg apologizes for their behavior, explaining that it is part of a stage they're going through. Dolly says she understands that "everything happens at the appointed time, all the changes take place as they're supposed to" (77) and compares these changes to NASA rocket launches: "All those events set in motion all that time ago, and then each stage proceeding on its own while the scientists sit back and watch" (77). Following this appraisal of how life always seems to follow its natural course, she thanks her family for "a very fine birthday" (77) and smiles.

unusual jobs. (AT, BL, CW, MP, SC) Tyler's characters make their livings in very odd ways. Macon Leary writes travel books for people who hate to travel, a job that was more or less dumped in his lap. Elizabeth Abbott stumbles upon her job as Mrs. Emerson's handyman. Ira Moran inherits his father's framemaking business without being consulted. Duncan Peck drifts through a kaleidoscope of jobs, while his wife Justine takes up fortunetelling. All these jobs reveal the multiplicity of ways in which Tyler's characters support themselves. Yet they also illustrate the ways in which people simply fall into their fates by chance, thus calling into question the ability of a person to change his or her destiny in even the smallest way, such as choosing an occupation.

V

---

vacations. (AT, LY, MP) Vacations, particularly beach vacations, provide Tyler's characters opportunities to escape their lives. Yet what they usually discover is that they are the same people on vacation as they are in their real lives. Therefore, the vacations often end disastrously, as in *Morgan's Passing* when Robert Roberts tries to drown himself and in *Ladder of Years* when Delia runs away from her family.

Valerie. (BL) Leroy Moran's friend who dreams that Leroy gets run over by a tractor-trailer.

Velma. (LY) Ramsay Grinstead's vivacious 28-year-old girlfriend; a beautician; Rosalie's mother.

Vernon. (LY) Delia Grinstead's cat.

Victor. ("Holding") the red-headed mechanic at the Exxon station, who has a tattoo of a carrot on his forearm.

Vietnam. (CW, DHR, SM) Tyler's Quaker pacifism is strangely absent in her novels. Except for indirect references to the Vietnam conflict, few references to the war itself or the social conflict that it engendered invade Tyler's Baltimore. Peter Emerson returns from the war in *The Clock Winder*, but he makes no comment about it. In *Saint Maybe*, Sister Lula's son, Chuckie, dies when he forgets to put on his parachute, but even that absurdity does not speak to the horror and carnage of the war. Even more pointedly, Ian Bedloe's non–life-threatening heart murmur allows Tyler to conveniently sidestep the issue, for it keeps Ian from being drafted.

Dr. Vincent. (DHR) the Tull family doctor.

Miss (Mildred) Vinton. (CN) longtime boarder at the Pauling house, who works in a bookstore.

violence. (AT, CW, "Misstep," SDL) Tyler takes an Aristotelian view of violence in her work. She does not display the violence openly. Instead, the violent action (Ethan's murder in *The Accidental Tourist*, Julie Madison's rape in "A Misstep of the Mind," or Evie Decker's self-mutilation in *A Slipping-Down Life*) all occurs outside the view of the reader. On the one hand, Tyler's decision not to portray the violence serves not to sensationalize it. More to the point, however, it reveals Tyler's true interest: not the violence itself but the effects of the violence on its victim(s).

Violet. ("Geologist") Maroon's sister, who has asthma.

Virginia. ("Woman") Corey and Ben's oldest child, who remains in Baltimore; Elise is Virginia's daughter.

vision. (CN, EP, IMEC, TCT) Sight is very important to Tyler's characters because it enables them to see the world and the people in it in new ways. This vision can take the form of Jeremy Pauling's artistic vision in *Celestial Navigation*, or the photographic eye of Charlotte Emory in *Earthly Possessions*, or of James Green in *The Tin Can Tree*.

W

Bertha Washington. (BL) overweight kitchen worker at the nursing home who finds Maggie Moran in the laundry cart and pushes her around the home with the help of Sateen Bishop.

Larry Watts. (LY) former renter of Belle Flint's, who was separated from his wife; he runs off with Katie O'Connell.

weddings. (AT, BL, CW, DHR, "Foot-Footing," LY, MP) Romance is almost never a part of Anne Tyler's world, so her weddings don't turn out to be fairy tale affairs. Instead they are often comical, pitting opposing characters in a formal situation and watching them fall apart. Most often, they also provide characters who aren't getting married with opportunities to evaluate their own marriages, as is the case with Delia Grinstead in *Ladder of Years* and Macon and Sarah Leary in *The Accidental Tourist*.

Eudora Welty. Anne Tyler's most significant literary influence, from whom Tyler learned the importance of character and specific detail in writing.

For Further Reading

Manning, Carol S. "Welty, Tyler, and the Traveling Salesman: The Wandering Hero Unhorsed." *The Fiction of Anne Tyler*. Ed. C. Ralph Stephens. Jackson: University Press of Mississippi, 1990: 110–18.

Tyler, Anne. "The Fine, Full World of Welty." [Rev. of *The Collected Stories of Eudora Welty*.] *Washington Star* 26 Oct. 1980: D1+.

———. "A Visit with Eudora Welty." *New York Times Book Review* 2 Nov. 1980: 33–34.

Juval Wesley. (LY) Leon Wesley's son; though set to join the navy, the boy is arrested for burglary.

Leon Wesley. (LY) the man who paved Zeke Pomfret's driveway; he comes in to discuss his son Juval's case with Mr. Pomfret.

Dominick (Dommie) Benjamin Whitehill. (CW) Elizabeth Abbott's old boyfriend in North Carolina; she leaves him at the altar; he is a pharmacist.

"Who Would Want a Little Boy?" *Ladies' Home Journal* May 1968: 132–33+. This poignant story reveals once again Tyler's ability to present children's viewpoints with great insight and sensitivity. Jason Schmidt's dilemma is indeed a strange one, for he is loved by many people. Yet circumstances do not permit him to stay with any one foster family long enough to establish permanent emotional ties. His mother's intensely jealous love for him and her attempt to maintain her burdensome regimen even in her absence prevent the small boy (and the succession of foster families he lives with) from establishing a life separate from his mother. Thus, left with only a box of photographs (a favorite Tyler motif) of his past families, Jason can never really escape from his mother-imposed isolation. In the end, the photographs simply allow him to remember his past near-connections while simultaneously reminding him of the impermanence of his present situation at the Burnses'.

Synopsis: The Burns family takes in Jason Schmidt, a 5-year-old boy whose mother has placed him in a series of foster homes. When 8-year-old Mary Burns arrives home from school one Friday afternoon and finds Jason sitting in the living room with his snowsuit on, she is at first surprised and a little jealous. Immediately she notices that the boy has strips of adhesive tape on his fingernails. Asking her brother Billy about the boy, Mary learns that he was left earlier by a woman. But when Mary questions Jason, he does not reply.

So Mary goes into the kitchen where her mother is fixing supper. Mrs. Burns tells her that Jason's mother, Mrs. Schmidt, dropped the boy off and that the tape is to keep the boy from biting his fingernails. Mrs. Schmidt has a "prescribed regimen" (157) that must be followed if the boy is to be allowed to stay with the family. Among other items listed in six pages of instructions, the regimen includes the tape, a bad-tasting purple solution on his fingers to keep him from sucking his thumb, and a napkin around his left hand to force him to use his right hand so that he won't be left-handed.

When Mary's father comes in, he takes off Jason's snowsuit and convinces the boy to eat some supper. Over the next few days, Mary learns more about

Jason's routine, including his required prayers in a foreign language. The family (especially the mother) grows increasingly attached to Jason. Gradually, Mrs. Burns stops following the regimen, but the tense visits of Mrs. Schmidt, who also loves Jason, create conflict. When she notices that Mrs. Burns has stopped putting tape on the boy's fingers because he doesn't bite his fingernails anymore, Jason's mother threatens to take the boy away, as she has in times past when the families the boy has stayed with stopped following her instructions.

Therefore, fearful of losing the boy she has grown so attached to, Mrs. Burns resumes the senseless regimen. Yet Mrs. Schmidt's increasingly frequent calls and visits over the next several weeks make it apparent that Jason is not going to be able to stay with the family indefinitely. At the end of the story, Jason, whom past experience has taught that his days with the Burnses are numbered, shows Mary a box of photos of him and his many "families." Mary, also realizing the truth, tells him that she doesn't like him anymore, but, as Jason knows, she doesn't mean it. He just looks at her and puts his pictures back in their box.

Becky Wiley. (DHR) Jenny Tull's daughter by her second husband, Sam Wiley; she develops anorexia nervosa.

Jenny Wiley. (DHR) See JENNY TULL.

Sam Wiley. (DHR) Jenny Tull's second husband and Becky's father; an irresponsible artist.

Mrs. Willard. ("Respect") older woman who owns the house Jeremy breaks into.

William. ("Common") Melissa and Joel's son, born April 30, named after Mr. Billy, his grandfather.

Mrs. Willis. (BL) Maggie Moran's supervisor at the Silver Threads Nursing Home.

Mrs. Willoughby. (SDL) the Deckers' elderly neighbor who is talking to Mr. Decker when he has his heart attack.

windows. (AT, "Flaw," "Geologist," "Saints") Tyler's windows act on two levels. On the one hand, they serve as observation posts from which a character can look out at the outside world before deciding to enter it (cf. Macon Leary in *The Accidental Tourist*). In addition, the windows serve as doorways into these new worlds, through which a character can start a new life.

Chester Wing. (MP) Liz Gower's husband.

Elizabeth (Liz) Gower Wing. (MP) See ELIZABETH (LIZ) GOWER.

Pammy Wing. (MP) Liz and Chester Wing's daughter; Morgan and Bonny Gower's granddaughter.

Barney Winters. (CW) Georgia veteran that P. J. Grindstaff Emerson knows who had visited home before being shipped to Vietnam.

"With All Flags Flying." *Redbook* June 1971: 88–89+. "With All Flags Flying" examines an old man's feelings about aging and losing his independence. Determined not to become a burden to his family, Mr. Carpenter sacrifices his happiness and decides to move into a nursing home. Mr. Carpenter's unexpected motorcycle ride to his daughter's house, however, belies his true feelings. Actually, he yearns for freedom and would prefer to maintain his independence. Yet, rather than burden his family, he moves into a nursing home when his opening comes up. Ironically, as his roommate Mr. Pond points out, Mr. Carpenter's desire to spare his family only proves his need (and his love) for the very family that he is leaving behind. Such are the complex, confusing, and often conflicting feelings associated with love of any kind.

Synopsis: Mr. Carpenter, 82, finally realizes that he's too weak to live alone in his small house out in Baltimore County. So early one Saturday morning, taking only the essentials (a change of underwear, a razor, and a little food), he hitchhikes (on a motorcycle) to his daughter Clara's home in Baltimore. He enjoys the ride, thinking it "a fine way to spend his last free day" (118) and imagining that the other motorists must envy the motorcycle's ability to move "hornet-like" in and out of traffic, "stripped to the bare essentials of a motor and two wheels" (118).

Arriving at the cluttered but happy home of his daughter Clara, who is astonished by the sight of her 82-year-old father arriving on a motorcycle, Mr. Carpenter tells her that he's decided to move into an old folks' home. He asks to stay with Clara's family while he waits for his name to come up on the home's waiting list. Clara's family is large—five sons and a daughter. The only daughter, Francie, 13, is Mr. Carpenter's favorite grandchild because she displays her feelings so openly.

The wait becomes longer not only because of the nursing home, but also because of Mr. Carpenter's family. Clara, her husband, and their children, as well as Mr. Carpenter's four other daughters, all try to convince him to stay with them. Although he is proud that his daughters have all turned out so well, "good, strong women with happy families" (121), he simply tells them that his decision is firm. He considers himself a lucky man.

As Mr. Carpenter contemplates the problems of growing old and the pathetic weakness of aging, he recalls an old school teacher of his (Lollie Simpson), who said she'd just sit and eat boxes of fudge and grow fat when she got old. He admires her spunk. As for himself, he chooses to remain independent, attempting to distance himself from his family so that he'll be able to make the break.

On the day that Mr. Carpenter finally moves into the home, Clara cries all the way there. At the home he meets his roommate, Mr. Pond, who had not wanted his family to put him in the home. Clara and Francie say good-bye, assured by Mr. Carpenter that he will call if he needs anything. Mr. Pond thinks that they've left him there to be rid of him, but Mr. Carpenter tells him that the move was his choice, to avoid the fate of others who "[hang] around making burdens of themselves, hoping to be loved" (125). Mr. Pond, however, asks a pointed question: "If you don't care about being loved . . . how come it would bother you to be a burden?" (126).

Instead of responding, Mr. Carpenter just watches out the window as Clara's car drives away. Then he lies down on his bed, listening to a "neuter voice" (136) which urges him not to give in at the end, to die gracefully. And he hopes fervently that Lollie Simpson is alive somewhere eating fudge and getting fat.

"A Woman Like a Fieldstone House." *Ladies' Home Journal* Aug. 1989: 86+. One of Tyler's best stories, "A Woman Like a Fieldstone House" captures the drama of what Tyler has called the most affecting event of all: the passage of time. The stages that Corey goes through in her life are mirrored by the reappearances of the seventeen-year locusts. With each return of the insects, Corey has moved into a different stage of life, with life-altering changes that she could never have imagined. These seemingly ordinary yet life-changing events have crept up on her imperceptibly. Therefore she doesn't even realize how important they are as they happen to her. Yet, with the retrospective view of time, Corey comes to understand her life more and more clearly, although never completely.

Synopsis: 1936—First Cycle: Young Corey becomes squeamish after being stung by something at her twelfth birthday party. Then in May, the seventeen-year locusts (cicadas) hatch out. Her father explains the insects as a cycle of nature just as her mother had recently explained the facts of life to her. Corey does not like the insects at all and spends the summer hopping around to avoid stepping on them. By mid-June, however, almost without her noticing it, the cicadas have gone.

1953—Second Cycle: Corey is now 29 and married to Ben, an insurance salesman. They have three children: toddler Dudley, 6-year-old Danny, and 8-year-old Virginia. While hanging out diapers one day, Corey discovers the cicada holes in her backyard and remembers when the insects had come seventeen years earlier. Now she does not mind the insects so much, although she has to keep a close watch on Dudley to prevent him from eating them. Danny and Virginia, however, love playing with the cicadas.

Corey's friend, Marilyn Holmes, is not so enthusiastic. She makes up several funny moves to avoid the creatures: the Locust Walk, Stomp, and Exit. Over the past seventeen years many changes have taken place. Corey likes some of these changes, such as air conditioning, which she does not have yet. That's OK, though, because she really prefers a breeze. Ben says that she is like his grandmother's old fieldstone house, which it takes the weather a while to get through. At this stage in her life, Corey is happy and busy raising a family.

1970—Third Cycle: Now Corey is 46. Her youngest child Dudley is in college. Ben is recovering from major surgery. The cicadas return, but, because of all the new malls and developments that have been built since 1953, they are having trouble emerging from their pupae. Thinking back to the insects' previous appearance, Corey wonders where her friend Marilyn is now.

Corey is relieved that it is Virginia (now married to Ted) who has to worry about keeping her granddaughter Hillary from eating locusts. Corey's pet cat Calvert enjoys catching and eating the bugs. Dudley bets his girlfriend Denise five dollars that she won't eat one of the bug's wings, but Denise does. Then a week or so later he bets her that she won't eat a whole one. For a few days they dicker the price of the bet up to fifty dollars, but by then the locusts are gone.

1987—Fourth Cycle: By the time the cicadas return, many changes have taken place. Ben is dead, and Corey is having to slow down herself. Now 63, she goes out walking to get exercise after a recent heart attack. On one walk she mistakes her new neighbor's cheese cloth covered tree for a statue of the Madonna. Every day Virginia calls to check up on her mother. But when Corey mentions the cicadas, Virginia says that she does not remember playing with the locusts as a child.

Elise, Virginia's youngest child and Corey's favorite grandchild, drops by. In spite of her fears because of what she has heard about the locusts, Elise bravely walks over to her grandmother's to read her the paper because Corey's eyesight is failing badly. Corey attempts to ease Elise's fears as best she can. Then they discuss the recipes for locusts that are printed in the paper.

Corey thinks of the changes that have taken place over the years. Dudley is now married (to Laura, not Denise) and living in California. Danny has moved around several times. Corey even has air conditioning now. As usual, the locusts leave in June. Late in September, however, while she is cleaning windows, Corey finds a dead insect stuck to a window screen. And for some reason she leaves it there.

worldview. (AT, BL, DHR, "Laps," SM) From time to time Tyler attempts to step back from her characters and present a larger worldview of life. In *The Accidental Tourist*, Muriel Pritchett wonders what Martians would think if they landed outside a hospital emergency room and saw how helpful human beings can be. In *Dinner at the Homesick Restaurant*, Pearl's memory of the perfect day has her enjoying "such a beautiful green planet" (DHR 277). In "Laps," Mrs. Bond wonders what Martians would think of the various body types represented at the neighborhood pool. And in *Saint Maybe*, Doug Bedloe reads a short story about aliens who split up two houses and juxtapose the halves of the two families to see if humans can cooperate with each other. When a child in one family gets sick, the mother reaches out to him, thus proving that humans can transcend family boundaries.

Joe Worth. (SC) partner in Eli Everjohn's detective agency in Caro Mill.

Maureen Worth. (SC) a neighbor of Justine and Duncan Peck's in Caro Mill.

Mrs. Wright. (BL) Daleys' neighbor, whose dog Maggie (Daley) Moran yells at for peeing on her mother's only rose bush.

writing. (AT) Macon Leary's occupation as a writer gives Tyler the opportunity to express her own love of writing and the challenges that it presents. Just as Macon struggles to express in words the essence of the places he visits, so, too, Tyler attempts to convey the essence of her characters.

X, Y, Z

"Your Place is Empty." *New Yorker* 22 Nov. 1976: 45–54. Another of
Tyler's stories about foreigners, "Your Place is Empty," transcends that
genre to convey a larger sense of any individual's isolation anywhere in the
world. Mrs. Ardavi's problem is not restricted to language or geography.
Like her son and daughter-in-law, she is simply struggling with the universal
human need to communicate and to make connections to the people around
her. Unfortunately, the limitations of language (any language) and the cultural differences she encounters work against her. Therefore the story ends
on a sad note that perhaps serves as a commentary on the inherent isolation
of the human condition in general.

    Synopsis: It has been twelve years since Hassan Ardavi has seen his mother,
so in October he invites her to come visit his family in America. Hassan's
wife, Elizabeth, an American, expects her mother-in-law to stay about three
months. Still knowledgeable of Iranian customs, Hassan anticipates a six-
month visit. Mrs. Ardavi, however, plans to spend a full year with her son's
family. In preparation for her mother-in-law's visit, Elizabeth learns some
Persian phrases so that she can communicate a little. Elizabeth and Hassan
also fix up a room on the third story of their brick colonial home so that
Mrs. Ardavi will have some privacy.

    Arriving at the airport and speaking no English, Mrs. Ardavi feels quite
strange in America. At first she doesn't even recognize Hassan because he
has changed so much. During the drive home, Hassan's mother, who has
stored up hundreds of stories to tell her son about Iran and his many relatives, is disappointed that he does not talk to her much; soon she, too,

becomes silent. Once they arrive home, to her surprise and relief, Elizabeth greets Mrs. Ardavi in Persian and makes her feel more at ease. First Mrs. Ardavi wants to see Hilary, Elizabeth and Hassan's daughter and her only grandchild. Mrs. Ardavi has brought Muslim medals for the child to wear on a necklace (for protection), even though Hassan no longer practices his religion and scoffs at her beliefs.

During the next month, Mrs. Ardavi begins to adjust to America as best she can, and life begins to fall into a routine. Hassan leaves very early each morning and works long days as a doctor. Left to themselves, Elizabeth and Mrs. Ardavi eat breakfast and talk, as much as Elizabeth's limited Persian will permit, mostly about Hilary. Then after breakfast Mrs. Ardavi writes letters to her many relatives while Elizabeth cleans house. Mrs. Ardavi tells her sisters about how organized America is and how terribly wasteful.

As Mrs. Ardavi observes her granddaughter's less than strict American upbringing, she recalls her own restrictive, unhappy childhood. Yet she still feels compelled to criticize the way Elizabeth is raising Hilary. Whenever Mrs. Ardavi sees something that she doesn't approve of, she starts saying, "In Iran. . . ." If Hassan is around, he comes to Elizabeth's rescue and retorts, "But this is not Iran, remember?" (47). Otherwise Elizabeth just has to grin and bear it.

Having settled in more, Mrs. Ardavi starts taking over the cooking duties from Elizabeth, who becomes a little upset but still doesn't say anything. Eventually all Mrs. Ardavi does is cook and then watch television and talk to her son. She begins to yearn for better language skills to express her personality, but only succeeds in annoying Hassan with her attempts to gain attention. As Mrs. Ardavi remembers her past life, she thinks about her three sons—Hassan, Ali, the oldest now dead, and Babak, whose wife is expecting their first child—and her husband, who had died just six years after they married, leaving her a widow for all these years. She also worries about death, not her own, but the deaths of her remaining sons, whom she fears will die before her.

After the new year, Hassan takes his mother to the dentist to see about her bad teeth. Before the dentist can work on her teeth again, however, it is February. By now Mrs. Ardavi is getting on Elizabeth's nerves so badly that Elizabeth is starting to withdraw. Matters come to a head one day when Mrs. Ardavi blames Elizabeth for making Hilary sick by taking her out on a cold day without covering the child's ears. When Hassan comes home, Elizabeth talks to him alone in their room. Then Hassan talks to his mother, and she finally sees how matters stand. Even though her other dental appointments have been scheduled, she tells Hassan that she misses her sisters and wants to return home. Hassan does not attempt to dissuade her. Mrs. Ardavi leaves on March 3, still looking "undeniably a foreigner" (54) as she boards her plane.

Zack. (CN) a boat mechanic.

Primary Bibliography

NOVELS

If Morning Ever Comes. New York: Knopf, 1964. Paperback: Bantam, 1965; Popular Library, 1977; Berkley, 1983; Ivy Books, 1992; Fawcett, 1996.

The Tin Can Tree. New York: Knopf, 1965. Paperback: Bantam, 1966; Popular Library, 1977; Berkley, 1983; Ivy Books, 1992; Fawcett, 1996.

A Slipping-Down Life. New York: Knopf, 1970. Paperback: Bantam, 1971; Popular Library, 1977; Berkley, 1983; Ivy Books, 1992; Fawcett, 1997.

The Clock Winder. New York: Knopf, 1972. Paperback: Bantam, 1973; Popular Library, 1977; Berkley, 1983; Ivy Books, 1992; Fawcett, 1996.

Celestial Navigation. New York: Knopf, 1974. Paperback: Bantam, 1976; Popular Library, 1980; Warner, 1983; Berkley, 1984; Ivy Books, 1993; Fawcett, 1996.

Searching for Caleb. New York: Knopf, 1976. Paperback: Popular Library, 1977; Berkley, 1983; Ivy Books, 1993; Fawcett, 1997.

Earthly Possessions. New York: Knopf, 1977. Paperback: Popular Library, 1978; Warner, 1983; Berkley, 1984; Ivy Books, 1993; Fawcett, 1996.

Morgan's Passing. New York: Knopf, 1980. Paperback: Berkley, 1981; Ivy Books, 1992; Fawcett, 1996.

Dinner at the Homesick Restaurant. New York: Knopf, 1982. Paperback: Berkley, 1983; Ivy Books, 1992; Fawcett, 1996.

The Accidental Tourist. New York: Knopf, 1985. Paperback: Berkley, 1986.

Breathing Lessons. New York: Knopf, 1988. Paperback: Berkley, 1989.

Saint Maybe. New York: Knopf, 1991. Paperback: Ivy Books, 1992; Fawcett, 1996.

Ladder of Years. New York: Knopf, 1995. Paperback: Fawcett, 1996.

SHORT STORIES

"Laura." *Archive* Mar. 1959: 36–37.

"The Lights on the River." *Archive* Oct. 1959: 5–6.

"The Bridge." *Archive* Mar. 1960: 10–15.

"I Never Saw Morning." *Archive* Apr. 1961: 11–14. [Reprinted in *Under Twenty-Five: Duke Narrative and Verse, 1945–1962*. Ed. William Blackburn. Durham: Duke University Press, 1963: 157–66.]

"The Saints in Caesar's Household." *Archive* Apr. 1961: 7–10. [Reprinted in Jessie Rehder, *The Young Writer at Work*. New York: Odyssey, 1962: 75–83; and in *Under Twenty-Five: Duke Narrative and Verse, 1945–1962*. Ed. William Blackburn. Durham: Duke University Press, 1963: 146–56.]

"The Baltimore Birth Certificate." *Critic* Feb. 1963: 41–45.

"I Play Kings." *Seventeen* Aug. 1963: 338–41.

"A Street of Bugles." *Saturday Evening Post* 30 Nov. 1963: 64–66. [Reprinted in *Saturday Evening Post* July-Aug. 1989: 54–57+.]

"Nobody Answers the Door." *Antioch Review* 24 (Fall 1964): 379–86.

"Dry Water." *Southern Review* NS 1 (Spring 1965): 259–91.

"I'm Not Going to Ask You Again." *Harper's* Sept. 1965: 88–98.

"As the Earth Gets Old." *New Yorker* 29 Oct. 1966: 60–64.

"Two People and a Clock on the Wall." *New Yorker* 19 Nov. 1966: 207–17.

"The Genuine Fur Eyelashes." *Mademoiselle* Jan. 1967: 102–3+.

"The Tea-Machine." *Southern Review* NS 3 (Winter 1967): 171–79.

"The Feather Behind the Rock." *New Yorker* 12 Aug. 1967: 26–30. [Reprinted in *A Duke Miscellany: Narrative and Verse of the Sixties*. Ed. William Blackburn. Durham: Duke University Press, 1970: 154–62.]

"A Flaw in the Crust of the Earth." *Reporter* 2 Nov. 1967: 43–46.

"Who Would Want a Little Boy?" *Ladies' Home Journal* May 1968: 132–33+.

"The Common Courtesies." *McCall's* June 1968: 62–63+. [Reprinted in *Prize Stories 1969: The O. Henry Awards*. Ed. William Abrahams. Garden City: Doubleday, 1969: 121–30.]

"With All Flags Flying." *Redbook* June 1971: 88–89+. [Reprinted in *Prize Stories 1972: The O. Henry Awards*. Ed. William Abrahams. Garden City: Doubleday, 1972: 116–26; and in *Redbook's Famous Fiction*. New York: Redbook, 1972: 84–87.]

"Outside." *Southern Review* NS 7 (Autumn 1971): 1130–44.

"The Bride in the Boatyard." *McCall's* June 1972: 92–93+.

"Respect." *Mademoiselle* June 1972: 146–47+.

"A Misstep of the Mind." *Seventeen* Oct. 1972: 118–19+.

"Spending." *Shenandoah* 24 (Winter 1973): 58–68.

"The Base-Metal Egg." *Southern Review* NS 9 (Summer 1973): 682–86.

"Neutral Ground." *Family Circle* Nov. 1974: 36+.

"Half-Truths and Semi-Miracles." *Cosmopolitan* Dec. 1974: 264–65+.

"A Knack for Languages." *New Yorker* 13 Jan. 1975: 32–37.

"The Artificial Family." *Southern Review* NS 11 (Summer 1975): 615–21. [Reprinted in *The Pushcart Prize: Best of the Small Presses*. Ed. Bill Henderson. New York: Pushcart Book Press, 1976: 11–18; in *Love Stories for the Time*

Being. Eds. Genie D. Chipps and Bill Henderson. Wainscott, NY: Pushcart Press, 1987: 137–46; and in *Selected Stories from the Southern Review, 1965–85*. Ed. Lewis P. Simpson, et al. Baton Rouge: Louisiana State University Press, 1988: 355–61.]

"The Geologist's Maid." *New Yorker* 28 July 1975: 29–33. [Reprinted in *Stories of the Modern South*. Ed. Benjamin Forkner and Patrick Samway, S.J. New York: Bantam, 1978: 343–54.]

"Some Sign That I Ever Made You Happy." *McCall's* Oct. 1975: 90+.

"Your Place is Empty." *New Yorker* 22 Nov. 1976: 45–54. [Reprinted in *The Best American Short Stories 1977: And the Yearbook of the American Short Story*. Ed. Martha Foley. Boston: Houghton Mifflin, 1977: 317–37.]

"Holding Things Together." *New Yorker* 24 Jan. 1977: 30–35. [Reprinted in *We Are the Stories We Tell: The Best Short Stories by North American Women Since 1945*. Ed. Wendy Martin. New York: Pantheon Books, 1990: 150–63.]

"Average Waves in Unprotected Waters." *New Yorker* 28 Feb. 1977: 32–36. [Reprinted in *Literature: An Introduction to Fiction, Poetry, and Drama*. Ed. X. J. Kennedy. 5th ed. New York: HarperCollins, 1991: 136–42.]

"Under the Bosom Tree." *Archive* Spring 1977: 72–77.

"Foot-Footing On." *Mademoiselle* Nov. 1977: 82+.

"Uncle Ahmad." *Quest/77* Nov.-Dec. 1977: 76–82.

"Linguistics." *Washington Post Magazine* 12 Nov. 1978: 38–40+.

"Laps." *Parents* Aug. 1981: 66–67+.

"The Country Cook." *Harper's* Mar. 1982: 54–62.

"Teenage Wasteland." *Seventeen* Nov. 1983: 144–45+. [Reprinted in *The Editors' Choice: New American Short Stories*. Vol. 1. Ed. George E. Murphy, Jr. New York: Bantam, 1985: 256–66; and in *New Women and New Fiction*. Ed. Susan Cahill. New York: New American Library, 1986: 133–45.]

"Rerun." *New Yorker* 4 July 1988: 20–32.

"A Woman Like a Fieldstone House." *Ladies' Home Journal* Aug. 1989: 86+. [Reprinted in *Louder Than Words: 22 Authors Donate New Stories to Benefit Share Our Strength's Fight Against Hunger, Homelessness and Illiteracy*. Ed. William Shore. New York: Vintage, 1989: 1–15.]

"People Who Don't Know the Answers." *New Yorker* 26 Aug. 1991: 26–36.

"The Runaway Wife." *Ladies' Home Journal* Apr. 1995: 130+.

CHILDREN'S BOOKS

The Tumble Tower. Mitra Modarressi, illustrator. New York: Orchard Books, 1993.

NONFICTION

"Because I Want More than One Life." *Washington Post* 15 Aug. 1976: G1+. [Reprinted as "Confessions of a Novelist" in *Duke Alumni Register* Feb. 1977: 20.]

"Olives Out of a Bottle." *Archive* 87 (Spring 1975): 70–90. [Reprinted in *Critical Essays on Anne Tyler*. Ed. Alice Hall Petry. New York: G. K. Hall, 1992: 28–39.]

"Still Just Writing." *The Writer on Her Work: Contemporary Women Writers Reflect on Their Art and Situation*. Ed. Janet Sternburg. New York: Norton, 1980: 3–16.

"Why I Still Treasure 'The Little House.' " *New York Times Book Review* 9 Nov. 1986: 56.

"Youth Talks about Youth: 'Will This Seem Ridiculous?' " *Vogue* 1 Feb. 1965: 85+.

IMPORTANT TYLER BOOK REVIEWS

Since 1972, Anne Tyler has written over 250 reviews of books by authors ranging from Vladimir Nabokov to Amy Tan. In addition to standard fictional works, she has reviewed a wide variety of books on subjects from photography to fairy tales, including several children's books. In these reviews she usually maintains a strict objectivity, but sometimes she slips and inserts an inkling of her personal views on a number of issues. Below are a few excerpts from some of her more revealing reviews.

"For Barthelme, 'Words Are What Matters.' " [Rev. of *Sadness*, by Donald Barthelme.] *National Observer* 4 Nov. 1972: 21. Tyler's view of people's isolation. "People keep failing. They fail at the usual things—love, change, family life—but more important, they fail to break through a certain insulation that lies between them and the world" (21).

"Of Bitches, Sad Ladies, and Female 'Politics.' " [Rev. of *Bitches and Sad Ladies: An Anthology of Fiction by and About Women*, edited by Pat Rotter.] *National Observer* 22 Feb. 1975: 31. Tyler's humanistic brand of feminism. The stories she likes best are "concerned not so much with the feminine condition as with the human condition, and to suggest otherwise diminishes them" (31). Tyler does not find female authors to be monolithic in their views, nor does she find any "shared quality that sets their work apart from men's" (31). Rather she sees "a surprising range of voices, styles and viewpoints," despite many of the women's stories treating similar situations (31).

" 'The Lonely Hunter': The Ballad of a Sad Lady." [Rev. of *The Lonely Hunter*, by Virginia Spencer Carr.] *National Observer* 16 Aug. 1975: 17. Tyler's reticence to talk about works in progress. Tyler is amazed that McCullers "would discuss her work at length with anyone, even in its embryonic stages—an act the very thought of which would make most writers [such as herself] shudder" (17).

Tyler's desire to live other lives through her writing. "Most writers . . . are not content to live only one life and must invent others on paper" (17).

"A Photo Album of Snips and Surprises." [Rev. of *Beyond the Bedroom Wall: A Family Album*, by Larry Woiwode.] *National Observer* 18 Oct. 1975: 21. Tyler's concept of plot. The book's plot is "almost nonexistent, but when you reach the end you realize that enormous events have taken place. It's a book that works approximately the same way life does, in other words" (21).

Tyler's view of time. "In books about families, the mere passage of time is often the most poignant event of all" (21).

Tyler's view of the ordinary. The book's author is "a master . . . at turning situations inside out—at showing us something so commonplace that it is almost hackneyed, then surprising us with what lies underneath" (21).

"Tales of an Apocalypse Served Up in a Tureen." [Rev. of *The Collected Stories of Hortense Calisher.*] *National Observer* 22 Nov. 1975: 21. Tyler on selfhood. "The warmest and most delicately wrought of these stories are the ones in which the division is between past and present—our present selves yearning over our past selves" (21).

"Women Writers: Equal but Separate." [Rev. of *Literary Women: The Great Writers*, by Ellen Moers.] *National Observer* 10 Apr. 1976: 21. Tyler and feminism. "There is no room in these [feminist] theories for the woman as mere individual" (21). "It's my personal feeling that only a portion of my life—and almost none of my writing life—is much affected by what sex I happen to be. And I can't imagine that even that portion would be affected in the same way for everyone" (21).

"Fairy Tales: More than Meets the Ear." [Rev. of *The Uses of Enchantment: The Meaning and Importance of Fairy Tales*, by Bruno Bettelheim.] *National Observer* 8 May 1976: 21. Tyler and fairy tales. Tyler claims to dislike fairy tales' "imperfect reasoning, haphazard plots, and apparently unteachable heroes, who always made the same mistake three times" (21). Yet she has found that "Beauty and the Beast" has become "incorporated into" her life in many ways (21).

[Rev. of *The Master and Other Stories*, by Sue Kaufman; and *Angels at the Ritz and Other Stories*, by William Trevor.] *New York Times Book Review* 11 July 1976: 7. Tyler's view of characters and the ordinary. Fully developed characters "give us a sense of layers unexposed, mysteries unsolved. . . . We are reminded that even the most ordinary situation can suddenly take a quarter-turn and assume a whole new meaning" (7).

[Rev. of *Crossing the Border, Fifteen Tales*, by Joyce Carol Oates.] *New York Times Book Review* 18 July 1976: 8+. Tyler's comments on the isolation of individuals. "The real borders are personal: the boundaries by which each individual defines himself and, rightly or wrongly, fends off other individuals" (8).

"Writers Talk about Writing." [Rev. of *Writers at Work: The Paris Review Interviews*, edited by George Plimpton.] *National Observer* 11 Sept. 1976: 19. Tyler's definition of a writer. A writer is "someone who works hard, treasures his privacy, and often acts a little befuddled from living in too many worlds. . . . He is not . . . a public sort of person, or even very social. He is too busy protecting what he considers to be his precarious good luck in having managed to create, from a handful of blank-faced and chaotic words, something wholly new and wholly his own" (19).

[Rev. of *A Sea-Change*, by Lois Gould.] *New York Times Book Review* 19 Sept. 1976: 4–5. Tyler's criticism of feminist literature. As the novel's main character evolves from "victim to aggressor," we see the "ultimate metamorphosis: woman to man. Except that we're going by a stunted definition of woman here, and an even more stunted definition of man" (5).

Tyler's opinion of feminist portrayals of the concept of male and female. She dislikes this book because it is "less a story than a statement—a generalization on the very nature of male and female. Generalizations of any kind tend to arouse a reader's suspicions; generalizations of this kind (men are brutal, and women love it) arouse out-and-out irritation" (5).

"Farewell to the Story as Imperiled Species." [Rev. of *Prize Stories 1977: The O. Henry Awards*, edited by William Abrahams; *Winter's Tales 22*, edited by James Wright; *The Sea Birds Are Still Alive*, by Toni Cade Bambara; *Yellow Roses*, by Elizabeth Cullinan; *Slow Days, Fast Company: The World, the Flesh, and L.A.*, by Eve Babitz; and *In the Miro District and Other Stories*, by Peter Taylor.] *National Observer* 9 May 1977: 23. Tyler's feelings about writing short stories. "The great joy in writing a short story comes from the fact that you feel free to take a few chances. If it doesn't work, you've lost a couple of days—not, as with novels, a couple of years" (23).

"Starting Out Submissive." [Rev. of *The Women's Room*, by Marilyn French.] *New York Times Book Review* 16 Oct. 1977: 7+. Tyler's defense of men against feminists. She dislikes the novel's female victim perspective, which gives men "no chance to tell their side of the story. Compared to the women—each separate and distinct, each rich in character—the men tend to blur together. They're all villains, and cardboard villains at that" (7).

"After the Prom." [Rev. of *Burning Questions*, by Alix Kates Shulman.] *Washington Post Book World* 26 Mar. 1978: G3. Tyler and feminism. Tyler sympathizes with the main character's plight because she is not merely struggling against victimization, but rather attempting to discover " 'how to live, how to be,' " in other words "a way of making the best use of her life. What she's struggling against, from childhood onward, is that cursory, pigeonholing glance that 'places' her and forgets her; and who wouldn't sympathize with that?" (G3).

"Looking Backward." [Rev. of *Victim of the Aurora*, by Thomas Keneally; and *The Caspian Circle*, by Donné Raffat.] *New York Times Book Review* 26 Mar. 1978: 12–13. Tyler's description of Iran. "We observe a culture trained to the most exaggerated formality and graciousness, but capable of comical family feuds and fistfights" (13).

Tyler and the objectivity of the narrator. What impresses her most about the book is "the stillness at its center: its narrator, wary and alert, condemned . . . to watch from a distance all the rest of his life" (13).

"Lady of the Lone Star State." [Rev. of *A Prince of a Fellow*, by Shelby Hearon.] *Washington Post Book World* 2 Apr. 1978: E4. Tyler's need for the reader to care about characters. Tyler's "axiom": "A book can have just about anyone for a heroine—even an outright villainess—as long as she assigns herself some worth that makes us want to identify with her. If she doesn't we stop caring" (E4).

"The Artist as an Old Photographer." [Rev. of *Picture Palace*, by Paul Theroux.] *New York Times Book Review* 18 June 1978: 10+. Tyler's genderless view of writing. Tyler praises Paul Theroux for "adopting the voice of a first-person woman narrator—apparently working on the assumption that women aren't all that different from men, which seems reasonable enough to me" (10).

"Woman Coping." [Rev. of *A Woman's Age*, by Rachel Billington.] *New York Times Book Review* 10 Feb. 1980: 15+. Tyler's view of the effects of the passage of time. "The mere progression of time, after all, is affecting in itself: the aging of someone we knew as a child, the reappearance of a character we thought long gone, the sight of a once purposeless woman gathering strength and coming into her own" (15).

"Everyday Events." [Rev. of *A Matter of Feeling*, by Janine Boissard.] *New York Times Book Review* 9 Mar. 1980: 10+. Tyler's appreciation of the ordinary. Even though the main plot of the novel concerns a love affair, "more important are the everyday events, sometimes non-events, of the household, weaving in and out of [the] story" (10).

"At the Still Center of a Dream." [Rev. of *The Salt Eaters*, by Toni Cade Bambara.] *Washington Post Book World* 30 Mar. 1980: 1–2. Tyler on dreams. "In dreams, a single detail from one scene can pivot the dreamer into another scene—something unrelated, incongruous in waking life but in sleep, possessed of a logic all its own. The transition is so seamless that the dreamer hardly notices" (1).

"Feminism and Power: A New Social Contract?" [Rev. of *Powers of the Weak*, by Elizabeth Janeway.] *Chicago Sun-Times Book Week* 8 June 1980: 12. Tyler's brand of feminism. Tyler admires the book's optimistic use of feminism "merely as an index to power relationships in general," an optimism that transcends "the victory-is-ours variety" to "[convey] a genuine hopefulness for the human race" (12).

"The Fine, Full World of Welty." [Rev. of *The Collected Stories of Eudora Welty*.] *Washington Star* 26 Oct. 1980: D1+. Welty's impact on Tyler. "For me as a girl—a Northerner growing up in the South, longingly gazing over the fence at the rich, tangled lives of the Southern neighbors—Eudora Welty was a window upon the world. If I wondered what went on in the country churches and 'Colored Only' cafes, her writing showed me, as clearly as if I'd been invited inside" (D7).

"The Stoics and Trudgers." [Rev. of *American Rose*, by Julia Markus.] *New York Times Book Review* 8 Mar. 1981: 9+. Tyler's view of family ties and her cyclical view of time. The novel conveys "the broader confusion that exists in every family: Each member always is, in fact, entangled with the others, and events do repeat themselves, and the succession of generations can appear less linear than circular" (9).

"The Glass of Fashion." [Rev. of *The Language of Clothes*, by Alison Lurie.] *New Republic* 23 Dec. 1981: 32+. Tyler's opinion of fashion. "I remain as baffled as ever by our lemming-like rush to shorter hemlines, or flatter bodies or whatever style seems subliminally implanted in our heads season by season" (34).

"Kentucky Cameos." [Rev. of *Shiloh and Other Stories*, by Bobbie Ann Mason.] *New Republic* 1 Nov. 1982: 36+. Tyler's sympathy for male characters. "It's heartening to find male characters portrayed sympathetically, with an appreciation for the fact that they can feel as confused and hurt and lonely as the female characters" (38).

"The Ladies and the Tiger." [Rev. of *Right-Wing Women*, by Andrea Dworkin.] *New Republic* 21 Feb. 1983: 34–35. Tyler and feminism. Tyler objects to the author's sweeping feminist generalizations about all women being exploited. Such a view leaves a "strangely limited view of men" (35).

"Male and Lonely." [Rev. of *Modern Baptists*, by James Wilcox.] *New York Times Book Review* 31 July 1983: 1+. Tyler's book reviewing methods. "Every reviewer, no doubt, has methods for marking choice passages in a book. Mine is a system of colored paper clips; yellow means funny" (22).

"He Did It All for Jane Elizabeth Firesheets." [Rev. of *Off for the Sweet Hereafter*, by T. R. Pearson.] *New York Times Book Review* 15 June 1986: 9. Tyler's description of *Southern*. "Certainly the constant straying from 'What Happened' to 'Who, Exactly, It Happened To' (and 'Who His Grandfather Was,' besides) seems distinctly if not uniquely Southern" (9).

"Marriage and the Ties That Bind." [Rev. of *Intimate Partners: Patterns in Love and Marriage*, by Maggie Scarf.] *Washington Post Book World* 15 Feb. 1987: 3+. Tyler's view of marriage. This book on marriage presents no "average" marriages, for Tyler asserts, "An ordinary, run-of-the-mill marriage has in many ways a more dramatic plot than any thriller ever written" (6).

"Bright Scraps of Fiction from Mary Gordon." [Rev. of *Temporary Shelter*, by Mary Gordon.] *Chicago Tribune Books* 29 Mar. 1987: 6–7. Tyler's view of short stories. These stories "perform that fish-and-loaves type miracle that the short story sometimes is capable of. They seem larger than the sum of their parts, bountiful, immense, anything but 'short' " (7).

"The Plodding Life: Dispatches from a Writer's Desk." [Rev. of *The Writing Life*, by Annie Dillard.] *Baltimore Sun* 17 Sept. 1989: M9. Tyler's view on the writing life. There is a paradox inherent in the life of a writer: "That in order to describe the world the writer must withdraw from it" (M9).

Secondary Bibliography

BOOKS

Croft, Robert W. *Anne Tyler: A Bio-Bibliography*. Westport, CT: Greenwood Press, 1995.

Evans, Elizabeth. *Anne Tyler*. New York: Twayne, 1993.

Kissel, Susan S. *Moving On: The Heroines of Shirley Ann Grau, Anne Tyler, and Gail Godwin*. Bowling Green, KY: Bowling Green State University Popular Press, 1996. 69–98.

Linton, Karin. *The Temporal Horizon: A Study of the Theme of Time in Anne Tyler's Major Novels*. Uppsala, Sweden: Acta Universitatis Upsaliensis, 1989.

Petry, Alice Hall. *Understanding Anne Tyler*. Columbia: University of South Carolina Press, 1990.

Petry, Alice Hall, ed. *Critical Essays on Anne Tyler*. New York: G. K. Hall, 1992.

Salwak, Dale, ed. *Anne Tyler as Novelist*. Iowa City: University of Iowa Press, 1994.

Stephens, C. Ralph, ed. *The Fiction of Anne Tyler*. Jackson: University Press of Mississippi, 1990.

Voelker, Joseph C. *Art and the Accidental in Anne Tyler*. Columbia: University of Missouri Press, 1989.

ARTICLES

Allen, Brooke. "Anne Tyler in Mid-Course." *New Criterion* 13 (May 1995): 27–34.

Bennett, Barbara A. "Attempting to Connect: Verbal Humor in the Novels of Anne Tyler." *South Atlantic Review* 60.1 (1995): 57–75.

Betts, Doris. "The Fiction of Anne Tyler." *Southern Quarterly* 21 (Summer 1983):

23–37. [Reprinted in *Women Writers of the Contemporary South*. Ed. Peggy Whitman Prenshaw. Jackson: University of Mississippi Press, 1984: 23–37.]

Binding, Paul. "Anne Tyler." *Separate Country: A Literary Journey through the American South*. New York: Paddington Press, 1979: 198–209. [Reprinted by University Press of Mississippi, 1988: 171–81.]

Bonifer, M. Susan. "Anne Tyler's Southernness: Pearl Tull's Reticence." *Bulletin of the West Virginia Association of College English Teachers* 12 (1990): 35–44.

Bowers, Bradley R. "Anne Tyler's Insiders." *Mississippi Quarterly* 42 (Winter 1988–89): 47–56.

Caesar, Judith. "The Foreigners in Anne Tyler's *Saint Maybe*." *Critique* 37 (Fall 1995): 71–79.

Carson, Barbara Harrell. "Complicate, Complicate: Anne Tyler's Moral Imperative." *Southern Quarterly* 31 (Fall 1992): 24–34.

Crane, Gwen. "Anne Tyler, 1941–." *Modern American Women Writers*. Ed. Lea Baechler and A. Walton Litz. New York: Scribner's, 1991: 499–510.

Eckard, Paula Gallant. "Family and Community in Anne Tyler's *Dinner at the Homesick Restaurant*." *Southern Literary Journal* 22 (Spring 1990): 33–44.

Evans, Elizabeth. " 'Mere Reviews': Anne Tyler as Book Reviewer." *Critical Essays on Anne Tyler*. Ed. Alice Hall Petry. New York: G. K. Hall, 1992: 233–42.

Gibson, Mary Ellis. "Family as Fate: The Novels of Anne Tyler." *Southern Literary Journal* 16 (Fall 1983): 47–58. [Reprinted in *Critical Essays on Anne Tyler*. Ed. Alice Hall Petry. New York: G. K. Hall, 1992: 165–74.]

Gilbert, Susan. "Anne Tyler." *Southern Women Writers: The New Generation*. Ed. Tonette Bond Inge. Tuscaloosa: University of Alabama Press, 1990: 251–78.

Inman, Sue Lile. "The Effects of the Artistic Process: A Study of Three Artist Figures in Anne Tyler's Fiction." *The Fiction of Anne Tyler*. Ed. C. Ralph Stephens. Jackson: University Press of Mississippi, 1990: 55–63.

Jones, Anne. "Home at Last and Homesick Again: The Ten Novels of Anne Tyler." *Hollins Critic* 23 (Apr. 1986): 1–13.

Madden, Deanna. "Ties That Bind: Identity and Sibling Relationships in Anne Tyler's Novels." *The Significance of Sibling Relationships in Literature*. Ed. JoAnna Stephens Mink and Janet Doubler Ward. Bowling Green, KY: Bowling Green State University Popular Press, 1993: 58–69.

Marovitz, Sanford. "Anne Tyler's Emersonian Balance." *Critical Essays on Anne Tyler*. Ed. Alice Hall Petry. New York: G. K. Hall, 1992: 207–20.

Nesanovich, Stella. "The Individual in the Family: Anne Tyler's *Searching for Caleb* and *Earthly Possessions*." *Southern Review* 14 (Winter 1978): 170–76. [Reprinted in *Critical Essays on Anne Tyler*. Ed. Alice Hall Petry. New York: G. K. Hall, 1992: 159–64.]

Petry, Alice Hall. "Bright Books of Life: The Black Norm in Anne Tyler's Novels." *Southern Quarterly* 31 (Fall 1992): 7–13.

Ross-Bryant, Lynn. "Anne Tyler's *Searching for Caleb*: The Sacrality of the Everyday." *Soundings: An Interdisciplinary Journal* 73 (Spring 1990): 191–207.

Shelton, Frank W. "Anne Tyler's Houses." *The Fiction of Anne Tyler*. Ed. C. Ralph Stephens. Jackson: University Press of Mississippi, 1990: 40–46.

Shelton, Frank W. "The Necessary Balance: Distance and Sympathy in the Novels of Anne Tyler." *Southern Review* 20 (Autumn 1984): 851–60. [Reprinted in

Critical Essays on Anne Tyler. Ed. Alice Hall Petry. New York: G. K. Hall, 1992: 175–83.]

Sweeney, Susan Elizabeth. "Anne Tyler's Invented Games: *The Accidental Tourist* and *Breathing Lessons.*" *Southern Quarterly* 34.1 (1995): 81–97.

Torres, Gerardo Z. "Rebuiding the Houses of Tull and Wingo." *Likha* 16.1 (1995): 71–87.

Voelker, Joseph C. "The Semi-Miracle of Time." *World and I* Feb. 1992: 347–57.

Wagner, Joseph B. "Beck Tull: 'The absent presence' in *Dinner at the Homesick Restaurant.*" *The Fiction of Anne Tyler.* Ed. C. Ralph Stephens. Jackson: University Press of Mississippi, 1990: 73–83.

Willrich, Patricia Rowe. "Watching through Windows: A Perspective on Anne Tyler." *Virginia Quarterly Review* 68 (Summer 1992): 497–516.

Zahlan, Anne R. "Anne Tyler." *Fifty Southern Writers After 1900: A Bio-Bibliographical Sourcebook.* Ed. Joseph M. Flora and Robert Bain. Westport, CT: Greenwood Press, 1987: 491–504.

INTERVIEWS

Ballantyne, Michael. "Novel No. 1 Published, No. 2 Typed, No. 3 Is Jelling." *Montreal Star* 21 Nov. 1964: Entertainments 4.

Brooks, Mary Ellen. "Anne Tyler." *The Dictionary of Literary Biography: American Novelists Since World War II.* Ed. James E. Kibler Jr. Detroit: Gale Research, 1980, vol. 6: 336–45.

Brown, Laurie L. "Interviews with Seven Contemporary Writers." *Southern Quarterly* 21 (Summer 1983): 3–22.

Cook, Bruce. "A Writer—During School Hours." *Detroit News* 6 Apr. 1980: E1+. [Reprinted in *Critical Essays on Anne Tyler.* Ed. Alice Hall Petry. New York: G. K. Hall, 1992: 50–52.]

Dorner, George. "A Brief Interview with a Brilliant Author from Baltimore." *The Rambler* 2 (1979): 22.

English, Sarah. "An Interview with Anne Tyler." *The Dictionary of Literary Biography Yearbook: 1982.* Detroit: Gale Research, 1983: 193–94.

Forsey, Joan. "An Author at 22." Montreal *Gazette* 2 Oct. 1964: 18.

Harper, Natalie. "Searching for Anne Tyler." *Simon's Rock of Bard College Bulletin* 4 (Fall 1984): 6–7.

Lamb, Wendy. "An Interview with Anne Tyler." *Iowa Journal of Literary Studies* 3 (1981): 59–64.

Lueloff, Jorie. "Authoress Explains Why Women Dominate in South." (Baton Rouge) *Morning Advocate* 8 Feb. 1965: A11.

Michaels, Marguerite. "Anne Tyler, Writer 8:05 to 3:30." *New York Times Book Review* 8 May 1977: 13+. [Reprinted in *Critical Essays on Anne Tyler.* Ed. Alice Hall Petry. New York: G. K. Hall, 1992: 40–44.]

Ridley, Clifford. "Anne Tyler: A Sense of Reticence Balanced by 'Oh, Well, Why Not?' " *National Observer* 22 July 1972: 23. [Reprinted in *Critical Essays on Anne Tyler.* Ed. Alice Hall Petry. New York: G. K. Hall, 1992: 24–27.]

Woizesko, Helene, and Michael Scott Cain. "Anne Tyler." *Northeast Rising Sun* 1 (June-July 1976): 28–30.

SELECTED REVIEWS OF TYLER'S NOVELS

If Morning Ever Comes

Gloag, Julian. "Home Was a House Full of Women." *Saturday Review* 26 Dec. 1964: 37–38.

Long, John Allan. " 'New' Southern Novel." *Christian Science Monitor* 21 Jan. 1965: 9.

Prescott, Orville. "Return to the Hawkes Family." *New York Times* 11 Nov. 1964: 41. [Reprinted in *Critical Essays on Anne Tyler*. Ed. Alice Hall Petry. New York: G. K. Hall, 1992: 61–62.]

Ridley, Clifford A. "From First Novels to the Loves of William Shakespeare." *National Observer* 16 Nov. 1964: 21.

Saal, Rollene W. "Loveless Household." *New York Times Book Review* 22 Nov. 1964: 52.

Sullivan, Walter. "Worlds Past and Future: A Christian and Several from the South." *Sewanee Review* 73 (Autumn 1965): 719–26.

The Tin Can Tree

Bell, Millicent. "Tobacco Road Updated." *New York Times Book Review* 21 Nov. 1965: 77.

Frankel, Haskel. "Closing a Family Wound." *Saturday Review* 20 Nov. 1965: 50. [Reprinted in *Critical Essays on Anne Tyler*. Ed. Alice Hall Petry. New York: G. K. Hall, 1992: 63–64.]

Gardner, Marilyn. "Figurines in a Paperweight." *Christian Science Monitor* 10 Feb. 1966: 7.

Ridley, Clifford A. "Spark and Tyler Are Proof Anew of Knopf Knowledge of Top Fiction." *National Observer* 29 Nov. 1965: 25.

A Slipping-Down Life

Edelstein, Arthur. "Art and Artificiality in Some Recent Fiction." *Southern Review* NS 9 (July 1973): 736–44. [Reprinted in *Critical Essays on Anne Tyler*. Ed. Alice Hall Petry. New York: G. K. Hall, 1992: 65–66.]

Lee, Hermione. "Frantic Obsessions." (London) *Observer* 29 May 1983: 30.

"New and Noteworthy." *New York Times Book Review* 3 Apr. 1977: 53–54.

The Clock Winder

Easton, Elizabeth. *Saturday Review* 17 June 1972: 77.

Levin, Martin. "New & Novel." *New York Times Book Review* 21 May 1972: 31. [Reprinted in *Critical Essays on Anne Tyler*. Ed. Alice Hall Petry. New York: G. K. Hall, 1992: 67.]

Smith, Catharine Mack. "Indian File." *New Statesman* 16 Feb. 1973: 240–41.

Celestial Navigation

Bell, Pearl K. "The Artist as Hero." *New Leader* 4 Mar. 1974: 17–18.

Clapp, Susannah. "In the Abstract." *Times Literary Supplement* 23 May 1975: 577. [Reprinted in *Critical Essays on Anne Tyler*. Ed. Alice Hall Petry. New York: G. K. Hall, 1992: 69–70.]

Godwin, Gail. "Two Novels." *New York Times Book Review* 28 Apr. 1974: 34–35. [Reprinted in *Critical Essays on Anne Tyler*. Ed. Alice Hall Petry. New York: G. K. Hall, 1992: 71–72.]

Pryce-Jones, Alan. "Five Easy Pieces: One Work of Art." *Washington Post Book World* 24 Mar. 1974: 2. [Reprinted in *Critical Essays on Anne Tyler*. Ed. Alice Hall Petry. New York: G. K. Hall, 1992: 73–74.]

Ridley, Clifford A. "Novels: A Hit Man, a Clown, a Genius." *National Observer* 4 May 1974: 23.

Searching for Caleb

Howes, Victor. "Freedom: Theme of Pecks' Battle Hymns." *Christian Science Monitor* 14 Jan. 1976: 23.

Just, Ward. "A 'Wonderful' Writer and Her 'Magical' Novel." *Washington Post* 10 Mar. 1976: B9.

Peters, Catherine. "Opting Out." *Times Literary Supplement* 27 Aug. 1976: 1060. [Reprinted in *Critical Essays on Anne Tyler*. Ed. Alice Hall Petry. New York: G. K. Hall, 1992: 80–81.]

Pollitt, Katha. "Two Novels." *New York Times Book Review* 18 Jan. 1976: 22. [Reprinted in *Critical Essays on Anne Tyler*. Ed. Alice Hall Petry. New York: G. K. Hall, 1992: 82–83.]

Updike, John. "Family Ways." *New Yorker* 29 Mar. 1976: 110–12. [Reprinted in *Critical Essays on Anne Tyler*. Ed. Alice Hall Petry. New York: G. K. Hall, 1992: 75–79; and in his *Hugging the Shore: Essays and Criticism*. New York: Knopf, 1983: 273–78.]

Earthly Possessions

Delbanco, Nicholas. *New Republic* 28 May 1977: 35–36. [Reprinted in *Critical Essays on Anne Tyler*. Ed. Alice Hall Petry. New York: G. K. Hall, 1992: 85–87.]

Johnson, Diane. "Your Money or Your Life." *Washington Post Book World* 29 May 1977: F1+.

Leonard, John. "A Loosening of Roots." *New York Times* 3 May 1977: 39.

Reed, Nancy Gail. "Novel Follows Unpredictable Escape Routes." *Christian Science Monitor* 22 June 1977: 23.

Updike, John. "Loosened Roots." *New Yorker* 6 June 1977: 130+. [Reprinted in *Critical Essays on Anne Tyler*. Ed. Alice Hall Petry. New York: G. K. Hall, 1992: 88–91; and in his *Hugging the Shore: Essays and Criticism*. New York: Knopf, 1983: 278–83.]

Morgan's Passing

Disch, Thomas M. "The Great Imposter." *Washington Post Book World* 16 Mar. 1980: 5.

Grier, Peter. "Bright Novel That Overstretches Credibility." *Christian Science Monitor* 14 Apr. 1980: B9. [Reprinted in *Critical Essays on Anne Tyler*. Ed. Alice Hall Petry. New York: G. K. Hall, 1992: 101–2.]

Hoffman, Eva. "When the Fog Never Lifts." *Saturday Review* 15 Mar. 1980: 38–39. [Reprinted in *Critical Essays on Anne Tyler*. Ed. Alice Hall Petry. New York: G. K. Hall, 1992: 95–97.]

Mojtabai, A.G. "A State of Continual Crisis." *New York Times Book Review* 23 Mar. 1980: 14+. [Reprinted in *Critical Essays on Anne Tyler*. Ed. Alice Hall Petry. New York: G. K. Hall, 1992: 98–100.]

Nesanovich, Stella. "Anne Tyler's *Morgan's Passing*." *Southern Review* 17 (Summer 1981): 619–21.

Prescott, Peter S. "Mr. Chameleon." *Newsweek* 24 Mar. 1980: 82–83+.

Towers, Robert. *New Republic* 22 Mar. 1980: 28+. [Reprinted in *Critical Essays on Anne Tyler*. Ed. Alice Hall Petry. New York: G. K. Hall, 1992: 103–6.]

Updike, John. "Imagining Things." *New Yorker* 23 June 1980: 94+. [Reprinted in his *Hugging the Shore: Essays and Criticism*. New York: Knopf, 1983: 283–92.]

Dinner at the Homesick Restaurant

de Mott, Benjamin. "Funny, Wise and True." *New York Times Book Review* 14 Mar. 1982: 1+. [Reprinted in *Critical Essays on Anne Tyler*. Ed. Alice Hall Petry. New York: G. K. Hall, 1992: 111–14.]

Gornick, Vivian. "Anne Tyler's Arrested Development." *Village Voice* 30 Mar. 1982: 40–41.

Mars-Jones, Adam. "Family Mealtimes." *Times Literary Supplement* 29 Oct. 1982: 1188.

McMurtry, Larry. "Tyler Artfully Mixes Domestic Fare, Tragedy." *Chicago Tribune BookWorld* 21 Mar. 1982: 3.

See, Carolyn. "The Family's Hold—A Caress or Grip?" *Los Angeles Times* 30 Mar. 1982, sec. VI: 6.

Seton, Cynthia Propper. "Generations at Table." *Washington Post Book World* 4 Apr. 1982: 7.

Sheppard, R. Z. "Eat and Run." *Time* 5 Apr. 1982: 77–78.

Updike, John. "On Such a Beautiful Green Little Planet." *New Yorker* 5 Apr. 1982: 189+. [Reprinted in *Critical Essays on Anne Tyler*. Ed. Alice Hall Petry. New York: G. K. Hall, 1992: 107–10; and in his *Hugging the Shore: Essays and Criticism*. New York: Knopf, 1983: 292–99.]

Wolcott, James. "Strange New World." *Esquire* Apr. 1982: 123–24. [Reprinted in *Critical Essays on Anne Tyler*. Ed. Alice Hall Petry. New York: G. K. Hall, 1992: 115–16.]

The Accidental Tourist

Eder, Richard. *Los Angeles Times Book Review* 15 Sept. 1985: 3+.

Mars-Jones, Adam. "Despairs of a Time-and-Motion Man." *Times Literary Supplement* 4 Oct. 1985: 1096.

Mathewson, Joseph. "Taking the Anne Tyler Tour." *Horizon* Sept. 1985: 14. [Reprinted in *Critical Essays on Anne Tyler*. Ed. Alice Hall Petry. New York: G. K. Hall, 1992: 123–25.]

McMurtry, Larry. "Life Is a Foreign Country." *New York Times Book Review* 8 Sept. 1985: 1+. [Reprinted in *Critical Essays on Anne Tyler*. Ed. Alice Hall Petry. New York: G. K. Hall, 1992: 132–36.]

Olson, Clarence E. "The Wonderfully Wacky World of Anne Tyler." *St. Louis Post-Dispatch* 8 Sept. 1985: B4.

Prescott, Peter S. "Watching Life Go By." *Newsweek* 9 Sept. 1985: 92. [Reprinted in *Critical Essays on Anne Tyler*. Ed. Alice Hall Petry. New York: G. K. Hall, 1992: 117–18.]

Updike, John. "Leaving Home." *New Yorker* 28 Oct. 1985: 106–8+. [Reprinted in *Critical Essays on Anne Tyler*. Ed. Alice Hall Petry. New York: G. K. Hall, 1992: 126–31.]

Yardley, Jonathan. "Anne Tyler's Family Circles." *Washington Post Book World* 25 Aug. 1985: 3. [Reprinted in *Critical Essays on Anne Tyler*. Ed. Alice Hall Petry. New York: G. K. Hall, 1992: 119–22.]

Breathing Lessons

Eder, Richard. "Crazy for Sighing and Crazy for Loving You." *Los Angeles Times Book Review* 11 Sept. 1988: 3.

Hoagland, Edward. "About Maggie, Who Tried Too Hard." *New York Times Book Review* 11 Sept. 1988: 1+. [Reprinted in *Critical Essays on Anne Tyler*. Ed. Alice Hall Petry. New York: G. K. Hall, 1992: 140–44.]

Klinghoffer, David. "Ordinary People." *National Review* 30 Dec. 1988: 48–49. [Reprinted in *Critical Essays on Anne Tyler*. Ed. Alice Hall Petry. New York: G. K. Hall, 1992: 137–39.]

McPhillips, Robert. "The Baltimore Chop." *Nation* 7 Nov. 1988: 464–66. [Reprinted in *Critical Essays on Anne Tyler*. Ed. Alice Hall Petry. New York: G. K. Hall, 1992: 150–54.]

New Yorker 28 Nov. 1988: 121.

Olson, Clarence E. "Odd Ties That Bind." *St. Louis Post-Dispatch* 11 Sept. 1988: F5.

Stegner, Wallace. "The Meddler's Progress." *Washington Post Book World* 4 Sept. 1988: 1+. [Reprinted in *Critical Essays on Anne Tyler*. Ed. Alice Hall Petry. New York: G. K. Hall, 1992: 148–49.]

Towers, Robert. "Roughing It." *New York Review of Books* 10 Nov. 1988: 40–41. [Reprinted in *Critical Essays on Anne Tyler*. Ed. Alice Hall Petry. New York: G. K. Hall, 1992: 145–47.]

Wolitzer, Hilma. " 'Breathing Lessons': Anne Tyler's Tender Ode to Married Life." *Chicago Tribune Books* 28 Aug. 1988: 1+.

Saint Maybe

Bawer, Bruce. "Anne Tyler: Gravity and Grace." *Washington Post Book World* 18 Aug. 1991: 1–2.

Cherry, Kelly. "The Meaning of Guilt." *Southern Review* 28 (Winter 1992): 168–73.

Eder, Richard. "Quiescence as Art Form." *Los Angeles Times Book Review* 8 Sept. 1991: 3+.

Gardner, Marilyn. "Ordinariness as Art." *Christian Science Monitor* 25 Sept. 1991: 13.

Kakutani, Michiko. "Love, Guilt and Change in a Family." *New York Times* 30 Aug. 1991: C21.

Morey, Ann-Janine. "The Making of Saint Maybe." *Christian Century* 20–27 Nov. 1991: 1090–92.

Parini, Jay. "The Accidental Convert." *New York Times Book Review* 25 Aug. 1991: 1+.

Ladder of Years

Caldwell, Gail. "The Marriage Fled." *Boston Globe* 7 May 1995: 47.

Eder, Richard. "Trying on a New Life." *Los Angeles Times Book Review* 7 May 1995: 3.

Gray, Paul. "The Intentional Tourist." *Time* 15 May 1995: 80.

Harrison, Kathryn. "Adventures of a Wayward Wife." *Washington Post Book World* 16 Apr. 1995: 1.

Lehmann-Haupt, Christopher. "Leaving a Life But Not Quite Escaping." *New York Times* 27 Apr. 1995: C17.

Oates, Joyce Carol. "Time to Say Goodbye." *Times Literary Supplement* 5 May 1995: 22.

Rubenstein, Roberta. "The Woman Who Went Away." *Chicago Tribune* 30 Apr. 1995, sec. 14: 1.

Schine, Cathleen. "New Life for Old." *New York Times Book Review* 7 May 1995: 12.

Shone, Tom. "Runaway." *New Yorker* 8 May 1995: 89–90.

Appendices

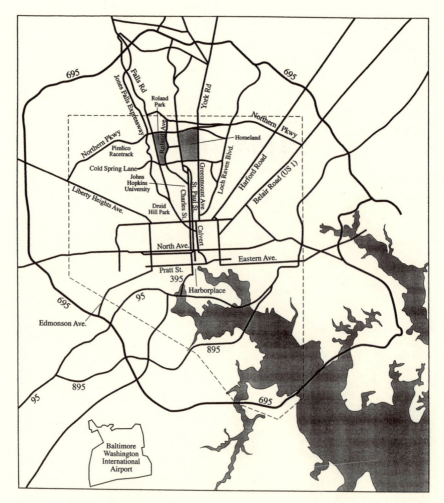

Anne Tyler's Baltimore

Appendix 1: Places in Anne Tyler's Novels

If Morning Ever Comes
New York
Sandhill, NC

The Tin Can Tree
Caraway, NC
Clancyville, NC
Graham, NC
Howrell, NC
Larksville, NC
Raleigh, NC
Rockland, NC

A Slipping-Down Life
Farinia, NC
Pulqua, NC
Tar City, NC

The Clock Winder
Baltimore:
*Cold Spring Lane
*North Charles St.
*St. Paul Street
*Wyndhurst Ave.

* denotes actual Baltimore locale

Partha, VA:
Quamikut Boatyard

Celestial Navigation
Baltimore:
*Roland Ave.
*Roland Park

Searching for Caleb
Baltimore:
*Falls Road
*Federal Hill
*Merchant's Exchange on Gay St.
*Roland Ave.
*Roland Park
*St. Paul Street

Blainestown, MD
Box Hill, LA
Buskville, MD
Caro Mill, MD
Guilford
Honora, MD
New Orleans
New York
Palmfield
Parthenon, DE
Parvis, MD
Peacham, LA
Philadelphia
Plankhurst
Polk Valley
Semple, VA
Wamburton, MD

Earthly Possessions
Clarion, MD
Linex, GA
Perth, FL

Morgan's Passing
Baltimore:
Beacon Ave.
City Hospital
Crosswell St.
*Druid Hill Park
Farley St.
Hartley St.
*Johns Hopkins Hospital
Mariana St.

Meller St.
Merger St.
*Pimlico Race Track
*St. Paul Street
*University Hospital

Bay Bridge
Bethany Beach, DE
Kent Narrows Bridge
Ocean City, MD
Rehobeth
Taney, VA
Tindell, MD

Dinner at the Homesick Restaurant
Baltimore:
Bolton Hill
Bushnell St.
*Calvert St.
*Charles St.
Prima St.
Putnam St.
*St. Paul Street
Sloop St.

Raleigh, NC
Wrightsville Beach, NC

The Accidental Tourist
Baltimore:
*Baltimore airport
*Baltimore train station
*Cold Spring Lane
Dempsey Road
Murray Ave.
*North Charles St.
*Pratt St.
Rayford Road
*St. Paul Street
Singleton St.
*York Road

Edmonton
London
New York
Paris
Philadelphia
Vancouver
Winnipeg

Breathing Lessons
Baltimore:
*Belair Road
*the Beltway
*Broadway
*Calvert St.
Daimler
*Eastern Ave.
Empry St.
*Erdman Ave.
*Franklin St.
*Harborplace
*Light St.
Mulraney St.
*Pimlico Race Track
*Pratt St.
*Route One
Whitside Ave.

Cartwheel, PA
Deer Lick, PA
Oxford, PA
Susquehanna River

Saint Maybe
Baltimore:
*the Beltway
Bolton Hill
*Charles St.
*Cold Spirng Lane
Dober St.
Govans Rd.
*Greenmount
Hampden
*Howard St.
Jeffers St.
*Lake Ave.
Lang Ave.
*Loch Raven
Waverly St.
*York Road

Cockeysville, MD
Greenspring Valley, MD
Portia, MD
Ruxton, MD
Sumner College, PA

Ladder of Years
Baltimore:
Bouton Rd.
*Calvert St.
*Charles St.
Deepdene Rd.
*Johns Hopkins University
*Lawndale St.
*Roland Park
*Roland Ave.
*Wyndhurst St.

Ashford
Baltimore–Washington Parkway
Bay Borough, MD
Bay Bridge
Bethany Beach, DE
Easton
Fenwick Island
Grasonville
Hwy. 50
Hwy. 97
Hwy. 380
Kellerton
Kent Narrows Bridge
Nanticoke Landing
Ocean City, MD
Salisbury, MD

Appendix 2: Songs in Anne Tyler's Novels

If Morning Ever Comes
"Life Is Like a Mountain Road"
"My Heart Belongs to Daddy"
"Nobody Knows the Trouble I've Seen"
"Whispering Hope"

The Tin Can Tree
"The Murder of James A. Garfield"
"Stardust"
"Sunshine on the Mountain"

A Slipping-Down Life
"The Blue Jeans Song"
"Honeypot"
"In the Garden"
"My Girl Left Home"
"Nobody Knows You When You're Down and Out"
"O Promise Me"
"St. James Infirmary"
"The Star-Spangled Banner"
"Trouble in Mind"
"The Walking Song"
"Young at Heart"—Frank Sinatra

The Clock Winder
"Be Still My Soul"
"Frere Jacques"

Celestial Navigation
"Stand Up, Stand Up for Jesus"

Searching for Caleb
"Blues in the Night"
"Bringing in the Sheaves"
"Broke and Hungry Blues"
"Broken Yo-Yo"
"Cane Sugar Blues"
"Careless Love"
"Chattanooga Choo Choo"
"Country Gardens"
"Doxology"
"Georgia Crawl"
"Good Night, Irene"
"Jogo Blues"
"Just a Lock of Hair for Mother"
"Mr. Crump"
"Nobody Knows You When You're Down and Out"
"The Pardon Came Too Late"
"Pig Meat Papa"
"Shut House"
"Stock O'Lee"
"Stone Pony Blues"
"The Stringtail Blues"
"The St. James Infirmary Blues"
"Wabash Cannonball"
"Whisky Alley"

Earthly Possessions
"Just As I Am"
"King of the Road"
"Little Things Mean a Lot"
"Love Lifted Me"
"Love Will Keep Us Together"
"Midnight in Moscow"
"My Life Is Like Unto a Bargain Store"—Dolly Parton
"Washington Square"

Morgan's Passing
"Clementine"
"Happy Birthday"
"I'm Walkin'"—Fats Domino
"June Is Bustin' Out All Over"
"Moments to Remember"
"Plastic Fantastic Lover"
"Sesame Street"
"Some Enchanted Evening"
"Steadily Depressing, Low-Down, Mind-Messing, Working at the Carwash Blues"

"What a Friend We Have in Jesus"—Guy and Ralna
"WPA Blues"

Dinner at the Homesick Restaurant
"The Ash Grove"
"Chattanooga Choo Choo"
"Greenfields"
"Greensleeves"
"I Can Help"—Billy Swan
"In the Sweet By and By"
"Le Godiveau de Poisson"
"Let It Be"
"Mack the Knife"
"Mairzy Doats"
"Me and Bobby McGee"
"Mister Rabbit"
"Nobody Knows the Trouble I've Seen"
"We'll Understand It All By and By"
"White Coral Bells"

The Accidental Tourist
"Baby's First Christmas"—Connie Francis
"Great Speckled Bird"
"Happier Days"
"I Cut My Fingers on the Pieces of Your Broken Heart"
"I'm Gonna Lasso Santa Claus"—Brenda Lee
"I Wonder If God Likes Country Music"
"My Little Gypsy Sweetheart"
"War Is Hell on the Home Front Too"
"We Gather Together to Ask the Lord's Blessing"

Breathing Lessons
"Afternoon Delight"
"Believe Me If All Those Endearing Young Charms"
"Born to Be with You"
"Camptown Races"
"Cassette Recorder Blues"
"Crazy"
"Davy Crockett"
"Death Is Like a Good Night's Sleep"
"Dust in the Wind"
"Friendly Persuasion"
"The Gambler"
"The Golden Road"
"The Great Pretender"
"Heartbreak Hotel"
"Help Me Make It Through the Night"
"Hound Dog"
"I Almost Lost My Mind"

"I Want You, I Need You, I Love You"
"Just a Closer Walk with Thee"
"King of the Road"
"Love Is a Many Splendored Thing"
"Love Me Forever"
"Lyin' Eyes"
"Microwave Quartet"
"Moonglow"
"My Prayer"
"Once to Every Man and Nation"
"On the Road Again"
"O Promise Me"
"Papa Loves Mambo"
"Que Sera Sera"
"Shall We Gather at the River"
"Sleepytime Gal"
"Stumbling Up the Path of Righteousness"
"This Old House"
"Tonight You Belong to Me"
"Truckin'"
"True Love"
"When Will I Be Loved"
"The Wichita Lineman"
"Yellow Rose of Texas"

Saint Maybe
"Abide with Me"
"Blessed Assurance"
"Blessed Jesus"
"Break Thou the Bread of Life"
"Down in My Heart"
"Happy Birthday"
"In the Sweet By and By"
"Leaning on the Everlasting Arms"
"Like a Prayer"—Madonna
"Love Divine, All Loves Excelling"
"Monday, Monday"
"Ramblin' Rose"
"Send Me the Pillow That You Dream On"
"Softly and Tenderly"
"Sweet Hour of Prayer"
"Winchester Cathedral"
"Work for the Night Is Coming"

Ladder of Years
"Blessed Assurance"
"By the Time I Get to Phoenix"
"Delia's Gone"
"King of the Road"

"Let It Be"
"Uncle Albert"—Paul McCartney
"Under the Boardwalk"
"Wedding March"
"We Three Kings"

Index

Pages in boldface indicate main entry.